LIFE AS A SIAMESE MONK

LIFE AS A SIAMESE MONK

Richard Randall

AUKANA
Bradford on Avon

Reprinted 1999
First published 1990

Aukana Trust
9 Masons Lane
Bradford on Avon
Wiltshire BA15 1QN

The Aukana Trust is a registered charity (No 326938)

Printed in Great Britain by Redwood Books, Trowbridge

Cover design by Paul Dudbridge
Cover printed by R A Blackwell & Partners, Bradford on Avon

A catalogue record for this book is available from the British Library

ISBN 0-9511769-2-7

Acknowledgements

The publishers extend their thanks for permission to
reproduce certain of the photographs in this book to
Mrs Jean Randall, Times Newspapers Ltd and
London Weekend Television Ltd.

CONTENTS

1

A MOMENT OF TRUTH

My decision to become a Buddhist monk was no sudden impulse. The idea had been germinating in what purports to be my mind for many years. Somehow or other, I could never bring myself to take the final step. There was always something, manufactured or otherwise, which I was able to use to myself as an excuse for procrastination. As I see it now of course, it was sheer lack of guts. In those days, to me, it was anything but that. There were so many loyalties, so many responsibilities, so many things to accomplish before taking the final step. Or so I thought.

I now know that my loyalties, ideals and responsibilities were largely handy excuses for doing nothing in particular. I was like a man forever calling at the doctor's surgery but refusing to take the physic prescribed.

* * *

It is generally conceded today that one's early environment and conditioning stamps the character and has a vast effect in later life. I am not too sure, however, that this holds true in my own case.

As a youngster I was maintained by the sweat of my mother's brow at what were known as respectable private schools, each of which was based upon Church of England ideas. Here I had the advantage – if so it may be called – of wearing the correct kind of cap and of being able to listen to nice little homilies on how to be good, how to be a little gentleman and so forth. Of education in the true sense I had little. What I learned was class-consciousness and an extremely odd variety of ethics and standards derived from the leftovers of a late Victorian Protestantism.

Fortunately for my long-suffering teachers – and for myself – a change in family fortunes decreed that I change my school. Such changes took place no less than fourteen times before I was turned loose to my own devices in the adult world.

At one time I attended a famous church school, and it was here, at the School of St Martins-in-the-Fields, that wider vistas were opened to me as I came under the influence of such men as the late Reverend Dick Shepherd and the Reverend W. R. Mathews, later Dean of St Paul's, and masters such as Wicks, Marsh and Reekie. It was here that I spent the happiest days.

The pupils were an utterly mixed lot, made up of Italians, French, Belgians, Irish, Spanish, Anglo-Indian, Anglo-Chinese, English and – as I was myself – Anglo-German. Here it was, in the rough-and-tumble conflicts between boys with different national characteristics (all of whom considered themselves utterly British), that I learned something of the broader values of life. It was in this environment that I developed a natural interest in religious history and the beginnings of philosophy.

Here, helped on untiringly by certain of my tutors, I began for the first time to think, to ask questions. Not only the 'whys' but the 'hows' as well. All manner of problems bothered me. Questions of values, morality and loyalties; patriotism and inequalities; the superiority of the Christian teaching; and so forth. All to me were things to be unravelled. None of them was, in those young days, which probably accounts for the fact that I left school and went into the jungle of earning my own living not as a Christian (which is what my education should have made me, if the environmentalists are correct) but as a firm agnostic. Or a quasi-rationalist, it might be even truer to say. But I am sure it was these very problems that shaped my life, and the answers I found to them that drove me to my decision.

The new experience of earning my living did nothing in any way to dull the problems with which I left school. If anything, the new situation accentuated them. Living in the West End of London as I did (I had lived in Whitcomb Street, between Pall Mall and Coventry Street, from early childhood), I met and mixed with all kinds of people from all strata of society. Some good, some bad, some indifferent and some who would be called by most people 'the dregs'. To me, however, they all had much in common. They were people, human beings, with problems not so very different from my own.

At night, when I had left my job and attended my session of night school, I would return home for a quick clean-up and then walk across Leicester Square to the cafés of Soho. Here, in this cosmopolitan and bohemian environment, so vastly different from what it is today, I found people with whom I could discuss the problems of ethics, politics, philosophy and religion. All the people with whom I talked were far older than myself, and many of them were brilliant, both men and women. They took in good part my tyro efforts and, at times, brutal directness in questioning. They guided me to the right books and introduced me to the joys of book-hunting in the Charing Cross Road.

I strove hard to make for myself a mind, a machine with which to reason; for reason appeared to me to be the answer to my restlessness. That is where my problems had led me: *restlessness*. It was during this period that I made the decision to study until 2.30 each morning. There was so much that I wanted to do and only twenty-four hours in a day, so I decided to pay for what I wanted in sleep time. During these night hours I read classical Western philosophy, logic, psychology and the rest. Comparative religion came as natural grist to the mill. Any new-found weapons and methods which I discovered in this way were tested in the cut-and-thrust of open discussion with my friends in Soho. I was overjoyed when I began to score points off them, but the elation was always short-lived: restlessness soon came uppermost once again.

I extended my studies to include Eastern philosophy, and became so enamoured of it that I determined to specialise in the subject – an undertaking which I succeeded in accomplishing. The ideas and subtleties of the Eastern mind appealed to me enormously. I gathered a working, though elementary, knowledge of Sanskrit and passed from there to Pali, the language of Buddhism. It was here that my mental search ceased. I found myself entirely at home with the philosophy and the world-view which it expressed. Here for me was the answer to all problems. I even went so far as to become a lecturer on the subject so that I might bring the glad tidings to others. But somehow I was still as restless as ever.

During all this time the question of success in life was ever-present. I suppose I might have been called a man with vast quantities of ambition but without the necessary sense of direction. My possibilities lay in a number of spheres, ranging from commerce to the arts. As fast as I decided on a particular direction and a field of interest upon which to direct my energies, and had almost attained success, another and more enthralling subject would attract my attention.

I could never keep myself pinned down to any one line of development or occupation. There was always the avid search for some experience or means of expression – for what, I knew not. I had a fear and detestation of the mediocre or humdrum. Success always beckoned, but when it was almost realised, the appalling finality of the situation made me turn off in a new direction.

I prided myself that I was finding out about myself. Life was a challenge, a series of situations which must be met and never shirked. No matter if it were successfully dealt with or not, the important thing was that I face the situation in question. It only gradually dawned on me that the situations were often created by myself where none need exist, producing a turmoil in my mind and social environment that estranged me from my friends and associates and, I am sure, brought unhappiness and uncertainty to those who were nearest and dearest to me.

From my twentieth year until the commencement of World War Two I ranged in occupation from branch-managership of an office machine organisation to freelance journalism and photography. Through all this time I was still pursuing my intellectual quest.

★   ★   ★

It was whilst I was in Exeter that I met and became friends with the only man who, up until that time, had the courage to show to me my ignorance and arrogance. I was just twenty then, slick and successful and, as I see it now, full of my own importance. He was in his early fifties. I happened to be in a café and he was sitting with three other fellows at a table opposite discussing marriage. Was marriage solely the concern of the church, or was it purely a matter of social contract? Without being asked, I walked over to them and immediately waded into the discussion with great heat, taking the stand that marriage had nothing to do with religion but was simply a social necessity covering physical and emotional acts between persons of opposite sex.

My tirade was cut short by the man in question. He asked me whether I practised what I preached. If I didn't, I lacked the moral courage to carry through my intellectual convictions. What did I know of the Christian ethic and marriage? Nothing, he presumed. Education and intellectual brilliance didn't come only from books and study, but from having the courage to test one's knowledge and theories in the process of daily life. He then introduced himself: George Marshall, one-time Antiquarian to Exeter City Corporation.

We met many times after that incident and for quite a time we lived in the same digs. He was kindness itself. He realised what were the blind spots in my education, and guided me to spheres of interest which uncovered them. He gave me my first taste of classical literature, a study which in my impetuous haste I had never undertaken, thinking it useless to my purpose. He introduced me to anthropology and to discoveries made through archaeological survey in both India and Egypt. All this, he taught me, was essential if I were determined to follow my particular line of intellectual development. For two years this fine man tutored and advised me, never forcing his own views upon me, never proselytising with any pet view he may have held.

Whatever views I arrived at were my own, based upon the research method he gradually managed to impart to me.

It would be true to say that George Marshall was one of the two men who had the greatest effect upon me – for the better, that is. The other was Frederik Henkle, a fine philosopher who took me in hand for three years and brought discipline into both my reading and my thinking.

Frederik was the only man that I had ever met who completely lived what he taught. He was the only man who managed to give me a clear understanding of Christianity and point me to its many beauties, whilst at the same time having the courage to bring to my notice the unreliability of the written records.

'Laddie,' he would say to me, 'you are one of those who must find your own way through the mystery we call life. Some can go through it fairly smoothly, accepting their social environments and religious backgrounds without question. You – and myself in my younger days – are the type who have to find their way by bitter experience. Your way will not be happy, but travel it with courage, for that is the only route by which you will be able to come to terms with yourself. Yours isn't a problem of the outer world – it's a problem of the inner world, the world of your mind. I came to terms with myself through the message of Jesus. You, I know, cannot do that. So you must continue to search. Go your way, and remember: keep on climbing, no matter how often you fall.'

I was fortunate indeed to have had the friendship and advice of these two grand fellows, but it was many years before their counsel and patient tuition bore fruit in my tangled life.

*   *   *

Up till and through the war years I continued to make an emotional and intellectual battleground of my life, still holding fast intellectually to Buddhist philosophy (I was a member of the Buddhist Society) but refusing to call myself a Buddhist. I was still struggling for commercial success through photography and journalism; I was moving with a fast set, drinking too much, neglecting my home, living a life cut off from everyone. It was a situation, I realise now, for which I was entirely responsible. My life was becoming unbearable to me and, I am sure, to those around me.

The only thing that had any steadying effect upon me, or gave me any rest from the turmoil of my mind, was the lecturing which I still managed to do. I was travelling to many parts of the country, speaking on the subject of Buddhist philosophy to undergraduates at places as far apart as Bristol, Liverpool, Hull, Cambridge and Oxford. Usually in

a state of despair and depression, probably pepped up with ben-
zedrine to counteract the drink of the day before, I would set off for one
of these cities and, during my lecture and the ensuing discussion,
attain the only peace that I knew. It was at one of these lectures that my
decision to become a Buddhist monk fructified.

On the night in question I was delivering a lecture to the Oxford
University Socratic Club. I had been talking for some time when I had
the strange sensation that I was standing back listening to myself. I
heard myself say: 'This is a completely rational way of life. It is
scientific in its approach. Here is offered no salvation through blind
faith. It's not something which one has to believe in first. Belief has no
part here. Here, in this philosophy, everything is a matter of facts – the
facts of life and experience. Everything about this philosophy may be
tested and proved to be true. It is the answer, I am sure, to all man's
problems. To put it to the test, all that is required is that one apply it to
oneself. It is something to be done, not talked about. Something to be
applied practically, not theorised about . . .'

The moment of truth had arrived. I stood before myself a weakling, a
hypocrite. After the usual discussion and the countless final cups of
coffee, I retired to the room set aside for me at Balliol. Not to sleep, as
was my usual bent after such an evening, but to think. In those few
hours before dawn I reviewed my life – a life of conflict, internal
conflict.

Part of me had spent years in intellectual excursions and had greatly
enjoyed the game called philosophy. I realised now that on the whole it
was pure sophistry, mere cleverness. I had met and mixed with like
minds who were concerned with the same games, but neither I nor my
associates ever got anywhere in any real sense. We were all, to a
degree, cynics, without rule or reasonable basis for accepting any form
of authority, moral or otherwise. I realised that my problems, my
unrest, were entirely of my own making, brought about because I had
never been able to come to terms with the various aspects of my
character. Never had I been able to strike the balance between intellect
and emotion, between austerity and sensuality.

I heard again what I had talked about that evening and I knew that I
had now to take the medicine which I had been prescribing for years – a
medicine not suitable for everyone, but the only one for me.

On my return to London that morning I literally left everything:
home, friends, family and business. I was determined to go East by one
means or another. My family made no efforts to deter me from my
decision, so that very morning I was off. After a number of vicissitudes
– such as wandering around London in winter for six days without
food or shelter – I managed to make my journey.

Here I was fortunate in two ways. Firstly, I had a friend at the Thai Embassy who, knowing of my plans, introduced me to a Thai *bhikkhu* (monk) who was paying a short visit to England. He, on hearing my story, promised that if I actually got to Thailand (then Siam), he would find a guarantor for me and arrange that I enter the Buddhist Order. Secondly, many friends and Buddhists throughout the country subscribed towards my passage to Thailand.

I left London Airport on a bleak morning in February 1954 with the thermometer showing fourteen degrees of frost, and two days later I arrived at Don Muang Airport, Bangkok, to a temperature of ninety degrees in the shade. My worldly possessions were precisely what I stood up in, a couple of books, and two pounds ten shillings in English money.

2

ARRIVAL AT WAT PAKNAM

I left the plane after cheery goodbyes from the crew and made my way to the Immigration Office. Here I was met by the bhikkhu to whom I'd been introduced in London – Thitavedo Bhikkhu. He stood there by the barrier, dressed in the thin golden-coloured cotton robes of a Buddhist monk, his face wreathed in smiles. 'Oh, so happy you come, sir,' he called out to me in his clipped sing-song English. I am sure that he could not have been any happier than I was to see him there to meet me. He was my only contact in this strange new environment. It was that moment of greeting, I think, which brought fully home to me the fact that I had travelled over nine thousand miles for this meeting, and that both my life and everything about it was not only past but also far away. There was now no means of turning back or escaping – I had no desire to do either.

It soon became apparent to me that my friend the bhikkhu was known and respected by all the airport staff. One word from him and all the difficulties of air travel in the East just melted away. Here at Don Muang I found myself at the receiving end of an efficiency and expediency which were, to say the least, amazing. Once through the formal side of my arrival, having had my hand shaken by every official with whom I had come into contact, I was shepherded through the airport building by Thitavedo.

At the main entrance a small group of people waited, and as we approached they came towards us, their hands raised palms together in greeting. These, said Thitavedo, were friends. He then proceeded to make introductions all round. There was Khun Sudhon Jungyampin, who was acting as my guarantor and who, I later learned, had deposited quite a large sum of money with the authorities as proof of his faith in my good behaviour. There also was his son, and two well-known businessmen, Khun Sanoh and Khun Suang.

These happy-visaged men told me that they had heard of me from Thitavedo Bhikkhu and had looked forward to my coming to their country. Many times they had met Englishmen who had come to their country on business, but never one who wished to enter the *Sangha* (Buddhist Order). I was a friend of Thitavedo Bhikkhu, therefore I was a friend of theirs and they would do everything in their power to help me. Would I now get into the car as we had a journey to make to the monastery where they had arranged for me to stay. It lay to the south-west and entailed passing through Bangkok where the traffic was very heavy.

Before entering the car I looked around me at the airport building, modern yet blending with traditional Thai architecture, and at the landscape in every direction – flat, with the earth a deep red-brown, shimmering in the glare of the afternoon sun under a cloudless pale blue sky. Giving no sense of distance or what lay beyond, it fitted in so well with my own mood. For me, the past was gone. As to what the future held, I could but wait and see.

As we drove off towards Bangkok I became for the first time conscious of the intense heat. Every pore from head to foot was exuding sweat. Sweat was running into my eyes and my head was aching like fury. For a while – I don't know for how many miles – I had difficulty in concentrating my attention on the passing scene. And what a rapidly changing kaleidoscope it was. Yet somehow I didn't feel the slightest bit strange or out of place. Nothing appeared to be new to me – I had an odd feeling of being at home.

The car sped on, and as I looked through the open windows I could see men and women in their native dress working in the rice fields as they had done for centuries past. On the road – by now a thin dusty ribbon carving its way through the countryside – were fast-moving modern cars. On the roadside was a bunch of people in Western dress. Others, far off in the paddy fields, wore large woven bamboo hats to protect them from the sun, looking like giant swaying sunflowers as they moved about their tasks. Round a bend in the road a river came into view, its banks besprinkled with open-sided teak and bamboo houses raised above the ground on stilts. Unconcernedly a young woman bathed stripped to the waist, while straddled across her hip a child suckled at one of her golden breasts. Unnoticing, the busy throng of the village went about their business.

I saw two small children, a boy and a girl, as naked and unashamed as the day they were born, frolicking in a pool of warm brown mud at the edge of the river, lolloping around like a couple of young hippopotami, screaming their delight at such freedom for all to hear. Then suddenly they left the pool and darted across the flat brown earth like two shining young birds in spring, their flight soaring and falling in an ecstasy. As I watched them disappear into the distance they fell to the ground as if through sheer exhaustion, and with a final flutter they seemed to dissolve into the very earth itself.

The road broadened and became well metalled as we moved through a small township. The streets were lined with open-fronted teak-built shops displaying all manner of goods. A busy, hustling, bustling scene. Yet amidst all this I saw a board bearing a legend that reminded me from whence I came: 'Drink Coca-Cola'.

Through narrow twisting streets we drove, amidst masses of strangely assorted vehicles: modern cars, man-drawn carts and barrows, three-wheeled taxis. Others, with more enterprising owners, were driven by lightweight motorcycle engines. One outfit was contrived with great ingenuity from a Norton 500cc. Back from the streets, the houses were packed tight: teak houses, bamboo houses, business houses, concrete houses stood cheek by jowl, the whole seething with a multitudinous mass of humanity, shouting their wares, singing their songs, arguing their prices.

We drove into and through Bangkok, city of contrasts and breathtaking pagodas, city of canals or *klong* – the Venice of the East. A city, this, of wide streets and modern buildings – a city of narrow tortuous ways between overcrowded hovels, of dried-up, stinking, black, muddied canals, of waterways and lakes bestrewn with lotus flowers, beautiful beyond imagination. A city of cinemas, loudspeakers, neon lighting, cafés, honky-tonks, opium shops. Above all, a city of beauty, the wondrous pagodas pointing their slim golden spires ever upward as if proclaiming the aims of the humanity which made their fantastic beauty possible.

We left Bangkok by the famous Chao Phraya Bridge spanning the Chao Phraya River – a river wide and teeming with all kinds of craft, from ocean-going merchantmen to the slim river-taxis so reminiscent of the Venetian gondolas. On over the bridge into the Thonburi province. Quickly the houses and shops began to thin until we arrived at the small town of Bhasicharoen. A sharp right turn of the road once through the town and the road ran out, blocked by a river. Thitavedo told me that this was where we left the car and proceeded on foot.

As I stepped from the car I saw that quite a crowd of people had gathered, many of them bhikkhus who lent a delightful splash of gold to the already colourful scene. Thitavedo, acting as interpreter, told me that all these people had been waiting to greet me and to escort me to the monastery which was about half a mile further on. Formalities here took some considerable time as everyone present wanted to welcome me personally. Eventually, the welcomes over, we proceeded on our way over the river by a narrow, high-domed bridge.

Every one of my, by now, very large party managed to negotiate the bridge with success except myself. To the enjoyment and amusement of everyone present I slithered and floundered on the glass-like surface, a surface which had been worn so smooth by untold thousands of bare feet. My feet, unlike most of the others', were clad in a pair of leather-soled shoes which gave me no grip whatsoever. With the stout aid of a couple of bare-footed laughing youngsters I made the journey to the other side without further mishap.

Here, before a tall-chimneyed building ('This,' I heard Thitavedo say, 'is place for burn body') was another large group of bhikkhus, another welcome committee. Again we set off along narrow tree-lined paths, dotted here and there with small teak huts. People lined the path on both sides, men and women, the old and young, some dressed in white, others in sarong and blouse. From them I heard a sound which passed from lip to lip and seemed to keep time with my tread: 'Farang – Farang – Farang'. A word which I learned meant European but which was to have a special significance for myself later.

The path opened out on to a large clearing and there before me stood the pagoda of Wat Paknam, with its white walls and red- and green-tiled roof and golden snake-head decorations, glistening like a jewel in the blazing sun.

Thitavedo led me across the compound to a two-storeyed brick-built house. This was to be my home, he informed me. On entering, I found that the ground floor consisted of three large rooms. In each of these, sitting packed as tight as possible on the teak floor, were more people to welcome me. But Thitavedo, making some rapid remarks to them in Thai, led me up the steepest flight of stairs that I had ever seen to the upper floor. This comprised one very large hall with two small rooms partitioned off at each end. The bhikkhu walked over to one of these, opened the door and beckoned me in.

I stepped into the room and he said, 'This is your home, brother. The place where you live and make ready your mind for when you become bhikkhu. Hope you very happy here. May you come by peace, by and by. Now you must have some rest. Drink some coffee and rest, because there are many people who want to see you, many senior bhikkhus you must pay respects to before you can say day is finished. Then we have to go to see the chief bhikkhu and after go to pagoda. Will leave you now, brother, and come again later.'

I looked around the room. Measuring about nine by six feet with white walls and two windows, it felt very peaceful. A low bed of teak boards, a chair and small table completed the furnishings. Looking out through the windows I was confronted with a profusion of trees. Trees of all kinds – banana, coconut, jackfruit, mango and many more I didn't recognise. Looking due east across a small stream I could see the pagoda. Yes, I thought to myself as I settled in the chair and took a cup of coffee, I shall find peace and happiness here.

★   ★   ★

Sleep must have overcome me because I was awakened by a light tapping on my door. I looked at my watch and saw that it was six-thirty in the evening, just half an hour since I had entered my room. On opening the door I found Bhikkhu Thitavedo waiting for me. We must go now and make all our visits, he informed me. Down those steep stairs to the lower floor – still the people were waiting – and out through the entrance into the pagoda grounds.

It was dark now, and the bhikkhu led the way carrying a torch. Our first visit, he said, would be to the abbot, who lived in a teak-built house across the compound. I was not to feel uncomfortable because customs here were unfamiliar – just follow him and do as he did and everything would be fine. The abbot had been looking forward to my coming and would understand that I knew nothing of Thai custom. We made our way toward the house and entered through a gate in the teak fence, which enclosed two sides of a small garden.

Inside the fence, the garden was dimly lit by oil lamps and an occasional stark and naked electric bulb which would glow fitfully with a faint yellow light. I removed my shoes as instructed by Thitavedo and proceeded across the garden to the front of a tumbledown house. Squatting on the ground facing it were about a hundred people, all chatting happily amongst themselves, smoking cigarettes and drinking the inevitable cups of China tea or coffee. Some were sitting closely packed round a yellow-robed figure who was seated cross-legged on a raised dais.

Thitavedo led me through the groups squatting in the garden until we arrived immediately in front of the dais. Following his every move I knelt down on both knees, joined the palms of my hands together and raised my arms till the palms were level with my forehead. I then bent my whole body forward from the hips until both forearms and hands were resting on the earth, elbows touching knees and forehead touching the ground between my hands. This procedure – which Bhikkhu Thitavedo explained in an undertone was the correct method of showing respect to a senior bhikkhu – was repeated three times. Each time I paid salutation to the figure on the dais I heard its voice repeat: '*Ayu vanno sukham balam*', a formula in the Pali language which I knew well, meaning 'May you have long life, health, strength and happiness'.

Salutations completed, still watching Thitavedo for a lead, I knelt back on my heels, keeping my hands chest high and palms together. The bhikkhu then proceeded to have a long conversation in Thai, a language of which I had not the slightest comprehension. This gave me the opportunity to scrutinise the yellow-robed figure on the dais for the first time.

He had a fine upright posture. His body, swathed in a thin yellow robe which left the right arm and shoulder bare, gave the impression of controlled strength. His strong, deeply-chiselled face had an air of kindness and peace about it. The eyes, surrounded by lines which could only have come through many years of laughing, were penetrating and bright. The head and eyebrows, shaven clean of hair as is the custom for Thai bhikkhus, finished for me a picture of a man majestic in his way, a man of strength and will-power, of kindness and understanding, of learning and experience – and, I imagined, a disciplinarian.

I was brought back from my thoughts by Thitavedo tugging at my elbow and intimating that we could now sit at ease. This entailed sitting with my left leg folded in front of me and my right leg folded back from the knee so that the foot was pointing back. This, he explained, was the polite way to sit at all times. I may say it was a posture that caused me much difficulty before I managed to master it.

When I had arrived at some semblance of the posture indicated, much to the amusement of the people seated around, Thitavedo pointed to the bhikkhu on the dais and informed me that this was the lord abbot. His name was Chao Khun Mangala Raja Muni. He was also a Maha Thera or Great Elder. Everyone here called him Lung Poh, which meant Great Father. I must listen now because Lung Poh wished to speak to me. Not to worry that I didn't understand the language – Thitavedo would translate for me.

The abbot turned and faced me with a smile. He pointed to me and then back to his own face as if intimating that I watch his face and proceeded to talk in Thai. When he spoke it was as if I knew exactly what was being said to me although I could not understand the language he used. And so it proved to be when Thitavedo translated the abbot's words.

'You come, my Western friend, from a far-distant corner of the world, and you are welcome. You may stay here and we will look after you. You are among brothers so be at peace. Have no pride or fear, forget your past now, put it behind you. If you are in doubt or difficulty, ask and we will try to help you. Ask anything you wish. We cannot give you the peace and insight which the Buddha taught – that you must find yourself. We can only point the way.'

As Thitavedo finished his translation I knew that the crucial moment of my visit to the abbot had arrived. It is the custom for anyone wishing to enter the Buddhist Sangha to ask a senior and learned bhikkhu to become one's teacher and guide. Looking up at Lung Poh, I could think of no man whom I would rather have as my teacher. Straight away I asked him to take me as a student. I completely forgot that he could not understand my language and words tumbled out of me in a torrent. I told him about my past, my studies and researches into Buddhism, about my reasons for wanting to become a bhikkhu under his tuition, about my future aims. I poured out in a mad profusion everything that had been pent up in me for years.

When I had finished I sat there trembling, just managing to retain control of my emotions. Lung Poh looked down at me and smiled again. He nodded his head as if to say that he understood, then he turned and said a few words to my friend Thitavedo, who in turn relayed to me that Lung Poh agreed to my request and would accept me as a pupil. When he found that I was proficient in my studies he would arrange for my ordination as a bhikkhu. But first we had to have many more talks.

Thitavedo then addressed the groups of people who had been squatting around and who had been an obviously interested audience. When he had finished, they made their way over to me and saluted me with raised palms, offered me cigarettes and coffee. Sleek brown-eyed children came and placed their hands on mine and uttered the one word of their language I so far understood: 'Farang', each with a tenderness and welcome in their tone. I could not understand why it was that I was receiving such attention until Thitavedo explained with an impish grin that Lung Poh had instructed him to translate the whole of our conversation together. We took our leave of Lung Poh and continued the round of official visits.

I visited five more elder bhikkhus, all living in different parts of the monastery grounds. In each case the salutation was the same and in each case the China tea, cigarettes and coffee were offered.

We had just paid our last visit when Bhikkhu Thitavedo said he thought it was getting much too late to go further and that we would have to visit the pagoda in the morning. It was better that we went back to our house because there were still many people who wanted to see me. And so it turned out to be. When we arrived at the house again, not only was the ground floor packed with patiently waiting people but they were sitting on the ground outside the house as well. This meant that I had to sit on the steps in front of the house whilst each and every one asked questions, and small boys produced from I knew not where an apparently inexhaustible supply of tea and iced coffee. When the last of my new-found friends had left it was one-thirty in the morning.

As I lay on the bench in my room trying to piece the day together I had difficulty in believing that I had only been in Thailand for a matter of hours, not even a full day. I tried to sleep but sleep would not come. I found my mind wandering over a day which, viewed in retrospect, seemed to be unreal. I turned to the past, my life, interests, loves, successes and failures. Even these had about them an air of fantasy. I felt detached, unreal. I could find no thought, no feeling, nothing to hang on to. In such a state I must have fallen asleep from sheer exhaustion, for I was awakened by the sound of a gong. It was the rhythm I think rather than the sound itself which aroused me – a *dang . . . . . dang . . . . . dang . . . dang .. dang . dangdangdangdang!!!!!!*

Rising from my bench I went to the window and looked out. It was not yet light. Looking to the east I could just discern a grey-green glow on the horizon. To the left of my window I could dimly make out a wooden tower. Perched on its highest point was a bhikkhu striking a huge bronze gong with a wooden baton.

With the sound of the gong the whole area sprang to life. Lights appeared in rapid succession all over the monastery. I glanced at my watch and found it to be 5 a.m. It was still too dark to see clearly but sounds told me that the monastery was a hive of industry. I heard splashings of water as the bhikkhus bathed, the clunk of buckets in the stream, the soft pad of bare feet as others came and went from the bathing place. But no sound of human voice.

As I watched I was gradually able to make out that a general exodus was taking place. Hundreds of robed figures, each with a metal bowl slung over one shoulder, were leaving the monastery area in all directions. Gradually the light of the early dawn changed to a bronzy green. Many strange sounds reached my ears. I had seen many dawns before but never one like this.

By 5.45 it was light. I was able to see the yellow-robed figures of bhikkhus and *samanera* (novices) returning to the monastery from their begging rounds and proceeding to the Dana Hall – the hall of gifts – to partake of their first food of the day. What a gracious sight that was in the early morning glow of the eastern sky. Hundreds of golden-clad bhikkhus coming from all directions and forming into a line beneath my window, proceeding on their way deeply wrapped in silent meditation. This vast blaze of rich gold gave off an atmosphere of almost perceptible warmth which quite overpowered me.

Then they were gone. The compound became deserted, and I was left with the sound of the far-distant chug-chug of river craft, the strangled crow of a cock, the last singing of cicadas, the hum of myriad mosquitoes. The irritable, frenzied bark of a pi-dog rose up. The cry was taken up by every dog for miles around until the very air seemed to vibrate to their hysterical yapping, whining and barking.

* * *

At 6.30 I was informed in sign language by one of the Thai 'boys' attached to my house that my breakfast was ready for me. These boys lived in the compound of my house, a common thing in Thailand. Mainly the boys attended the Wat Paknam school or took a large part of their education from the bhikkhus, or in some cases attended schools in the district. They were usually placed by their parents in the care of a bhikkhu when they came of school age.

I went to the lower floor and found a table laid for me and about a dozen people sitting on the ground. These, I later learned, had supplied the meal for me. What a meal it was! Someone had conceived the idea that it would be a good idea to provide me with an English breakfast. I sat down and looked around the table at an assortment of dishes numbering a good twenty. Many of them I did manage to recognise as to content – squid, bird's-nest soup, curry and rice. But most of the dishes contained food with which I was quite unfamiliar.

The one thing that really interested me at the time was the plate which had been placed before me by a dear old lady with cropped greying hair, grubby white sarong and blouse and betel-blackened teeth which she parted in a wide and generous grin as she pointed to the plate, to herself and then to me, uttering '*Farang – Farang*' again and again, intimating that she had supplied this particular dish of food.

I looked down at the plate. It contained, very tastefully laid out, two rashers of bacon, two fried eggs, fried potato chips and a slice of fried bread. An English breakfast indeed, I thought to myself as I attacked it with spoon and fork. It was not until I had conveyed the first spoonful to my mouth that I realised that the whole concoction had been liberally sprinkled with caster sugar.

Fortunately my confusion was covered by the fact that Thitavedo came into the room at that precise moment. Laughing, he explained that sugar on such a meal was quite common and please would I eat it as the people had been very kind and it would not be good to make them feel that their food was unwelcome to me. The old lady in particular had walked many miles to come and cook for me.

Pointing to the other dishes, he also said that I would have to sample something from each, even if I only dipped my spoon into them. I realised that I was beginning to learn something about 'face' and how not to lose it. Keeping a smile on my face and making appreciative noises I sampled every dish on the table and delightful they were, except for one which brought tears to my eyes and practically stripped the skin off the roof of my mouth. Everybody in the room laughed at my efforts to relieve my discomfort. One of the boys ran forward with a slice of mango and in desperation I began to push it away, but Thitavedo would have none of it. 'You eat, stop the hot very fast. Mango or sugar very good for stopping the too hot.' I took one bite of mango and the burning in my mouth subsided.

The meal was topped off by two large glasses of black Thai coffee, a drink to which I became somewhat addicted. It was made, I discovered after some questioning, by roasting the beans in butter. They were then ground to a coarse powder, more butter was added, then they were roasted again on an iron plate over a charcoal fire. When finished the powder was placed in a bag and boiled for a considerable time in water, and finally poured into a glass or cup with a lot of sugar.

The meal at long last came to an end. Cigarettes were handed round, I conveyed my thanks to my numerous hosts, then retired to my room on the upper floor once again. I intended to sit quietly and if possible get some rest, but the lure of the open windows and the many strange sounds coming in through them proved too much for me. I moved over to the window facing due east which had previously given me such a good view of the pagoda. It was fortunate that I did, as I saw for the first time bhikkhus and samaneras making their way to the pagoda.

They came from all directions, old and young. Some in brown robes, some in yellow, some in orange, some in ragged robes, some in new – all making their way towards and into the pagoda, each with right shoulder and arm bare, barefooted. I had read of such scenes but this panorama before my eyes surpassed any description I had met in my studies.

Some four hundred bhikkhus entered the pagoda that morning, with some two hundred or more sitting on the ground outside. All had entered, I learned, for the morning chanting of the *Sutta* – Discourses of the Buddha in Pali – and to hear instruction on the discipline, philosophy and practice of the bhikkhu life by Lung Poh.

As I listened to the surging, swelling sound of those massed voices, I recognised the opening stanza of the Metta Sutta – the instruction on the practice of loving-kindness. I knew this sutta so well that I found it impossible to resist the temptation to join in. The glorious sound vibrated over the whole area as the choir of Thai voices chanted: '*Karaniyam atthakusalena yan tam santam padam abhisamecca.*' 'This is what should be accomplished by the man who is wise in his own good and would attain peace.'

My mind began to bring up old scenes, scenes of home and England, of friends and family whom I had left so abruptly, and for a while I was almost overcome by a bout of self-pity and loneliness. I fell to asking myself what perversity of character it was that had driven me half across the world to a culture and religious outlook so foreign to that which had been my own. I had heard chanting many times before from some of the finest churches in England, both Church of England and Roman Catholic. But never had I been affected as I was by the chanting of these massed bhikkhu voices. The wave of loneliness passed quickly, and I realised with its passing that whatever it was in my character that had brought me to this far corner of south-east Asia, it had brought me to a place, a people and a teaching with which, for the first time in my life, I felt thoroughly at home.

3

TOUR OF THE MONASTERY

Later that morning my friend the bhikkhu took me on a conducted tour of the monastery territory. 'Monastery' of course is not the term which strictly fits a description of this place. Wat Paknam had not the slightest likeness to a Western monastery. Here there were no walled enclosures cutting off the inhabitants from the world. Every inch of the area – about three-quarters of a square mile – was open to the public, who used and passed through it at all hours of the night and day. Some had even settled on the land round the pagoda, building for themselves small teak or bamboo houses from which in some cases they also maintained small businesses, supplying food, drink and cigarettes. Others were undertaking the strict training of the white-robed lay follower. *Arama* would be the better designation for Wat Paknam or for that matter any other Buddhist pagoda area. This is an ancient term used in the time of the founder of the Buddhist brotherhood to denote a park, a park set aside where bhikkhus may live.

Even the bhikkhus bear little resemblance to their Western counterparts, the monks. Bhikkhus, for instance, do not take life vows as do Western monks. They are not striving for the same ends, although many well-meaning Western writers would have it otherwise. Whilst the Western monk, undertaking poverty largely as a penance, strives through the grace of God for forgiveness, salvation and at-one-ment in the end with God the Father, the bhikkhu has no such concepts. Neither does he have the concept of a creator God. He has no doctrine of original sin. Whatever be the error of his ways, there is no one who can forgive him. He takes to poverty not in any sense as a penance, but purely because the ownership of multitudinous goods would be an impediment to his self-chosen life.

Again, the Western monk inhabits a walled monastery all the year round. And in some orders, when he is travelling abroad he is allowed to doff his monkish attire and wear lay clothes. The bhikkhu on the other hand undertakes to be a wanderer for nine months of the year, begging his food as he goes, once a day only. At no time nor under any circumstances may he wear lay dress. Should he do so, his ordination is at an end and no matter how many years he has spent in the robe he would have to enter the Order again, beginning as samanera or novice once more. Only during the season of the rains does the bhikkhu remain in one arama attached to a pagoda. Here he stays for three months, receiving further instruction and spending his time in meditation. At no time may he beg money, no matter for what cause.

These differences stood out stark and clear to me as I made my way round the territory known as Wat Paknam. I realised one thing with great clarity: whereas monasticism in the West had developed and then receded into a comparatively few cenobitic establishments (owing undoubtedly to secular demands and education), here in Thailand monasticism in the form of the Buddhist Sangha had gone on – with a few notable exceptions – exactly as it had done throughout the two and a half millennia of its history.

An abrupt halt was called to these thoughts as Thitavedo Bhikkhu touched my arm and said, 'Come, brother, we go and show you how many bhikkhus live here. Come see Thai bhikkhu house!'

I shall never forget that excursion into the life and accommodation of Wat Paknam. I had taken my house and my room as the standard for the area, but such was not the case. Whereas my house was brick-built, I found that every bhikkhu house I visited was built of teak. Each was simply a small wooden hut built on stilts which raised it four or five feet above ground level. Beneath were pools of stagnant, stinking water surfaced with a thick green slime, the habitat of innumerable insects. Even in daylight mosquitoes swarmed in hordes. In these huts there were no benches to serve as beds, no chairs or tables.

We were now in the *vipassana* section of Wat Paknam. *Vipassana* or insight meditation was that for which Wat Paknam had become famous throughout Thailand, Cambodia and Vietnam. A good two-thirds of the area was given over to these small huts, officially intended to accommodate one bhikkhu or samanera and laid out in such a manner that each bhikkhu could spend his time completely alone and undisturbed. Some of them were closed, and I was asked by Thitavedo not to knock on the door or in any way disturb the occupant who, he informed me, was certainly within. Others were open with a bhikkhu sitting outside. Some of these I was able to question.

One I found to be a man ninety-two years of age who had spent fifty years as a bhikkhu. He seemed a happy old man. When I asked him what he did and what he studied he replied that his time was running out so he spent all his time in meditation. He did this so that he might come to an understanding of himself and be conscious of his last moments, and so die at peace, with no hankering after life, no suffering that he was leaving life. He was a delightful old man. I saw much of him and learned much by watching him in my later days at Wat Paknam, until his last day came. He died sitting in meditation in the peace of his hut just as he had wished.

During that morning I was able to cover the whole area. Four hundred bhikkhus and two hundred samaneras lived in the territory, I discovered, many of them living not one but two to a hut. In the scholars' and students' quarters conditions were especially crowded.

The ground surrounding Wat Paknam was surrounded on all four sides by water, the north-eastern corner being bounded by the junction of a swift-flowing river and a wide, deep klong or canal. It was from this junction where two rivers meet that Wat Paknam derived its name some three hundred years ago. One of the rivers was diverted and made to form a link with the then existing canal system, but the place is still known as 'where the two rivers meet'.

Facing along the river front were situated the pagoda kitchens where the begged food was cooked and warmed up. These were long, low, teak-built sheds leading straight on to the water's edge: a necessity, I quickly discovered, where water is scarce for nine months of the year.

I went inside the cooking sheds and found them to be a hive of industry. Huge cauldrons of boiling rice and other foods were simmering over charcoal fires tended by smiling Thai women of every age. All were dressed in white sarong and blouse, with a white shoulder-scarf thrown over one shoulder, most with the right shoulder bare. All were shaven-headed. These, I learned from Thitavedo, were *upasika*, the female equivalent of bhikkhus. Although they had not the official status of the bhikkhu they led more or less the same kind of life. Some were preparing food of various kinds. Others were fanning furiously at fires which were loath to come to life. Still others were carrying water from the river to be used for cooking. Going out on to the river frontage I found others squatting down at the waterside washing utensils, vegetables, meat and various cooking cloths. Just below the cooking sheds were two more young women taking a bath and below them still, two children and an old woman attending to the calls of nature, all in the same river.

I discovered from Bhikkhu Thitavedo that there were as many as three hundred of these upasikas resident in the area. Some of them spent their lives in service to the pagoda and arama, while others, under the watchful eye of Lung Poh, spent their whole time in meditation and study.

In the days of Siddhattha Gotama, the founder of the Buddhist Sangha, the Order comprised bhikkhus and samaneras (the male fully-fledged monk and the novice), and *bhikkhuni* and *samaneri* (the female equivalent). Bhikkhunis had to be ordained both by a chapter of bhikkhus and then by a chapter of bhikkhunis. In the course of the five hundred years after the Buddha's death the Bhikkhuni Order died out. It has never been possible to admit women to the Order by the founder's two prescribed ordinations, so these white-robed women whose official position is but that of female lay followers take it upon themselves to uphold as many rules of the original Bhikkhuni Order as they can. Many of them I found to be extremely erudite, and quite often groups of them were sent from Wat Paknam to distant parts of Thailand to instruct in both Buddhist philosophy and meditation techniques.

Set back from the cooking sheds in a grass compound stood the pagoda, facing due east. Around it was a low wall with four openings at the cardinal points. Inside the wall the whole ground area was paved with large flagstones worn smooth by the tread of many feet. The pagoda, a long high building painted white, had a steeply pitched roof covered with highly-glazed Chinese tiles in red and green. The roof dipped in the middle and rose at each end of the ridge, giving it a sway-backed appearance. At the eastern and western ends the ridge ended in a rampant cobra coloured with gold leaf. The pagoda was situated along a line running west to east with the main entrance at the eastern end. Hanging from the eaves were little brass and silver bells which at each gentle breeze would tinkle out an extremely pleasant sound.

When we arrived at the main entrance of the pagoda Thitavedo indicated that I should take off my shoes before entering – one of the ways by which one showed respect in Thailand.

I found the interior to be spacious and lofty. Hanging from the roof were oil lamps and a couple of electric bulbs. The floor was completely clear, there being no necessity to provide seats here, where all sitting was done on the floor. Immediately facing the east and situated at the far end of the pagoda was a large figure of the Buddha raised on a platform about three feet in height. The figure itself was about fifteen feet tall, made of bronze and covered with gold leaf. On either side stood figures of the Buddha's chief disciples: on the left Sariputta and on the right Moggallana. Rising in two tiers from the raised platform were two rows of smaller Buddha figures, roughly three feet tall and each covered in gold leaf.

In front of this platform and its numerous figures, a third of the floor space was taken up by a raised wooden platform one foot in height and covered with rugs. Thitavedo told me that we must go on to this platform and pay our respects to the Buddha. As if aware of my resistance to any kind of bowing down to images, he reassured me saying, 'Remember, brother, do not make difficulty in your mind. We are not bowing down before an image. That would be very silly and waste much time. It is only metal and stone and has no power. We do like this to pay respect to the memory of our founder and teacher Gotama, who became Buddha. We bhikkhus try to keep him alive in our minds all the time. We think of his life and try to come to the great understanding just as he did.'

We went forward, knelt and paid respects just as we had to the abbot, touching the head, hands and arms three times to the ground. Having paid our respects in this time-honoured and traditional manner, we left the pagoda and returned to our own dwelling.

* * *

Later that day I was visited by Lung Poh who, using Bhikkhu Thitavedo as interpreter, proceeded to question me on my knowledge of Buddhist literature and philosophy. At the end of some four hours he was satisfied, and from Thitavedo I gathered that he was very pleased with my knowledge and studies.

The one thing that interested him, however, was how I had come by such knowledge, living in the West as I had. He was agreeably surprised when I was able to explain that in England we were fortunate to have the whole collection of works which we know as the Pali Canon, comprising all the *Sutta* or Discourses of the Buddha, all the books on *Vinaya* or Discipline and legal codes for bhikkhus, and the whole of the *Abhidhamma* or Philosophy. And as well as the complete collection in the Pali language, all but three of the books had been translated into English. He was even more delighted when he learned that the Pali Text Society was continuing its original good work of producing the whole collection in both Pali text and translation by the issue of regular reprints; and that Pali could be studied at the School of Oriental and African Studies at London University.

He then wanted to know from me why it was that I had come to Thailand and not some other Buddhist country. Here I decided to be completely frank. I explained that I had no romantic ideas about the East and that I expected to find just as many mixed customs and ideas prevalent in the East about Buddhism as there were in the West about Christianity. I had realised in my years of study that many of the customs in Buddhism had nothing whatever to do with what Gotama had taught but were hangovers from an indigenous Hindu civilisation and culture. In much the same way, in the West, pagan customs had been absorbed into what was now known as Christianity. My main requisite had been to find a country which had developed at its own pace and which had not come under European domination and colonisation. This had had a disastrous effect in the Buddhist countries where it had prevailed, as witness Ceylon and to a lesser degree Burma. Here in Thailand this had not happened, and I hoped that here I would find that for which I was searching.

This again satisfied him. He thanked me for my frankness and with a chuckle agreed that I would find much that was not strictly Buddhist practised by the people. He said I was not to let that worry me at all, as people were people wherever one went. He then went on to discuss my becoming a bhikkhu. Which kind of bhikkhu did I wish to become? Which group did I wish to join, the *vipassana dhura* (meditation group) or *gandha dhura* (the group which studied the books)? I had seen enough of books, I told him. I now wanted to apply their instructions: to become a meditation bhikkhu. That was the sole reason I had asked him to instruct me: he was famous as a teacher of meditation.

Lung Poh then proceeded to tell me that I had made the right choice. There was only one way to understand the Buddha's teaching and that was by doing what Gotama himself had done. He had come to understanding by meditation – I could do the same. The books were all very fine but it would be of no use to believe them – they had to be tested and proved. The only way in which they could be proved or disproved was by the meditational methods laid down by the Buddha himself.

He then told me that he would see that I first became ordained a samanera and that later he would arrange and be responsible for my final higher ordination as a bhikkhu. But to begin with he wanted me to undertake meditational instruction as a layman. It would be necessary therefore that I officially take upon myself the precepts and rules of training of a lay Buddhist and this we would do immediately. Would I kneel down in front of him and repeat everything he said after him?

I rose from my mat on the floor, knelt before him and bowed my head three times to the ground in salutation. Then, sitting back on my heels with my hands raised palms together, I repeated after him:

> 'Namo Tassa Bhagavato Arahato Samma Sambuddhassa.
> Namo Tassa Bhagavato Arahato Samma Sambuddhassa.
> Namo Tassa Bhagavato Arahato Samma Sambuddhassa.
> Buddham saranam gacchami.
> Dhammam saranam gacchami.
> Sangham saranam gacchami.
> Dutiyampi Buddham saranam gacchami.
> Dutiyampi Dhammam saranam gacchami.
> Dutiyampi Sangham saranam gacchami.
> Tatiyampi Buddham saranam gacchami.

Tatiyampi Dhammam saranam gacchami.
Tatiyampi Sangham saranam gacchami.
Panatipata veramani sikkhapadam samadiyami.
Adinnadana veramani sikkhapadam samadiyami.
Kamesu micchacara veramani sikkhapadam samadiyami.
Musavada veramani sikkhapadam samadiyami.
Sura meraya majja pamadatthana veramani sikkhapadam
  samadiyami.
Imani pañca sikkhapadani samadiyami.
Imani pañca sikkhapadani samadiyami.
Imani pañca sikkhapadani samadiyami.'

These I translated into English to Bhikkhu Thitavedo who had been
instructed to see that I thoroughly understood what I had undertaken:

'Praise to the Lord, the Arahant, the Self-Enlightened
  Buddha.
Praise to the Lord, the Arahant, the Self-Enlightened
  Buddha.
Praise to the Lord, the Arahant, the Self-Enlightened
  Buddha.
I go to the Buddha for refuge.
I go to the Teaching for refuge.
I go to the Order for refuge.
For the second time I go . . .
For the third time I go . . .
I undertake the rule of training to refrain from killing
  living creatures.
I undertake the rule of training to refrain from taking that
  which is not given.
I undertake the rule of training to refrain from wrongful
  indulgence in sensual pleasures.
I undertake the rule of training to refrain from lying,
  slander and gossip.
I undertake the rule of training to refrain from sloth-
  engendering liquors and drugs.
I take upon myself these five rules of training.'

The precepts taken and Thitavedo having informed Lung Poh that I
had understood them perfectly, Lung Poh went on to explain the initial
approach to meditation.

'First we have to learn to fixedly concentrate the mind so that it may
be brought to peace. This is not easy. The human mind is like a mad
monkey on a many-branched tree being chased by a swarm of angry
wasps. As soon as you start the exercise you will realise how difficult it

is to control the mind. But control it you must if you are to make any
progress. To do this it is necessary to withdraw the mind from the
outer world of the senses and to turn it within itself. To help you to
attain this withdrawal I want you to use your imagination in this
manner.

'Sit comfortably in a position which you can hold for hours if
necessary. Then fold your hands in your lap. Your right hand should
be on your left, with the index finger of the right touching the thumb of
the left. Close the eyes and try to imagine that you are concentrating
the mind in the opening of the right nostril. I want you then to repeat
the words *samma arahan* three times. Next, concentrate the mind at the
inside corner of the right eye and repeat the words as before. Next, try
to concentrate your whole attention in the centre of the skull. Then to
the back of the mouth just above the uvula. Then to the bottom of the
throat. Then right down to the navel. And finally at a position two
finger-breadths from the navel. At each of these positions you are to
repeat *samma arahan* three times, but when you come to the last
position you should keep on repeating the words. If you find that the
mind wanders come straight back to the final position: do not go
through all the positions again. From this you will learn much. If you
have success you will be conscious of a pinpoint of light seen as if in the
mind's eye.

'Now I must tell you to forget all the books. You are not to do any
reading at all – spend all your time at this exercise. The only time you
may break is when you are taking food or attending the calls of nature.
Even during those times try not to let the mind wander, try to keep it
withdrawn. Try hard. Bhikkhu Thitavedo will look after you and if
there are still questions which you may wish to ask he will deal with
them until I see and talk with you again.'

With those final words he rose and left my house.

When Thitavedo had returned from escorting the abbot back to his
quarters, we sat and talked and drank coffee far into the night. I was
somewhat disgruntled at the exercise which Lung Poh had given me,
and when Thitavedo asked me what I thought of it I expressed my
thoughts in no uncertain terms. I said that I had come all this way to
undertake meditation and by that I meant *Satipatthana* or the Four
Ways of Mindfulness. According to the Buddha's own words in the
Satipatthana Sutta, this was the one and only way to final understanding. Yet here I was with an exercise which fitted, I thought, more easily
into the field of kundalini yoga. If I had wanted to study yoga I would
have gone to India. What I wanted was strictly Buddhist meditational
methods as laid down in the books of the Pali Canon.

Thitavedo listened patiently to my grumbling and fault-finding. When I had finished he leant forward in his chair and offered me another glass of coffee and a cigarette. He looked at me intently for about a minute without the slightest sign of expression on his face. Then he smiled.

'Trouble, brother, is that you make too much study, know too much books. Think you are very clever, but head too big, too full of pride, not much room for wisdom. Lung Poh very wise and has much experience after fifty years as bhikkhu and nearly all those years as vipassana bhikkhu. You just come and not even a bhikkhu yet. Think you know more than Lung Poh. Your mind must be trained before you can start to practise the four ways of mindfulness. That will come, but first you must practise the exercise given by Lung Poh. This is strictly Buddhist method as you will find when you have gained some experience. You must test this method. You do not have to believe me or Lung Poh. You have to test and find out for yourself. If you find it not a good way then you can find fault.'

As I listened I realised that every word he said was so true. I was, and had been, proud of my knowledge of my subject and was not easily given to listening. I knew all about the theories of the teaching but had not an atom of practical experience. I realised that I had been something of a fool.

Without more ado I told the bhikkhu that I had been ungrateful and a fool and that I knew that I was a 'big head' as he had put it. Thitavedo laughed and said, 'Your head big but have known bigger. My head very big at first, but much shrunken since Lung Poh teach me.'

His remarks and humour did much to restore me to a more reasonable frame of mind. We continued to chat for some time until he said that it was time we retired. One thing he must remind me about was that from tonight onward we would have no conversation in the social sense. I must spend all my time at the exercise. He would arrange that my door was knocked upon at meal times. 'Now goodnight, and try hard!'

I retired to my room and shut the door. Before going to bed, thinking over all that had happened in my short time at Wat Paknam, I decided to call my room 'the head-shrinking department'. This name was to be used by both Thitavedo and myself for many a long day. As yet I was unaware of its full import.

4

EARLY MEDITATION EXPERIENCES

I awoke at four the next morning, bathed by pouring a bucket of tepid water over myself and returned to my room determined to apply myself to the exercise which Lung Poh had prescribed. Having managed to get myself comfortably seated squatting on the floor I closed my eyes and tried to fix my whole attention in the opening of the nostril as instructed. I failed completely. I tried again and again but could not do it. I tried to help myself by visualising the nostril but no sooner had I arrived – after much effort – at a mental picture of the nostril than I found it fading and my mind drawn to some sound or other.

I became aware of innumerable sounds which I had not heard before. The more I struggled to attain even the slightest degree of concentration on the nasal area, the more I became conscious of some sensory stimulation. My mind wandered everywhere but where I wanted it to be. I remember feeling that I was just on the point of success when I heard what I took to be the sound of a river-boat in the distance. Immediately I was caught up in a mental game of conjecturing how far away it was, what type of boat it was. I became so involved that I was not even aware when I left that mental playground. The next time I caught myself I was going through in mind the act of boarding a number nine bus in Piccadilly Circus.

Again I tried to clear the mind. I brought myself back to the task in hand only to become conscious of the pain in my legs. I determined that I would not move until I had arrived at some semblance of concentration. Then I became painfully aware that I was being bitten by what appeared to be hordes of mosquitoes. Try as I might I could not put the thought of mosquitoes out of my mind. My hands and feet, I thought to myself, must surely be swollen beyond recognition. Grasping at this excuse, I got up from the floor and lit a candle, as it was not yet daylight, to see just how badly I'd been stung. The damage was surprisingly small considering the fact that I had inadvertently left both windows unshuttered during the night.

By this time I had become furious with myself. I had always prided myself upon my powers of concentration and will. Again I seated myself on the floor, calling myself a long string of uncomplimentary names during the process. I applied my mind to the exercise once more, and was progressing very well, as I thought, when I heard a knocking on the door. I opened my eyes and found that I was lying on my side on the floor. I had obviously been fast asleep.

Opening the door I found that a table had been laid with my breakfast. I went over to it and sat down. Pouring out a large glass of coffee I began to drink. For a moment I closed my eyes and immediately I was conscious of a clear mental picture of my right nostril. I became so absorbed that I was beginning to feel quite conscious of my own nostril – when the fact that I had attained this small degree of success dawned upon me and the whole experience was gone. Try as I might, it would not come again.

I was rather chastened as I finished my cold breakfast and coffee. I puzzled over a mind such as mine, so perverse that it could not gain any success at the exercise whatever effort was used. Yet when occupied with something else and apparently not trying at all, it had suddenly produced the thing demanded of it. As I went back into my room I realised that I might know a lot about an awful lot of things but I understood absolutely nothing about the thing which thought about them, the something I called 'my' mind.

For three days I saw no one and talked with no one. I just sat in my room and tried to get some mastery of the exercise. I began to detest my own company and would have done anything just to talk with one of the boys, even though we would not have been able to understand one another. Anything, I thought, would be better than trying to master this restless and uncontrollable mind of mine. I spent ages just looking out of the windows at the passing scene before I caught myself and dragged my mind back to the exercise with much recrimination.

★   ★   ★

One evening I thought I had found a loophole which would give me some relief from my own unbearable company. I decided that I was doing too much sitting, that I was not getting any exercise – which after all was a very bad thing. So when it was dark I left my room in my bare feet and strolled along the various paths of Wat Paknam. I did this twice and although I felt rather like a schoolboy playing truant, I kept telling myself that exercise was very necessary. After all, one could not just sit day after day.

About two hours after I had returned from my second night stroll Thitavedo came to my room and called me out. I was quickly out and greeting him profusely, telling him that there was much for us to discuss, many questions I wished to ask. Please would he come and sit down and have some coffee with me and let me talk for a while?

He looked at me with not a smile and said, 'Brother, you very foolish man. Lung Poh tell you stay in your room and work hard at exercise, but you go out. Very foolish not to do as Lung Poh says. He can send you away – then what you do? Also very foolish to go out at night without light and shoes. Many dangerous snake live here. You tread on him, him bite and you die. Now go to room and work. I come and tell you when you can stop work and when you can walk out. Remember, brother, you ask to come here, you ask Lung Poh to teach you. Lung Poh and myself not ask you to come. The more you not work, the longer it take before you become samanera. If you can't do meditation Lung Poh not ordain you.'

Then he smiled and took my hand.

'Very hard business you take on, brother. Just keep on trying. You will come to understand that it is not good for me to answer your questions. You find the questions – also you have to find answers. Now go to your room and not to come out till I tell you.'

With that he left, and I wandered disconsolately back into the room which I had thought a haven of peace but which was nothing more or less to me now than a torture chamber.

★ ★ ★

During the next two weeks I remained in my room, only leaving it for bathing and other natural functions. I even had my meals in the room, brought by one of the boys, who never made any attempt to talk to me. During this period I gradually began to attain some semblance of calm. The one thing I had learned, if nothing else, was that struggle and strife in the mind, based upon pride in mental achievement, was no way to attain success in mastering the meditation techniques which the abbot had given me.

Gradually it dawned upon me that the times when I had the best success were when the mind appeared to have tired itself out and could find nothing else to titillate itself with. It would then fall back automatically into the meditation exercise. In this way I learned not to be upset when the mind darted from one thing to another in rapid succession. After all, I would tell myself, this is but the nature of mind.

Step by step in this way I was able to master each position of the exercise down to the final position just above the navel.

I ran into more trouble, however, when I fell to wondering what was the reason for the continual repetition of *samma arahan*. I knew what the terms meant in Pali. *Samma* meant best, highest, supreme. *Arahan* equated with the one who was fully enlightened. The Buddha was often referred to as arahant. To me, the terms meant 'supremely enlightened one'. But considering what it was that was enlightened – in this case, the mind – the words could be made to mean 'supreme pure mind' – a mind which was free from ignorance of things as they are, from egocentricity and pride. I decided on the definition 'supreme pure mind'.

But where did that get me? Why not repeat 'number nine bus' ad infinitum? After all, there was no magic in just words. Again, was this not just the same as the technique used in the Jesus Prayer by some Christian orders? If so, what advantage had Buddhism over Christianity in my case? I had always resisted the Christian teaching and yet here I found in Buddhism a technique of meditation which seemed so very similar.

Again and again my mind argued back and forth, somehow determined on conflict, doubt and scepticism. Any calm which had been gained over the past few days rapidly disappeared. Surely, I argued with myself, the tenets of Christianity and Buddhism were fundamentally different. Discounting the question of which held the Truth, they were utterly different in aim and content. Christianity was based upon the concept of a creator God. Jesus Christ was his son and one with God the Father through the Holy Ghost, the three making the Holy Trinity. It was a doctrine of first causes and beginnings. Of the sinfulness of man – all men were born sinners. Smirched with original sin, they could come to salvation only through the intercession of Jesus Christ, in whom one had to believe and have faith, and the grace of God the Father. One could do nothing of oneself to attain salvation other than supplicate of God for his saving grace through prayer.

The whole doctrine was based upon Christ's Sermon on the Mount, with the Commandments of Moses added. Both of these were God-given commands, Christ himself being God, and Moses receiving direct from the Voice of God the Father the Ten Commandments. It was a doctrine of acceptance and faith, of vicarious salvation through the sacrifice of Jesus, of everlasting perdition, or heaven, as the case might be.

The teaching of Gotama Buddha was so utterly different. It held no concept of a creator God, of original sin, of vicarious salvation through a saviour. No doctrine of eternal heaven or hell and no commandments uttered by the authority of God regulating the behaviour of man. Here Gotama, stepping aside completely from the henotheistic Brahmanism of his time, taught something unique in the history of man's thinking. Had he not taught the doctrine of Dependent Origination which had so appealed to me in that it removed the necessity for dealing with first causes? Thus it destroyed forever, for me, the infinite regress of ever finding preceding causes for first causes.

And yet, at that moment, I found myself longing that I could have faith in the Christian teaching. Just to have faith and to place myself in the hands of the Lord – surely this would bring peace if one could attain it! What had I done with my life? I had never considered myself a religious man. I had denied the existence of the God of my mother and father, the God of my early childhood, the God which my early teachers had assured me was surely there. But my questioning, unbelieving mind had turned away from such things as untenable. Now here I was in a far-distant land, searching for the ultimate truth of the Buddha's teaching and finding myself trying to practise a meditation exercise which was on all fours with Christian teaching.

I decided to put the matter to the test and for hours replaced *samma arahan* with the words 'number nine bus'. All that happened was that I caught myself saying *samma arahan*.

* * *

It was in this state of mental turmoil that I awoke one morning feeling extremely ill. I hadn't been feeling too well for days but had put it down to my state of mental distress and the heat to which I was not accustomed. This morning, though, I felt particularly ill. I had great difficulty in breathing and was, to some degree, light-headed. Every time I breathed it was accompanied with great pain. To escape this I fell back on the practice of the meditational exercise and for brief spells was able to get away from the pain. This in its turn began to give way to violent fits of coughing which brought gulps of blood to my mouth.

When this happened for the first time I realised with a strange lack of panic that I was indeed ill. I also had a fairly good idea as to what I was suffering from. I had had pneumonia in the past during the war, but never to this extent. I could not lie down owing to the pain in my ribs so I sat on the floor and applied myself to the meditational task. I found that no effort was necessary – I just fell back on the exercise as the only thing to do. I knew that even if I called one of the boys I could never make him understand that something was wrong with me. As the morning wore on I found that I had not the slightest interest in whether I got well or not.

I must have fallen into a stupor for I came round to find Thitavedo shaking me by the shoulder. 'Brother,' he said, 'you not well. What matter with you?'

I explained as best I could and pointed to the spittoon. He looked again at me and then at the contents of the spittoon. His face full of concern, he said, 'So sorry, brother, you very sick. Must call Lung Poh and try find doctor. Not to worry. You and me very closely like. We like brothers from same mother. I not leave you long. Back very fast. Just go fetch Lung Poh.'

He hadn't been gone more than a few minutes when I became aware of the murmuring of voices outside my window. I pulled myself painfully upright and staggered to the window and looked out. Below, people had gathered – men and women, boys and girls, bhikkhus and samaneras. Some were looking up at my window, others were seated on the ground in the attitude of meditation. The news had travelled fast indeed: Farang was ill.

When Lung Poh arrived I was again sitting in the meditation posture. As he entered my room I attempted to rise and pay him salutation in the traditional manner. But smilingly he placed his hands on my shoulders and held me back and waving aside my efforts, sat himself down in front of me. Thitavedo sat to one side and placed a hand reassuringly on my knee. When the abbot began to speak to me I was once again conscious of a strange rapport between him and myself. His whole manner spoke of compassion and understanding. So much so that I forgot my pain and the mental tumult of the past days. For the first time in my life I felt completely relaxed and at peace.

'You, my friend, have had a very bad time for many days now. Your mind has been in distress. You have had many doubts and fears. You have tried all manner of ways to escape from the task which I set you. You have not been able to escape, neither have you been able to run away from yourself. There has been for you much suffering.

'The First Truth which the Buddha taught us is that life, all life, is a state of suffering. You have experienced the truth of that statement and you now know that the suffering which you have experienced was not of the world of material things. It was of your world, your mental world, the world of your mind. Here, through the constituents of your character and your ignorance of the truth of things as they are, you have created your own suffering. The teaching of the Buddha allows us to cease from this self-made suffering. He taught a way by which we can escape from the wheel of life, the wheel of *samsara*, the wheel of coming to be in a realm of suffering and unrest. This wheel is but the mind of man clouded by ignorance. An ignorance so vast that man is not conscious even that he is ignorant. We might almost call it a cloud of unknowing.

'You have learned in the past days since you arrived here – on my instructions, being left entirely alone night and day – that your trouble is not with the world at large but with your inner world, the world which you yourself create and destroy every moment. Your present thoughts have arisen dependent upon past thoughts and desires. Your future thoughts will arise dependent upon your present thoughts and desires. It is no good for you to worry and think about the past or to try to envisage the future. That is the way to more suffering and unrest. You must control your thoughts *now*. You must bring your mind to peace and tranquillity *now* – and you will be sowing the seeds for like thoughts in the future. That is why I gave you the exercise to practise. When you can master this your mind will be at peace temporarily. All the agitation of your mind will stop for a short while because it has become focused upon that point of light about which I spoke to you.

'Now you are very ill it is more important than ever that you practise the exercise. You could die now, and it is better if one is to die that one die with the mind at peace, in a state where it is neither clinging to the past nor grasping at a future. We are going to bring a doctor for you but that will take time. I want you not to go to bed nor to lie down. That would not be good for you. Spend your whole time at the exercise. Go over it again and again. Go to sleep sitting where you are doing the exercise. When you wake, let your first thought be the exercise. This way you will get results. Work as if the next moment were your last. For such it may be.

'There are many lay people here who think that I have some magic power which will cure all illness. People all over the world have such beliefs and in some cases so strong is their faith that they recover from their ills. You, I know, have no such ideas or faith in the power of magic but I assure you that there are many here who sincerely believe in such possibilities. Several of them have already asked me if they may come and sit in your house deep in meditation so that they may send you their healing power. Let them come, my friend, they can do you no harm, and it is good to know that one has friends and well-wishers close at hand. You and I know that the Buddha did not teach such things – but remember he did teach us to be tolerant of others' ideas.

'I must leave you now. I will call to see you often and I trust that you will soon recover because I want to ordain you samanera soon. I will send the message for the doctor, but be patient and work hard all the time.'

When the abbot had left, Thitavedo returned to my room bringing with him a large pot of coffee and two cups on a tray which also held a large number of small packages. He poured coffee for us both, then pointed to the packages and said, 'These cures for you. All sent by people who know how to make you well. Everyone different but one thing in common. Everybody want to make you well. Better don't to take them, brother, but to take the thoughts of these kind people.

'Lung Poh very wise,' he continued, 'knows your mind very well. He knows how you think and what you go through for many days. He sit and think about you all the time. Always he talk about you. He say he has been waiting many years for man like you to come from the West. He very sure you will make success and do much work with him. I also think about you all the time. I feel like you my brother. First time I see you in London I like you and knew we understand each other. Sometimes I have to be very fierce with you and look very stern – but only to help you. I would like to spend time talking with you all day but that would be bad for your progress. First you get good with exercise because soon you have to learn all about ordination ceremony. Then you will have to divide time between learning ceremony and making practice. Remember, brother, this only beginning. Much more, many much more Lung Poh is going to teach you. Must leave now. Will come to see you again by and by. Do much practice.'

That evening six shaven-headed white-robed women – upasikas – came to meditate in my house. Outside sat others. It was three days before the doctor arrived. During that time Lung Poh and Thitavedo called to see me two or three times a day and whilst my physical condition had deteriorated considerably and breathing had become something of an agony, my mental state had improved enormously and I found myself able to cope with the situation with some degree of success. This I am sure was due largely to the effect of talks from both Lung Poh and Bhikkhu Thitavedo.

The doctor – a navy man – examined me and pressed me here and there. My grunts and groans, no doubt, gave him the answers he required, for we neither spoke the other's language. Then he looked into the spittoon, raised his eyebrows and produced from his bag a large hypo and an equally large phial of penicillin. Having filled one from the other he proceeded to give me the benefit of the marriage first in one buttock and then the other.

The next day he came again, this time accompanied by another doctor who spoke excellent English. They both examined me thoroughly and agreed upon a joint diagnosis. The English-speaking doctor, upon my asking if I had pneumonia, agreed that this was so and that I had it in both lungs. He felt sure that the penicillin would arrest it, although he was afraid that it was going to be given in rather large doses. So it proved to be. After two days of injections the pain had subsided and the bleeding eased considerably. By the third it had completely stopped. On the fourth day I received two more injections and the doctors told me that I was out of the wood and that they would not be calling again. I saw much of these two fine chaps during my stay. We became quite firm friends and, I hope, still are to this day.

By the end of that week, apart from a little shakiness in the legs, I was feeling fairly fit and beginning to enjoy food again. I had managed to learn one expression in Thai which meant 'thank you' so I was able to go to all the people who had been meditating for my recovery as they left and simply say '*Kop jai*'. As I saw the answering smiles on their faces I even began to think that my illness had been worth it. After all, I found myself thinking, who cares about the pros and cons of magic when everyone is so kind? In any case, where does one magic begin and another leave off? Had penicillin been discovered centuries back, it would undoubtedly have been called magic. The man who applied it would have been called a wizard and the hypo his magic wand.

5

ORDINATION AS A NOVICE

The day following the departure of the doctor and the upasikas who had meditated for my recovery, Lung Poh came to me and informed me that he would ordain me as samanera on the coming Saturday at 1 p.m. I should therefore divide my time between practice of the exercise and memorising the Pali and general instructions for the carrying out of the ordination ceremony.

I had spent much time before coming to Thailand in memorising both the samanera and bhikkhu ordinations, both from the aspect of intonation of the Pali and traditional sequence and also, which mattered more to me, from the aspect of the legal and other import of both ordinations. I had studied the Vinaya Pitaka or collection of books dealing with the discipline and legalities for all members of the Sangha. Much midnight oil had been burnt in becoming completely at home with all that was involved in those five volumes.

These thoughts running through my mind, I informed Lung Poh that I was already well-practised and could repeat the ceremony from memory without any necessary further work. He, however, with a smile, told me that first, before I made up my mind that I was sure of myself, I must study the Pali of the ceremony which Bhikkhu Thitavedo would place in my hands.

Whilst this point was being discussed, Thitavedo left the room and returned with a sheaf of neatly typed papers. These contained the whole of the ceremony transposed from Thai to Roman characters. On glancing at them I realised immediately that there were minor differences between my memorised version and that now in my hands. The general tenor was the same, but there were slight differences in the sequence and pronunciation. Considering the type of mind I had, I knew this would entail my erasing completely from my memory that which I had learned so patiently and re-learning according to the papers I had just received. I remember letting out a long sigh at the work which I could see before me, a sigh which was also weighted with the knowledge that once again I had thought I knew the answers, had crossed bridges before arriving at them and was therefore still, to use Thitavedo's words, a 'big head'.

Glancing up at both Lung Poh and the bhikkhu I raised my hands and held them widely spaced from my head, rather like a fisherman recounting the size of the one that got away, indicating to both that I realised my mistake. They both appreciated the joke and joined wholeheartedly in the ensuing laughter. Lung Poh then held forth on the necessity of retaining a sense of humour, how a sense of humour could help one to accept and deal with one's faults. Laughter was a good thing. Just because one was a bhikkhu or a samanera it didn't mean that one had to go around with a long face. The bhikkhu life was supposed to bring peace, happiness and understanding to a man. To bring a man to understanding of himself. A bhikkhu with an unhappy face was an unhappy bhikkhu. But on the other hand, it was also bad to laugh unnecessarily, to be uncontrolled in laughter. That could lead to hysterical behaviour and more suffering, because in such a state one could say and do things which one might later regret.

After the abbot left, Thitavedo and I spent some time in conversation together. There were many questions I wished to ask in reference to the ordination, particularly concerning the correct pronunciation of Pali. I had heard both Sinhalese and Burmese reciting Pali and to my ear they sounded different. The Sinhalese have a rising and falling, sing-song method of chanting Pali, fitting in grace notes and lengthening vowel sounds as and when the mood takes them. The Burmese on the other hand chant in a plain tone, rather nasally and without any apparent lip movement. From what I could gather from the code of discipline, Gotama had laid it down that the *Dhamma* or teaching should only be chanted in plain tone. If a man should be interested in the tune he made, he would be more concerned with that than with the meaning of the words. This rather led me to favour the Burmese method.

My questions were soon answered by Thitavedo who promptly chanted a long passage in Pali so that I could be sure of the pronunciation and tone required. He then requested that I also chant. This I did, and he appeared to be perfectly satisfied. So much so that he said, 'Brother, you sing Pali very fine. Have big voice. On ordination day you must use big voice then everybody very happy.'

I understood the latter part of his remarks very well. What he meant was that Thai people in general have rather high-pitched and quiet voices whereas my own was rather low-pitched and had plenty of volume, thanks to years of lecturing and public speaking without the aid of a microphone. His term 'big voice' meant simply that I had a strong voice.

He then continued to speak about the forthcoming ceremony and told me that he would come to see me on Friday, the night before the ceremony, accompanied by the first and second assistants to the abbot. These two would test me and ask questions, making quite sure that I knew both the whole of the ceremony and the full import of the life I would be undertaking. Meanwhile it would be best if I kept my mind in meditation for periods as long as possible.

During the rest of that week I divided my time so that I spent the morning, afternoon and early evening in practising the meditational exercise and the nights until 2 a.m. memorising for the ceremony. During meditational practice I discovered that odd things were beginning to happen. I found it increasingly easy to withdraw my attention to the final and seventh position, just above the navel. I also found that I could maintain quite sustained concentration on that area, until an irritating fear would arise in my mind that I was going to lose consciousness. Every time this happened I panicked. Sweating and trembling, I would go and look out of the windows before commencing again.

Gradually I managed to get beyond this fear and held concentration for much longer periods. This brought me to a point where I began to think that I was seeing things. Coloured designs, swirls, circles, even scenes and strange faces floated before my mind's eye. It was during one of these sessions that I had my first experience of the pinpoint of light which Lung Poh had intimated was to be found and concentrated upon.

I had been going through a particularly fantastic period in practice when momentarily everything went black. Then suddenly, there in the blackness stood a most brilliant point of light rather like a bright distant star. My attention automatically became riveted upon this. I had the impression that from the point of light came another, and another, and another, and so forth. How long that particular period lasted I am not sure. When I eventually opened my eyes I found that whilst I could see perfectly, for a moment I had no sense of feeling whatsoever. I could move neither arm, leg, head nor body. Feeling returned rapidly, however, together with the knowledge that I had severe cramp in both thighs.

With continued practice I found that I was able to sit for quite long periods and that all the fantasy ceased. I quickly found myself concentrated upon the point of light. Even during moments when I was taking refreshment I found that the mind would fall back to its state of withdrawal, focused on the point of light. I completely lost count of time and was quite surprised when Thitavedo banged on my door and announced that it was Friday evening – please to come out now as I must meet the two Theras or Elders who were the assistants to Lung Poh.

I opened the door of my room. Thitavedo stood waiting for me. He looked intently into my eyes for a moment, then placed his hands on my shoulders and said, 'Oh brother, you make Thitavedo very happy. You have made strong practice and have succeeded with exercise. You have found bright light. I know. Now you can go on very fast with Lung Poh. He be very pleased when I tell. Now we must go see Theras downstair.'

On the ground floor I met the two Elders. Each had been a bhikkhu for more than twenty years and was entitled to the affix Maha Thera, meaning Great Elder. They both looked extremely young with hardly a line on their faces. I remarked upon this and learned that they were each forty-two years old and had spent most of their lives in the Sangha. Each had become a samanera at the age of twelve.

I spent some four hours being questioned and instructed by these two Elders. Eventually they were satisfied and we all relaxed for a while over coffee and cigarettes. Before they left me that night they stressed the advice of Lung Poh and Thitavedo that I should hold my mind in meditation all the time now until the ordination was over. Thitavedo also left, and I settled down to a session of meditation which lasted throughout the night.

At 6.30 the next morning I was visited by a junior bhikkhu. Thitavedo told me that he had come to shave my head in preparation for the ordination ceremony. I went to the lower floor and sat on a stool close to a large water container, having first stripped to the waist.

The young bhikkhu came forward and raised his hands palms together level with his head. I was somewhat taken aback by this, as it was not the usual practice for a bhikkhu to pay this high form of respect to a layman. Traditionally, the respect of the layman went to the bhikkhu and never the reverse. Rising from my stool I intimated to the young bhikkhu that I could not receive his respect. Going down to my knees I bowed once to the floor in front of him. Again I sat on the stool and again the bhikkhu raised his hands in salutation. I turned to Thitavedo in desperation and found myself saying, in words similar to his own quaint English, 'Brother, what to do? Not proper for bhikkhu salute layman. How come he salute me?'

Thitavedo laughed outright and replied, 'Not to worry, brother. This Thai custom. He got to shave head with sharp knife and may break skin so some blood come. He raise his hands first to say sorry for damage which might come. Also in Thailand head highest part of body and we do not touch unless ask first.'

With this explanation I was somewhat relieved. The young bhikkhu began to sharpen his open hollow-ground razor on a stone. When he was satisfied with the sharpness of the edge he poured a scoop of water from the large earthen vessel over my head and began to shave.

With the first cutting sweep of the razor across my scalp I began to realise – I think for the first time – the kind of life I was about to undertake. Never again whilst in the robe would I be able to wear hair or eyebrows or beard. I had always thought that the loss of these things would mean nothing to me. Yet as my thick mop of hair began to disappear, I found myself concerned with what I would look like. With the hair-laden water dripping off my nose and mixing with the sweat of my body, I realised what I was giving up.

I was taking on a life of poverty and celibacy. Never to be allowed to possess money nor anything other than three cotton robes, a begging bowl, razor, needle and cotton, drinking filter-cup and girdle. To be satisfied with food begged once each day as I walked barefoot. To sleep at the foot of a tree or on a low hard bench. To be satisfied with cow urine, honey, ghee or clarified butter and fruits as medicine, if required. All these things passed through my mind with great clarity as the shaving was completed. I wondered if I could stand such a life.

The young bhikkhu finished his task. I removed the rest of my clothing and washed all the loose hair from my body. Bhikkhu Thitavedo then handed me a set of white robes consisting of a sarong, white blouse and a shoulder cloth. The sarong, a garment of about seven feet in length and three feet in width, was worn around the body extending from the navel to just about level with the middle of the calves. The garment was wrapped around the body, the two open ends being brought together edgewise and then, by a series of concertina folds, brought to the front of the body and tucked into a belt. The shoulder cloth was worn loosely under the right shoulder and over the left.

I managed at long last, to the great amusement of both bhikkhus, to get myself properly attired in these unusual garments. I was now dressed in the traditional manner of a male lay follower of the Buddha. It was usual when a young Thai was going to be ordained that he deck himself out in all his native finery on presenting himself for the ceremony. With him would come his clan, celebrating with music, song and dance the great occasion. In my case, there were no representatives of my family or race, so it had been decided that I present myself in this simple white dress.

I took my leave of the young bhikkhu and with Thitavedo returned to my upper room. Thitavedo explained to me that the ceremony would be very quiet and that not many people would be present. He then said that it would be better that I take my meal and then wait in meditation until some of my Thai supporters and friends came to fetch me. I was to follow them and they would tell me what to do. He himself would be in the pagoda all the time during the ceremony and would translate where necessary. With that he left me to my own devices.

At 12.30 he returned to inform me that it was time for me to leave for the ceremony. On the ground floor I found waiting for me the friends who had met me at the airport. They had brought their families with them and made a very colourful scene. Everyone was smiling and appeared to be very happy. Khun Sudhon, my guarantor, Khun Sanoh and Khun Suang led me out of the house. Lined up in front of the entrance were some fifty white-robed, shaven-headed upasikas. Each bore flowers and small gifts. Behind these were about a hundred lay people, men, women and children. My friends and Bhikkhu Thitavedo led me to the rear of this gathering and then placed in my hands lotus flowers, lighted tapers and sweet-smelling joss sticks. These I had to carry between my joined palms which were raised chest high.

Thitavedo told me that my party, led by the upasikas, would now move off to the pagoda, or *bot* as it is known in Thailand. We would make a procession three times round the bot keeping our right shoulders towards the building. I would then enter by the eastern door, first having knelt before the *sima* stone. This stone was one of six which marked the legal boundaries of the bot. Here I was to ask for permission to enter.

'Not to worry,' my friend said, 'you remember everything. But keep the mind, brother. Keep the mind on bright mark all the time. Not to let the mind wander or watch the people. Keep the mind fixed in meditation so when you come to Lung Poh mind at peace and easy to talk to. Not to suffer, brother. Not to feel all by yourself now. I look after you and Lung Poh very kind and very closely by like with you. When you finish ordination then you wear robe like me and we can have much more closely by like in same language of brothers. So, now you go. I hop around like firefly all time not far from you.'

The procession began to move off. For a moment, as I gazed down at the flowers, tapers and joss sticks in my hands, I struggled with almost overpowering emotion. Except for this fine bhikkhu, a man I had known for such a short time yet who treated me like a brother, I had no one in the world to whom I could turn in this great moment, a moment of literally stepping off into the unknown.

I looked down again at my hands and focused my attention on the lighted taper. Almost immediately there came into my mind the words *samma arahan*, followed by the pinpoint of light. From there on I was as a man who walked as two. One part of me walked and acted as required automatically. The other listened and watched in a completely detached manner, registering all that went on but in no way reacting from a personal point of view. The sensation was as near as I had ever come to date to equilibrium or equanimity. There was an awareness of large crowds, of movement. Of hot paving stones under my bare feet – stones heated by a tropical sun yet causing no pain. I could feel the sweat coursing down my body, running down my back and between my legs, the white robes sticking to me and impeding my movements. Yet I had no feeling of discomfort.

As lotus petals were strewn in my path the procession eventually halted at the eastern entrance to the bot, having completed three circumnavigations. A hush fell over the crowd as I came to my knees before the sima stone. Placing my flowers, joss sticks and tapers beside me, I proceeded to make the triple salutation, bowing my head to the ground each time. I remember standing and hearing my voice as if from a great distance begin to chant: '*Ukasa vandami bhante, sabbam aparadham khamatha me bhante. Maya katam puññam samina anumoditabbam; samina katam puññam mayham databbam. Sadhu, sadhu, anumodami.*'

These words were so important to me. I had always had an affinity with the sounds both of Pali and Sanskrit. Something in me warmed as I listened to or uttered the vowels and consonants of these ancient languages, which in some respects were like Italian. Whilst the sounds of this beautiful language could be translated, the result would never carry the warmth and feeling of the original: 'Allow me, I respect and salute you, venerable sir. May you, venerable sir, pardon me all my faults. Benefits obtained by me should be shared by you, venerable sir. Whatever benefits are attained by you should be shared with me. So be it, it is good, I will so share.'

As I uttered those words I was standing not before an edifice built to house an image in replica of a famous teacher, but in a jungle glade facing a clearing bounded and marked out by six trees. My words were uttered to Siddhattha Gotama, the teacher and founder of the Way. In paying my respects to him, I was uttering my willingness to share everything of the life to come with him, asking him to put aside any faults of mine which had arisen through lack of understanding or respect.

I was led from the sima stone, still with the feeling of being back in the time of the founder of this way of life I was about to undertake, through the eastern entrance of the bot. The whole floor area was crowded with people. Seated on the raised platform were twenty-four senior bhikkhus, facing each other twelve a side. Between these two rows of yellow-robed figures, as if at the head of an avenue, and directly below the huge Buddha figure, sat Lung Poh, abbot of Wat Paknam.

My friends and supporters led me to the right-hand side of the platform facing the Buddha figure. Again I knelt and paid triple salutation. Then I rose to my feet and repeated the same Pali words I had spoken at the sima stone. I was directed to the eastern end of the platform, which I mounted, sitting down on the carpet facing the mass of lay people. I came to my knees and raised my hands in salutation to the assembled gathering, bowing my head to the ground. Holding out my hands I received from my supporters and friends in the assembly a set of yellow robes. The act signified my utter dependence in future on the goodwill of the laity for my means of sustenance.

Having received the robes I turned about and made my way through the two ranks of bhikkhus until I came face to face with the abbot. Still on my knees and still holding the robes resting across my open hands, I moved in close and offered the robes to Lung Poh. When he had taken them I bowed three times to the ground. Then rising to my feet I repeated the incantation in Pali for the third time. Any act or motion in the Sangha had to be uttered three times before it became legal. If the assembly of bhikkhus remained silent the act was then accepted and legal. If, however, someone questioned any point of order before the triple saying was complete, then the whole process had to be gone through again, or the applicant refused permission to go further at the moment.

In my case the assembly remained silent through each of the incantations, so I was instructed to proceed. I knelt in front of the abbot, saluted once again, then rose to my feet. Raising my hands, palms joined, to my head, I chanted in Pali: '*Ukasa karunam katva pabbajjam detha me bhante.*' Then, coming to my knees: '*Aham bhante, pabbajjam yacami. Dutiyampi aham bhante pabbajjam yacami. Tatiyampi aham bhante pabbajjam yacami.*' 'Venerable sir, may you have compassion on me and grant to me the novitiate. With your permission, venerable sir, I beg admission as a novice. For the second time, venerable sir, I beg admission as a novice. For the third time, venerable sir, I beg admission as a novice.'

Still kneeling and facing the abbot I pointed to the robes which he held and chanted: '*Sabbadukkha nissarana Nibbana sacchi karanatthaya imam kasavam gahetva pabbajetha mam bhante, anukampam upadaya.*' 'Venerable sir, will you take these yellow robes and grant me the novitiate for the purpose of ending all suffering and attaining Nibbana thereby.'

Holding out my hands I then chanted three times: '*Sabbadukkha nissarana Nibbana sacchi karanatthaya etam kasavam datva pabbajetha mam bhante, anukampam upadaya.*' 'Venerable sir, give to me the yellow robes and the novitiate for the purpose of ending all suffering and attaining Nibbana thereby.'

The abbot placed the bundle of robes across my outstretched arms. Holding my hands he uttered the words, '*Samma arahan, na?*' This I knew to mean that I must now strive to attain concentration in preparation for receiving the traditional *Kammatthana* or object of meditation. All Buddhist meditation revolves around the concepts of impermanence, unrest and soullessness, pertaining to all phenomena mental and physical, and the traditional objects for meditation based upon release from these states are the man's own body and mind.

I looked up into Lung Poh's eyes as he began to chant the words which I had to repeat word for word, backward and forward, after him. '*Kesa – Loma – Nakha – Danta – Taco. Taco – Danta – Nakha – Loma – Kesa.*' 'Hair of the head – Hair of the body – Nails – Teeth – Skin.'

As these words were uttered and repeated by myself I had the feeling that I was as if peering down a microscope into a pool of bright light. I saw clearly and much magnified the hairs of the head and body, the teeth and skin, and became utterly absorbed in contemplation of a single hair and its construction.

From that point onward my mind moved through a process for which it had obviously been conditioned by the initial exercise. As if by choice I came back to the original meditation mark, a pinpoint of light. Out of it grew a body which I accepted naturally as my own. Again back to the mark and again a body. This process took place sixteen times in all, appearing to happen at four different levels, with four points of light followed by the sense of seeing or being aware of four bodies. At the final level the first two bodies were still what I would call my own. The third, however, was that of my teacher, Lung Poh. He appeared to be smiling and pointing onward.

Again my mind turned to the pinpoint of light and from it bloomed forth like a flower a figure of the Buddha. It was nothing like the images which I had seen so many times. The figure was so utterly human, the face smiling and kindly. For a while it seemed to me that some interchange was going on between the figure and myself, not in words as such but in a sense of complete understanding. When the figure disappeared I knew not.

I was just becoming aware of a sense of having been at utter peace, a feeling that I had indeed never existed, that the whole of what I called my life was but a dream, a dream which I had taken with such seriousness to be reality – when suddenly my eyes were open and again I saw before me the abbot and around me the twenty-four bhikkhus. Every one of them, including Lung Poh and Thitavedo, appeared to be very happy with whatever had been going on.

I now knew that I must rise, pay my respects to the assembly of monks and retire so that I might change from the white robes of the layman to the yellow robes of the novice. I found that I could not move. I looked down at my legs folded in the meditation posture. I struck them with my hands, but could feel nothing. They felt utterly dead and completely beyond my control. Two bhikkhus and two laymen came forward and literally carried me to the back of the bot behind the great Buddha figure. Here my legs were massaged back to life. I was stripped of my lay robes, the sweat was wiped from my naked body, and then I was dressed in the three yellow robes, with my right shoulder left exposed. I was then led back to the eastern end of the bot to proceed with the ceremony.

I knelt down before a Maha Thera (the senior of the two who came to test me) and paid respects three times. Standing, I asked of him, just as I had of Lung Poh, that he might forgive me any faults in my attitude towards him, and that we might share the gains of my new life. Then came the process of asking for the three refuges and the ten precepts or rules of training for a novice. I again knelt and began to chant the requests and responses in Pali.

I repeated three times after the officiating bhikkhu: *'Namo Tassa Bhagavato Arahato Samma Sambuddhassa'* 'Praise to the Lord, the Arahant, the Self-Enlightened Buddha.' The bhikkhu then asked: *'Ya maham vadami tam vadehi?'* 'Are the respects and salutations complete?' I replied: *'Ukasa ama bhante'* 'By your leave, yes, venerable sir.' The bhikkhu then began to chant the *Sarana* or refuges, which I repeated after him three times, taking refuge in the Buddha, the Teaching and the Sangha. He again questioned me with *'Saranam gamanam nit-thitam?'* 'Are the refuges complete, finished?' To which I responded once again: 'By your leave, yes, venerable sir.'

Then followed the rules of training, the first five being the same as the lay precepts with the exception of the third. Instead of stating *'Kamesu micchacara veramani sikkhapadam samadiyami'* 'I undertake the rule of training to refrain from wrongful indulgence in sensual pleasures', it became *'Abrahmacariya veramani sikkhapadam samadiyami'*. This could be best described as meaning 'I undertake the rule of training to refrain from any form of sexual indulgence.'

Then followed the five extra rules: *'Vikalabhojana veramani sik-khapadam samadiyami.'* 'I undertake the rule of training to refrain from taking a meal at the wrong time' (literally, taking a meal after midday by the sun).

'*Naccagitavadita visuka dassana veramani sikkhapadam samadiyami.*' 'I undertake the rule of training to refrain from attending places of entertainment, shows, singing, dancing and plays.'

'*Malagandha vilepana dharana mandana vibhusanatthana veramani sikkhapadam samadiyami.*' 'I undertake the rule of training to refrain from adorning the body with garlands, perfumes, powders or jewellery.'

'*Uccasayana mahasayana veramani sikkhapadam samadiyami.*' 'I undertake the rule of training to refrain from using high and luxurious beds' (literally, to use a hard low bed or the ground).

'*Jata rupa rajata pattigahana veramani sikkhapadam samadiyami.*' 'I undertake the rule of training to refrain from using or amassing gold or silver' (literally, not to possess or handle any form of money or store any form of wealth).

With these precepts completed to the officiating bhikkhu's satisfaction I repeated three times: '*Imani dasa sikkhapadani*' 'I undertake these ten rules of training.'

I again moved through the lines of bhikkhus and presented myself kneeling before the abbot. I asked of him: '*Ukasa karunam datva nissayam detha me bhante.*' Literally: 'Please, venerable sir, out of compassion give to and explain to me the supports or modes of living for the bhikkhu life.'

Lung Poh then proceeded to explain to me that I should always try to be satisfied with whatever conditions I found myself in. To be content if necessary with robes made from rags gathered from the burial ground, for such were the robes of Gotama. To be content with food gathered once a day by begging my way barefoot. Whilst there were invitation meals from kind lay people and at times food would be brought to me, I was to maintain the ideal of the begged meal. Food was but fuel for the body. I must learn to take rich and poor food, and sometimes go without food, with equal equanimity, always bearing in mind the words 'I take this food not for sensual pleasure but just to keep the body going that I might strive for enlightenment'. Further, I should be prepared where necessary to be satisfied with the medicines cow urine, honey, ghee and fruits. To be satisfied with a sleeping place at the foot of a tree in the jungle.

Having listened intently to my instructions from Lung Poh I then asked of him: '*Upaccayo me bhante hohi*' 'I ask you, venerable sir, to be my teacher.' To which he replied: '*Opajikam pasadike na sampadehi*' 'There is no impediment if such be your wish.' To which I responded: '*Sadhu bhante*' 'It is well, so be it, venerable sir.' With this last utterance the ceremony as such was completed and I sat before the bhikkhus and the abbot as a samanera, a novice in training prior to becoming a bhikkhu.

For the first time, I was able to look round the interior of the bot. I realised that the ordination ceremony had not after all been such a small and private affair. Most of the available floor space was taken up and the place was fairly packed with people.

I was beckoned by an elderly man to come to the far end of the platform. Thitavedo told me that I must now go as requested so that I might receive gifts from the lay people as was the custom on such occasions. I went over and sat down in front of the old fellow – I later learned that he was known as Khun Ek, an elder of the lay committee who helped to maintain Wat Paknam. Here I received small gifts such as toothbrushes and paste, cigarettes, matches, candles and a bathing cloth. Small gifts were then offered to all the bhikkhus who had officiated at the ceremony. As each gift was given the donor bowed three times before me in respect and salutation. It was only the restraining hand of Thitavedo which prevented me from returning the salutations in like manner.

'Not to do like this, brother. All the time just say to everyone "*Ayu vanno sukham balam*". This mean, "May you have old age, good complexion, happy and plenty strong".'

On hearing this I laughed outright, laughter in which everyone in the pagoda joined, including Thitavedo. He then turned to me again and enquired, 'You understand, brother?'

'Yes, I understand, sir. You mean, "May you have long life, health, strength and happiness".'

Thitavedo laughed again and said, 'Brother, you translate my English very well. Now, you say to the people like I tell you. Use big voice then everybody very happy.'

At each salutation or gift I uttered in tones loud enough for all to hear, '*Ayu vanno sukham balam*'. And indeed everyone was happy. Every face in that pagoda had a smile. It seemed to me that every smile was a smile of welcome, of understanding. It was as if they were trying to tell me that they had taken me to their hearts. That from now on I was truly one of themselves.

Again I returned to the centre of the platform and sat facing the assembled bhikkhus and Lung Poh. Thitavedo placed a large glass of water in my hands and instructed me that I must pour this in a steady stream into a glass bowl, whilst the bhikkhus chanted *Anumodana*, the thanksgiving for gifts. He explained that the water represented the pure mind, and that whilst the chant was going on I should hold in mind the thought that I was sharing my good fortune with everyone, and bear in mind my parents, family and the many friends who had helped to make this day possible for me.

The bhikkhus began to chant:

> 'Yatha vari vaha, pura paripurenti sagaram.
> Evam eva ito dinnam petanam upakappati.
> Icchitam patthi tam tumham khippam eva samijjhatu.
> Sabbe parentu sankappa.
> Cando pannaraso yatha.
> Mani jotiraso yatha.
>
> Sabbitiyo vivajjantu; sabba rogo vinassatu.
> Mate bhavat vantarayo; sukhi dighayuko bhava.
> Abhivadanasi lissa niccam vuddha paja jino,
> cattaro Dhamma vaddhanti;
> Ayu vanno sukham balam.'

The water flowed in a steady stream from jug to bowl and with it my mind turned back to my parents, to my life prior to these moments. Names and faces in a never-ending stream flooded my mind. People I had known and loved. People whom I had disliked. Friends and acquaintances. All were there. I knew in that moment that all these had helped in their own way to make this experience possible. I acknowledged my good fortune and my debt to these people present in my world. And my mind was at rest and at peace.

The ceremony ended, and all the assembled bhikkhus turned and faced the figure of the Buddha and three times paid their respects, as I did myself. Then, led by Lung Poh, we left the bot, myself as the most junior of the gathering coming last.

As I left the bot men and women bowed before me. Some placed their foreheads on my bare feet and stroked them with their hands. Little children took my hands in theirs, chanting in sing-song fashion: 'Phra Farang, Phra Farang' – 'Phra' being a term of great respect usually reserved for the bhikkhu. Literally it meant 'lord'.

In such a way I was led back to my house across the pagoda compound. When I arrived I found the ground floor packed with people waiting to see and talk with me. Thitavedo came to my rescue by telling them that I must have some rest. Escorting me to the upper floor he made me sit down in a chair and called one of the boys. He then told me that I must be very tired as the time was late. It was 6.30 in the evening and the ordination had been one of the longest he remembered. Lung Poh had seen that my mind was right and had given me a very long instruction in meditation which had taken me very far and had lasted four hours. He explained that the abbot did not usually do this and must have thought very highly of my potential to take me so far.

I told him that I had very little understanding of what had gone on, only that I had felt impelled to follow some sort of command. Was it he who had translated the instructions for me? No, it was not he who had instructed me. Whilst he had been there to act as interpreter, it appeared to him that I always immediately obeyed Lung Poh's command without waiting for the translation. Even before he had the opportunity to begin to translate I was already giving the signal with my hand that I understood, and that I had arrived at the point to which I had been instructed. But no more talk – I must drink some coffee and rest for a while.

Two of the boys brought coffee and China tea. The latter was in a beautiful cloisonné pot carried in a bucket-shaped outer container lined with thick quilted silk, the whole completed by a beautifully embroidered and quilted cover. Both boys knelt before me and three times bowed to the ground. Then, pouring both tea and coffee, they presented me with both cups and offered me both the coffee pot and the container of China tea. Taking each article in both hands they gave them to me. This was done not only with the coffee and tea, but also with cigarettes and matches. They then retired a few feet and sat smiling at me.

My mind was absolutely bursting with questions but each time I made any attempt to talk Thitavedo held up his hand and stopped me. 'You rest now. Make the mind rest. Plenty time to ask question. Still have busy time to come later.'

I settled back in my chair and swilled my mouth with the tea and spat it out into the spittoon. Then I took a long draught of hot and sweet black coffee, lit a cigarette and fell into a drowsy reverie. The past appeared to be utterly unreal, the present so real and yet so fleeting. Somehow the only real thing about my life was the past few days. I felt utterly at home with both the people and the country in which I now found myself, more at home than I had ever felt in my life. I said to myself that I would remain with these kind and tolerant people for the rest of my life. And immediately realised that such a promise was nonsense.

The two boys came over to me and began to massage my legs and I realised once again how painful they were. I tried to stop them, to get them to leave me in peace, but they just smiled and continued. Thitavedo explained that it was necessary for me to feel well, and that my legs were being massaged as I was not used to sitting for a long period as I had that afternoon. I must be got ready, he said, as soon I had to go down to the people who were waiting in the main room downstairs.

The massage completed and my legs feeling much more as if they belonged to me, I went to the lower room with Thitavedo. It was crowded with men and women both old and young, children of both sexes and babies in arms. My friend the bhikkhu and I sat down before the gathering, and one after another they came forward and paid their respects. Mothers and fathers brought their babies and asked me to touch their children's heads. Such golden creatures they were, mainly naked except for a silver or golden chain around the waist, ending in a tiny silver or gold apron across the pubic area.

One old lady asked Thitavedo that I might chant again, as my chanting in the pagoda had made her so happy. Please, could Phra Farang chant some more and make her more happy. When the bhikkhu informed me of the request I was only too happy to comply. I could not as yet speak to these people in their native tongue but at least I could speak to them in the language of their Buddhist way of life. I began to chant the Metta Sutta, the sutta of amity, of loving-kindness, a sutta which had always brought great peace to my own troubled mind. Automatically my voice began to make the sounds which were mere words but which to me and my new friends meant so much more.

'*Karaniyam atthakusalena – yan tam santam padam abhisamecca.*
Sakko uju ca suju ca – suvaco c'assa mudu anatimani.
Santussako ca subharo ca – appakicco ca sallahukavutti
santindriyo ca nipako ca – appagabbho kulesu ananugiddho.
Na ca khuddam samacare kiñci – yena viññu pare upavadeyyum
sukhino va khemino hontu – sabbe satta bhavantu sukhitatta.
Ye keci panabhut' atthi – tasa va thavara va anavasesa
digha va ye mahanta va – majjhima rassaka anukathula,
dittha va ye va adittha – ye ca dure vasanti avidure,
bhuta va sambhavesi va – sabbe satta bhavantu sukhitatta.
Na paro param nikubbetha – natimaññetha katthacinam kañci,
vyarosana patighasañña – nañña maññassa dukkham iccheyya.
Mata yatha niyam puttam – ayusa ekaputtam anurakkhe,
evam pi sabbabhutesu – manasam bhavaye aparimanam.
Mettañ ca sabba lokasmim – manasam bhavaye aparimanam
uddham adho ca tiriyan ca – asambadham averam asapattam.
Tittham caram nisinno va – sayano va yavat' assa vigatamiddho
etam satim adhittheyya – brahmam etam viharam idha-m-ahu.
Ditthiñ ca anupagamma silava – dassanena sampanno
kamesu vineyya gedham – na hi jatu gabbhaseyyam punar eti' ti.'

'This is what should be accomplished by he who is wise in
his own welfare and would attain calm.

He should be upright, strenuous and sincere in his ways,
without pride and easily contented.

He should not be encumbered with things of the world. He
should be wise but in no way arrogant, his senses under
control. He should beg his round without greed.

He should do no mean thing nor act in any way that wise
men might reprove him. May all beings live happily with
minds at peace.

All living beings, no matter if they be weak or strong or in
any size or shape; whether they be visible or invisible,
near or far, born or to be born. May all beings live happily
with minds at peace.

Let him not deceive another nor despise a person in any
state. Let him not wish harm to another in anger or
hatred.

Just as a mother would protect her only child at the risk of
her life, even so should he cultivate limitless goodwill in
his mind for all beings.

His thoughts of amity and kindness should encompass the
whole world without limit. So let him cultivate an infinite
goodwill.

Whether he be standing, walking, sitting or lying down,
during all his hours awake he should be mindful, for this
way of living, they say, is the best in the world.

Giving up vain discussion, of good habit and insight, freed
from attachment to sense desires he comes not again to
birth.'

As I finished the chant the people showed their appreciation with
'*Sadhu, sadhu!*' 'It is good, so be it!' Everyone in the room looked happy,
all were smiling. One dear old lady sat rocking herself backward and
forward, smiling valiantly through a cascade of tears which were
coursing unrestrained down her age-creased cheeks. Why, I asked
Thitavedo, was she crying? The old lady and my friend exchanged
some words. He turned to me and said that she was crying because she
was so happy. She had a feeling of great *piti* or overpowering joy. Tears
are like that, I suppose. When the mind and body are thrust beyond all
reasonable means of expression by the extreme of either happiness or
anguish, the only outlet left is tears.

6

MEETINGS WITH
THAI PEOPLE

We remained in that room on the lower floor of my house until eleven
that evening, a happy evening spent answering the direct and
uninhibited questions of an intensely interested audience. When the
last visitor had left Thitavedo and myself retired to the upper floor.
There were many questions which I wanted to put to him in respect of
the meditation period during the ordination ceremony.

As soon as we reached the upper floor I took over the duties of a
junior. A samanera is junior to all bhikkhus. I saw to it that his room
was tidy and ready to be slept in, drew a chair to the table, asked him to
sit down and gave him coffee. Having seen to all his wants I also sat
down with coffee and a cigarette.

A number of Westerners would, I suppose, think it strange and out
of keeping that a bhikkhu or samanera should smoke. Yet it is purely
through ignorance of the bhikkhu life – and of course the ever-present
desire of many Westerners to project on to others austerities which
they think they should apply to themselves and yet have not the
courage to carry out. There is no rule which says that a samanera or
bhikkhu may not smoke. Whilst he is literally a beggar owning nothing
and not allowed to deal with money, he may still accept gifts. And
should someone give him cigarettes, he will accept them, either to be
smoked by himself or if he is a non-smoker, to be given to someone
who does.

Smoking is of course much older in the East than the West. Long
before the days of Sir Walter Raleigh forms of smoking were being
indulged in throughout India. Even in the Bhikkhu Vinaya or Bhikkhu
Rules of Discipline (a work which in its present form dates from the 5th
century B.C.) can be found the words: 'Anujanami Bhikkhave,
dhumanetta dhumam pathum' 'Bhikkhus, I allow you to inhale smoke
through a smoking pipe.' There can of course be over-indulgence, but

this is controlled by the dependence upon the freely given gift. No gifts of cigarettes – no smoking. No food – no eating. As simple as that.

All the time I had been carrying out my duties for Thitavedo he had sat with a quizzical smile on his face. And when I had taken my seat he said, 'Brother, not necessary to do like this. We very closely by like brothers and you older than me, not to feel like servant to me.'

To me rules were rules and had to be carried out, and I said so in no uncertain terms. He laughed for quite a time at my remarks, then said, 'Brother, you very absolute, know Vinaya very well. But I had to make some test to find if you understand and if you willing to carry out rules complete. But, brother, you not completely under Vinaya, you only samanera yet. But you do good to carry out full Vinaya. Good experience for when you come bhikkhu like me.' I thanked him for his advice and then began to ask the questions which had been in my mind ever since the ordination ceremony had been completed.

Why had Lung Poh kept me in meditation for four hours? What was the purpose of what appeared to me to be four levels of fantastic experience carried out through what was to me a purely imaginary sixteen bodies? Why had I seen the Buddha? Everyone knew that he had died two and a half thousand years ago. Surely I was not going to be asked to believe that he was still alive in some remote realm and that I should therefore treat him as a god?

Thitavedo smiled at my outburst. He explained that of course no one expected me to believe that the Buddha was living in some heaven or that I had to believe in him as a god. Such a question did not arise. Even Gotama Buddha himself had said that he was not to be treated as a god and that the question of whether he lived or did not live after death was ridiculous. No, that was not the purpose of the meditation during the ceremony. It was purely that Lung Poh had seen that my mind was well concentrated and had taken the opportunity to give me direct instruction whilst I was in a peaceful frame of mind and not my usual questioning and argumentative self. The very basis of the experience was to guide me to the levels of my own mind. The various bodies were to be searched for so that even more intense concentration could be gained.

He could not tell me more, however. He had told me enough. What I now had to do was to practise the new exercise time and time and time again. By so doing I would make the necessary discoveries for myself. When I did make what I thought to be discoveries I could go to him and tell him what I had found out, both about myself and the teaching itself. The way of the Buddha was not just a way which had to be believed. Belief did not enter into it. Everything had to be tested, and the only way in which it could be tested was by means of meditation.

Books and theories were all very well, but the Dhamma, the law or teaching of the Buddha, was a matter of personal experience. I must come to my own personal experience through meditation. Even supposing that we agreed upon philosophical theories concerning the teaching, I would still be no nearer understanding myself. All that I would have was that two men agreed that such and such was true concerning some aspect of the teaching. But agreement between us did not necessarily make it true. The teaching of the Buddha was for application to oneself and not a matter of theories. The best thing for me to do was to work hard at meditation.

I should also remember that I now had to learn completely the Pali for the bhikkhu ordination of *Upasampada*. There was no saying when Lung Poh would set the date of my final ordination, but I should be ready. The best thing for me at the moment, however, was that I went to bed as the time was very late. I must remember also that I was a robe-wearer now and that I could not waste too much time in sleep. The more time spent in meditation practice the better.

Also I must remember that now I was a samanera I would have to practise a special meditation every time I put on and took off my robes. The same applied when I was retiring to my bench to sleep and when I arose; whenever I partook of medicine or food or was receiving food into my begging bowl. I must be up in the morning before dawn so that I would be ready when Thitavedo or some other bhikkhu took me out for the first time on the begging round. All the time when I was begging food, no matter where I was – city, town, village or jungle settlement – I was to keep the eyes on the bowl and carry out the meditation. Even when people gave me food I was not to look up from the bowl, neither was I to thank them. I must try always not to speak or break concentration during the whole round.

I took my leave of the bhikkhu and retired to my room at 1.30 a.m. It was only then that I realised fully how tired I was. Taking off my *civaram* or outer robe I laid myself down on the teak bench, well and truly ready for sleep. But sleep would not come. The mind appeared to be more intent on again going over the events of the day, trying to reason out the processes involved in my new meditational experience. I managed with a struggle to drag the mind away only to lie awake listening to innumerable new sounds.

I was in the middle of trying to make up my mind what kind of animal it was that kept making a noise which sounded like 'Tu-kow, Tu-kow' when I realised that I had already forgotten some of the things which Thitavedo had impressed upon me before retiring. I had taken off a robe without any thought and thrown myself on my bed with even less, the only concern in my mind being sleep. There was nothing for it but to get off the bed and start all over again. I carried out the set meditations as instructed and again went back to bed. I must have fallen asleep straight away, for the next thing I remember was waking again and finding that it was already 4.30 in the morning.

Knowing that I only had an hour in which to carry out both meditation duties and get ready for the morning begging round, I resisted the desire to go back to sleep, rose somewhat stiffly from my hard bed and then bathed. Having carried out the duties as well as I could remember I decided to robe myself ready for going out.

Struggle as I might I could not get the robe to go on correctly. I had counted the proverbial ten more than once and my patience was becoming somewhat ragged. I cursed myself roundly for not being able to master getting dressed. To make matters worse the efforts I had made with robing had made me sweat very heavily, so much so that the robes stuck to my body as if glued in place. The more I tugged and pulled the worse matters became. The fact that I was trying to put on only two robes – I was allowed to lay one aside after dawn – made not the slightest difference.

I was in the middle of another attempt when Thitavedo came to my room asking if I were ready yet. I let him in and taking one glance at my state, he laughed until the tears came to his eyes.

'Not so much trouble putting on robe, brother,' he said. 'You just watch. You see I do very quick.'

He stripped himself of his civaram, a large but lightweight patch-work robe, and said, 'You take off robe like me and we start together to put him on again.' I stripped off my robe and watching Thitavedo, tried to emulate everything he did.

Firstly he turned the robe inside out and then placed it round his body, bringing the two open ends together in front of him. He then proceeded to roll the ends together across his chest from left to right. I tried to do likewise. When the robe was firmly rolled tight to his chest, he wriggled it down to his feet, turned the roll outwards and then under his left foot. He then pulled what had been the bottom of the robe up level with his chest and taking the open end, he rolled it inwards from left to right. Pulling the now tube-like structure up above his head, he held it by the roll in his left hand and, with his right hand inside the robe, began to tighten the roll so that the whole robe came tightly to the body. Pulling up the robe from the bottom, with his right hand he arranged the roll so that it came to position on the left side of the body. Then gripping the roll under the left armpit, he turned the rest of it round the left arm in a kind of sleeve. When he stood erect, the robe completely covered him from neck to ankle, the right arm under the robe, the left outside but covered by the twined sleeve.

During the whole of this process I had tried to carry out every step which the bhikkhu had taken, hoping of course that I would arrive at the point where he was now – in a perfectly wrapped robe. On looking down at myself I realised that I resembled nothing better than a dishevelled bundle of rags. To make my discomfiture even worse, at that precise moment I felt my girdle come undone and my undergarment (or *sabang* as the Thais call it) fell in a heap at my feet, leaving me standing precariously covered with one very insecure robe.

Thitavedo looked at me in mock despair, shook his head and said very seriously, 'Brother, I make no magic. I do just like you see me do and my robe on perfect. Trouble with you is that you too angry and don't watch closely like or your robe fine like mine.'

This was the final straw to the camel's back of my mind and I exploded. I protested that I wasn't angry – not me – I never lost my temper. I had paid strict attention to everything he had done. I made all sorts of excuses for my failure to robe myself. When I paused for breath to continue my outburst I happened to look up at the bhikkhu. He was sitting there looking at me in a highly amused fashion, his face literally creased with smiles.

Before I had the chance of saying another word he pointed to me and said, 'That much better, brother. Most of your anger out now. Nothing wrong in being angry or making to admit that you are. Thing to remember is that when angry, can't think straight. Angry making very dangerous, can get into all sorts of big bother. Now, the anger gone like steam in boiler too long. You feel better now. Come close by to me and I help you with the robe.'

With his expert assistance I was quickly robed. Placing my iron begging bowl over my right shoulder hanging by its carrying strap, I followed Thitavedo down to the lower floor and out into the open.

As we stepped out from our house I could hear the first gong telling us that the sun had been seen above the horizon and that we could go on our rounds. The gong, about two feet in length, was situated at the top of a wooden tower forty feet above the ground. Here a bhikkhu or samanera would station himself each morning, facing the east. As soon as he could see the rim of the rising sun just above the horizon he would begin to beat the gong with a heavy wooden baton, at first with slow even strokes, then gradually working up the speed until there was a continuous sound. He then let the beating cease, only to start again from the beginning. Three times the process took place, after which he would come down from his lofty vigil and take his place with the rest on the begging round.

I did not have to go far for food that morning. In fact only half a dozen steps, for people had come specially to place food in my bowl.

With bowed head and keeping my eyes on the ground I followed Thitavedo until he stopped by the first group. Here, I did as he. I lifted the robe and drew my bowl round to the front of my body. Removing the brass lid and placing my two heels together I leant forward and presented the open bowl. All I saw from then on was hands, all kinds of hands. Old hands, young hands, clean hands, dirty hands, the hands of men, women and children – all placing with great care some kind of food in my metal bowl.

As I walked my silent way the words of the meditation on food hummed through my mind continuously. 'I take not this food for sensual pleasure, nor to glorify the body that it may become strong and good to look upon. I take it just to keep the body going in health, that I might strive with energy for the enlightenment which I seek.'

That morning on which I first begged, as Buddhist bhikkhus and samaneras have begged for over two and a half thousand years, something happened which had a very deep and lasting effect upon me. Returning from my very short round and picking my way carefully along the path to try and save my bare feet from as much damage as possible, I came to a small white-robed figure squatting by the side of the pathway. On looking closer I found it to be an old, very old woman, who was undoubtedly offering me food. I leaned forward, keeping my eyes on the proffered bowl, and into it I saw enter two scrawny old hands which dropped rice into the bowl. Next they produced a few morsels of dried fish. I then noticed that these same old hands were rummaging around in the food contained in the bowl in an effort to remove the dirt which had been carried there by them.

For a moment my stomach turned and I felt quite sick. Then I remembered that Lung Poh had instructed me that I must always accept food from a woman, no matter how old or young, as if I were accepting it from my mother. It mattered not whether the food was good or bad – the important thing was that it was a gift. I must learn to accept as it would be good for me, as I was a very proud man. It was good also for the giver because it taught them to think of others as well as themselves. I must remember that a man following the bhikkhu life was utterly dependent upon the lay folk for his welfare. Therefore I should learn to accept from all with equal poise and strive to be a bhikkhu strict in carrying out the rules and strong in learning and meditation. In this way were the lay folk repaid.

Yes, something happened to me that morning. I felt for the first time the interdependence which exists between people. To me there had been an overflowing of these people into my world. For the first time my barriers were down and with them went some of the blindness that had kept me in many ways apart from my fellow beings. It had come about through two old hands and the owner's sense of joy at giving, through Lung Poh's instruction and the sudden closeness – through his use of the word 'mother' in reference to all women – of my own mother.

We entered the compound of our house and Thitavedo and I sat on the ground and ate our meal from the bowls in silence. The meal finished, we rinsed out the bowls and turned them up to dry. We were just about to enter the house when three people came into the compound. It was Khun Ek, the old man who had helped me so much the day before, with his two sisters. They brought with them three large thermos flasks and glasses. Having paid their respects they poured out glasses of coffee from the flasks and presented them to us. Khun Ek then offered the inevitable cigarettes.

As we sat there chatting, other people were walking past the house, but on seeing that the bhikkhu and I were sitting out in the compound with visitors, they also came in and joined the party. This went on until there was a steady stream of people coming into the compound. As I looked around the continually enlarging gathering I realised that I had obviously become something of a showpiece – these people were coming mainly to have a look at the strange sight of a European in the yellow robes of a Buddhist.

One old fellow I remember particularly because he came and sat down immediately in front of me and proceeded to thoroughly examine me with his eyes from head to foot. What he saw apparently amused him very much. First he began to smile, finally he laughed outright. He pointed to my nose and then his own and indicated that my nose was longer than his. Thitavedo was also enjoying the situation. He said, 'Brother, old man think you look very funny. He also want to know what you think he look like.'

I looked again at the old man and found the impish twinkle in his old slanted eyes too much to resist. Turning to the bhikkhu I replied, 'Tell him that I think he also looks very funny.' This was translated to the old man and in fact to the whole gathering. On hearing this he laughed even more and I joined with him in the laughter. He then came very close to me and stroked my feet – a great compliment as I realised, for to a Thai the lowest part of the body is the foot. He then bowed his body low and three times brought his forehead down until it reached my feet. Taking my two hands in his he shook them warmly, and departed. That was the beginning for me of a long friendship. As the old boy left I felt how fortunate I was to have the opportunity of living among such frank, good-natured and uninhibited people.

We rose and entered the house after Thitavedo had explained to the people that I had much work to do and that I must now get back to my meditation. He said that it wasn't good for me to be disturbed too much as this would interfere with my concentration.

When we had arrived at our upper quarters and I had taken Thitavedo's robe and bowl and placed them safely away, I told him that I could see difficulties ahead for me if there were going to be crowds of people wanting to see me all day. I said that at the moment I didn't want to enter into social contact as it would waste a lot of my time. I wanted to spend all my time in meditation practice so that I might make as much progress as possible. I also wanted to work hard so that I might attain my higher and final ordination as a bhikkhu at the earliest possible date.

The bhikkhu agreed with everything I said and told me he was glad to hear me speak as I had. It was very easy to get caught up in social pursuits. Some bhikkhus did get so caught and spent most of their time talking with the people. But whilst the people were always happy to talk with a bhikkhu, and Thai people were very sociable, they greatly appreciated a man who was intent on mastering meditation. In fact they had much more respect for him. He would inform everyone of my wishes and they would understand and not encroach on my time.

7

VISIONS AND VOICES

From that day onward for a period of some five months I was not
disturbed. The local people even arranged for food to be brought to me
and presented at the house to save me time and trouble. I spent the
whole of that five months at meditation practice in my room, and left
the building only three times in a period of six months.

* * *

After Thitavedo had gone on his way, I entered my room and prepared
myself for practice. I found that I settled down easily to the first type of
exercise, attaining the pinpoint of light very rapidly. When, however, I
tried to continue with the process which had been given me during the
ordination ceremony, I failed dismally. I tried right through the
morning and far into the afternoon without success. I then decided to
give the matter some thought – to try to think out the system, to try to
find some clear-cut procedure which would impress the various steps
of the exercise indelibly on my mind so that it would take them without
being driven to it. I had learned from my practice of the initial exercise
that sheer brute force never brought results. I knew that it was no good
asking questions any more, and that even if I did ask Thitavedo would
only tell me to practise the new exercise without question. He would
say that I had to find my own answers, that of truth they would come
through the meditation alone and in no other way.

I remembered that Lung Poh had given names to the various levels
of the meditation which I undertook during the ceremony. As I sat and
thought about what had been said the names came to mind. The first
was *dipaya kaya*, the second *rupa brahma kaya*, the third *arupa brahma
kaya*, and the fourth *dhamma kaya*. The Pali terms and their values I
knew well enough, but as to their import I was completely in the dark. I
decided therefore to work out a verbal repetition which would impress
itself on my mind – a process which I had found to be successful at the
beginning of my training. This followed each pinpoint of light followed

by its respective body at each level, right up to the fourth and final level.

Throughout that night I kept up the repetition. Through the next day and night and the day and night which followed – until all that I could hear or think of was the repetition. On the third night, partly I suppose through lack of sleep, things began to happen. Each step of the exercise began to take form clearly in my mind. Even with my eyes open I could see the pinpoint of light and also various aspects of my own body projected in front of me. I got to the point where I could strip the body in stages of its skin and flesh and various organs until I was finally left with the skeleton. I even took that apart until there was nothing. Then I panicked. For a moment I felt that I had disappeared completely.

I sprang up and rushed to the window and looked out, only to find that I could see nothing as it was dark. But I heard a sound, loud and clear as if in the very room itself: 'Tu-kow – Tu-kow – Tu-kow'. I took this noise to be part of my now nightmare state. Surely this could be no animal cry? Realising that I was letting things get out of control I forced myself to sit down again and tried to attain some semblance of calm. To stop the quaking and trembling of my limbs and the pounding of my heart. All that happened was that my mind began to carry out the repetition, and I found myself back at the first level of bodies.

Again I opened my eyes, hoping to break away. I became aware that I was apparently not alone, for in the corner stood an old man. I yelled at him and he disappeared, only to be followed by other apparitions. At one point I saw myself out there with them, arguing with them and then being chased by them.

How I got out of my room I do not know but get out I did. I lit candles and poured myself coffee, dreading the thought that eventually I would have to return, no matter what happened. At one point I decided that I would wait for Thitavedo and ask him what was the cause of my situation. As quickly as I came to the decision I knew that it was the way to defeat. If I didn't go back to my room on my own at once and face out the situation I would never be able to make the attempt to follow the exercise again.

I went into the room with a candle and my coffee, sat down and lit a cigarette. Again my mind fell into a highly concentrated state. Opening my eyes I saw the figure of Lung Poh, smiling and reassuring. He spoke to me, or at least so it seemed.

'Now do you understand, Tan William, *dipaya kaya?*' – William being one of my lay names and *tan* meaning brother – '*Dipaya* means double or fantasy. *Kaya* means body. So the first level could mean the area where the double of your physical walks, the body you use when dreaming. It could also be called in your language the psychic area.

'All over the world there have been people who say that they can see and converse with spirits. Here such abilities are called *iddhi*. They are developed from this area of mind, knowingly or unknowingly. It is best not to get entangled in this sphere of mind. There is nothing clever in being able to operate in the psychic sphere. Quite often people who are of subnormal development are extraordinarily gifted in what might be termed psychic attributes. They are often most misguided, however, believing everything they supposedly see and hear in these states and quite often doing untold harm by telling credulous people all sorts of nonsensical things.

'If you are to make good progress it is essential that you have experience of this area of the mind's function. We call this the area of fantasy. If you practise hard with this sphere you will begin to have some understanding of reality – to be able to know the real from the unreal. To know where these visions and voices come from and who or what is responsible.

'This meditation system is a mixed one. As you know there are two kinds of meditation in the Buddha's teaching. One by way of *samatha* or tranquillity requires that one practise and attain the four mental absorptions or *jhana*. The other is by way of vipassana or insight. The practice which you are undergoing involves both systems. In this way you will be enabled to attain extreme concentration which will stand you in good stead when you begin to practise for insight.'

With those words the apparition faded. I looked around my room and found that everything was in order. The fact that there were no ghostly visitors present probably accounted for the feeling of peace and well-being which flowed over me after the fear and panic which I had suffered off and on for days past.

* * *

I spent many days after this thinking about the philosophy – if so it may be called – of Gotama's teaching in relation to my own experiences. For a while I was somewhat confused as to the reason for my being thrown so completely on my own company in what seemed at times to be an utterly self-concerned meditation. Gradually, however, the picture became clearer as I brought to mind all that I had learned intellectually about the teaching.

I realised that my real problem lay in trying for the first time to apply a philosophy to the process of actual living – a philosophy so utterly different from our approach to life in the West and yet one to which I had been drawn intellectually for years. I suppose this question of practical application is the main difference between the Eastern and Western approaches to philosophy. In the West we are conditioned to think in terms of individual permanence, of soul unchanging, of life after death, of the going on unchanging of the something we call 'me'. Even if we become something of an intellectual or in any way a free thinker, the subconscious behaviour patterns come through and we behave in daily life in a manner which completely belies our intellectual protestations.

We in the West – if we take any interest in philosophy as such and are given to any attempts at deep thought or original thinking – keep it on the intellectual level only. Rarely indeed does one of our philosophers apply his philosophical view or theory to his life – unless indeed he be a Bertrand Russell, the most outstanding example in the past fifty years, I would say, of a man with the courage to live as he thinks. How few of our philosophers have lived their lives in accordance with their stated opinions and theories! The last of the Greeks so to do – if Plato be right – was probably Socrates. From then onward the Western philosophical eye appears to have turned outward, to things. This was first noticed, I think, in Aristotle who, it would appear to me, set the standard for our more materialistic approach to life, aided and abetted by the neo-platonism of the established churches.

Even in the cases of Schopenhauer and Hume, two philosophers of later times who have in some way approached the Eastern viewpoint, we find the statement of the view arrived at and lip-service paid to the theory in general – but no attempt made to test the theory in life itself. Schopenhauer based his *World as Will and Idea* on a poor translation of some of the *Upanishads* and apparently considered Buddhism his ideal philosophy. But he remained what he was, a highly irascible man who, if report be right, ill-treated his old landlady abominably.

Hume, in his *The Nature of Human Understanding*, stated practically word for word the psychological findings of Gotama as to the nature of mind in relation to a self, and to a degree by somewhat similar methods. Yet at the end it would appear that Hume threw his discovery to one side with a 'Well that's all right but we have to go on living!' and carried on his life a disappointed man, because he did not get the public acclaim to which he thought he was entitled.

Not that I would find fault with these two great minds, for I had for years done precisely the same thing. What I came to realise as I thought about these things was that Gotama had become the Buddha through *applying* his philosophy to his own life. In this I stumbled on what I feel sure is the fundamental difference in the approach to philosophy in East and West.

In the East and in India in particular, philosophy grew out of the jungle settlements, which were a tradition dating back some thousand years before the time of Gotama. Here men lived disciplined lives applying to themselves a philosophy which was allied to their religion. Here they lived out the theories and tried to attain the fruits in this life of the particular philosophy they professed.

They were mainly concerned with man – his body, his mind, his spirit. Not much time was wasted on the objective world. They felt sure that man in some way did not see the world aright – that he saw it and believed it, while in fact what he saw was an illusion. The purpose of their philosophy and their lives was to penetrate this illusion and come to see the Real. To do this, a man had to come to know himself, to control firstly his body, then his mind, the general thesis being that if one could come to rights with oneself all would be right with the world. The one thing they did was to apply their theories to themselves.

In the West our history has been a history of knowing more and more about more and more and less and less about the something which knows these things – the mind of man. We appear to be on a never-ending chase ever outward for more things to discover and control. Yet we have discovered nothing much new about man. It would appear that Western man, driven by a fear of finding out about himself, strives always to find more things in the world which he can bring under control – disease, the elements, other nations, wealth, politics. He is unaware that the more he strives to bring his particular order into the world at large, the more undisciplined he appears to become himself. He little knows that to bring discipline and order into the vast and complex series of relationships which is the world, there must be discipline and order in the mind of man – who, after all, is but one of the relationships involved.

* * *

Such thinking, however, did not do much to relieve my situation. In fact, I felt pretty small in my own estimation. The very process of thinking things out was but an escape from the task in hand, the task of coming to grips with my own character.

I knew that Gotama had taught by the use of four statements fundamental to his way of life. He had stated that all life was in a state of unrest or suffering; that there was a reason for this unrest; that the unrest could be brought to an end; and that there was a path which led to that end. All things, he had said, were transient, impermanent. All things were without a permanent abiding entity – man included. Things were always becoming something other, ceaselessly. Nothing ever remained the same.

Yet I felt much the same to me as I sat and thought. My body was still there. My legs still hurt. My mind was still worried. It was all very well for the teaching to state that there was nothing permanent and that there was no abiding entity such as the something I called 'me' – but I very much felt a 'me' about. It was *me* surely that got unhappy, fearful and worried. It was *me* who got hungry and tired. It was *me* who wanted to undertake the bhikkhu life so that I might have better understanding of *me*. If there was no *me*, what was all the struggle and fuss about? Why didn't I throw the whole thing up? Even if did, on the assumption that there was no *me*, who was it then who had decided to abandon the struggle?

So I went, on and on, round and round in circles, coming back finally and sadly to the realisation that the only way in which I could get answers to the questions and heartsearchings was to continue with the practice as laid down by the abbot.

I struggled for hours on end to bring myself back to practise. I found myself fluctuating between desire on the one hand to look out of my windows or at the antics of the small house lizards and insects with which my room was infested, and aversion on the other for any action or thought which would bring ideas of meditation in their train.

Hours were spent in listening to and watching the lizards. It was not long before I began to understand what their chirpings were about and to imitate them successfully. Their calls – in some ways similar to the chirrupings of small birds – had three main functions, so far as I could make out. A soft high-pitched excited note was used by both male and female during courtship – a pastime which with them appeared to vie in importance even with eating. A lower-pitched and slower sound they made when they were friendly, and a harsh chirrup if they were angry or frightened.

They moved around the walls and ceiling of my room at great speed, swallowing insects by the score. Whenever I made any attempt to get close to them they would bolt off and hide themselves in some crack in the wall. Gradually I managed to get them to trust me by making their friendly call. Eventually, after I discovered their taste for sweet black coffee, I was able to call them so that they would come down off the wall or ceiling on to the floor with me and take coffee off the end of my finger. At first they would fight and the largest of them – a big old male – would drive the others away so that he had his coffee first. Not until he had finished would the rest dare come close. Later on, however, I managed to have them sitting there half a dozen at a time, each taking it in turn to lick the coffee from the end of my finger.

I managed to bring this about by taking hold of the big fellow on one of his visits – in such a manner that he couldn't get away – and then calling the others with the friendly call. As soon as they saw that the big fellow could do them no harm they came down with alacrity. When they had all settled down I wetted one finger with coffee and held it out to them and they all came forward and sat around my finger in a ring and began to lick in unison. I then – still holding him of course – introduced the big fellow to the coffee session. After a few struggles the coffee became too much for him to resist and he settled down and licked away merrily with the rest. After two days of this he came down with his companions with no trouble whatsoever.

Even in the middle of a fight – and these creatures fight very viciously, quite often taking a leg or a tail off each other – I found that if I called them they would stop the fight and come down to me. I remember on one occasion when a fight had been going on, I looked up just in time to see the big fellow biting off the rear leg of his adversary. I called as loudly and quickly as I possibly could, but the leg was severed. That being accomplished, both came down to the floor with the rest and partook of their coffee. The fellow with three legs was pushing and shoving greedily with the rest in his efforts to get his fair share of what was going.

I learned a terrific amount about myself and life in general watching these little creatures. Their whole lives were spent in reproducing their kind, going in fear and dread from snake, rat or fellow lizards; and staying alive to carry out this function on food which consisted of literally thousands of insects per day. It was a life of kill or be killed, never at peace, watching all the time for attack, searching for food, food which always cost a life. It was a life of looking for a mate, often killing to get her and at times, having got her and wooed her, being killed by her as well.

I had seen it happen on more than one occasion that after the suitor had gone through the act which most human beings would call love, his consort would turn and rend him limb from limb. If he was lucky, he would crawl away on two remaining legs with a stump of a tail. She, coquettish as ever, would flounce around again in wait for the next male with enough desire to approach her. Watching these creatures, and to a degree making friends with them, showed me graphically that all life is unrest and suffering indeed.

8

THE MAGICAL NAGA

Just three weeks had passed by when I was again visited by the abbot.
Accompanied by Thitavedo he came into my room and sat himself
down on a rug which I spread for him. The usual salutations and
formalities over, he began to question me, Thitavedo interpreting, on
various aspects of Buddhist thought. What was the compilation of the
Pali Canon? How many sections were there? What was the form of the
higher or bhikkhu ordination? Did I know the words required for the
ceremony? Did I know the Rules of Discipline for a bhikkhu? Was I
conversant with the whole Vinaya or Discipline section of the Canon?

I answered all his questions to the best of my ability. Fortunately, I
have an almost photographic memory and was thus able at times to
reproduce almost word for word certain sections relating to the
questions. I was able to recite from memory the whole of the Pali
required for the higher ordination and to give the sense of the two
hundred and twenty-seven rules which control a bhikkhu's life. I was
also able to name every section in the Canon and to give a fair idea of
the contents of each.

When I had finished answering his questions, and frankly was
hoping that there would not be any more that afternoon, Lung Poh
looked across at me – by this time shifting my position as often as
possible because I was so uncomfortable sitting in the correct Thai
manner. He put out his hand and laid it upon my knee. Smiling, he
asked how many books, including commentaries, there would be in
the English translation of the Pali Canon. To this I was able to reply that
to the best of my knowledge there were about thirty-three volumes in
the collection. Lung Poh then turned to Thitavedo and had some
conversation with him in Thai. It was quite obvious that I was the
object of their talk.

Thitavedo then said to me, 'Brother, Lung Poh very pleased with
your knowledge and with answers you give. Now he wants to know

how you come by all you know so soon. How come you know bhikkhu ordination so well? Where you get him from?'

I explained that I had not come by the knowledge very soon, as he put it. That it had come through some twenty-five years of study. The bhikkhu's ordination requisites I had studied and memorised from the Pali before I left England. I explained again that the trouble with me had been the fact that whilst I had a very sound knowledge of Buddhist scriptures, I had never during all those years of study made any attempt to apply them.

Lung Poh, having listened to my replies to his questions, then announced through Thitavedo that he was going to arrange for me to be ordained bhikkhu in just five days from now. The ordination would take place at 1 p.m. on the day of the full moon of *Vaisakha*. This was a day of great celebration among Buddhists as it was the day upon which Prince Siddhattha Gotama had been born. It was also the day, years later, when he gained his complete enlightenment. At the end of his life it was also on this day that he died.

As my ordination was so close Lung Poh wanted me to come into the bot several times during some of the forthcoming bhikkhu ordinations so that I could study the way in which things were carried out. Also I would have to prepare a lecture that I would deliver after the ceremony. This he knew would make me very busy and take away some of my time from meditation. I would have to organise my time so that I managed to get everything in during the course of the day. It would be a large and important ceremony, and large numbers of people would be present. The word had already gone out about my ordination so that people would come from all parts of the country to be present on that day.

The one thing which I wanted to stay away from was large crowds, and I particularly did not want any special treatment. I mentioned this to the abbot but he would have none of it. He told me that the people wanted it that way, and so did the lay committee of the pagoda. Everyone had watched me very closely since I had arrived and had noticed that I spent all my time in my house applying myself to meditation, even refusing invitations to visit many famous places in Thailand. This had made me very popular with them. Also, it so happened that I would be the first Englishman to be ordained a bhikkhu in Thailand, and the fact that I had come to their country solely for that purpose had caused a great amount of interest throughout the land. The people wanted to honour me by organising a big celebration. I must understand, and let them have their way. The best thing for me to do was not to worry – everything would be all right on the day.

After Lung Poh had left, Thitavedo returned to my room. When I had attended to his wants, having placed China tea at hand and poured myself coffee and lit a cigarette, he placed a hand on my shoulder and said, 'Brother, you very lucky fellow. Lung Poh love you very much, think about you all the time. He pay you a great honour by ordaining you on Vaisakha day. No other ordinations on that day – you the only one.

'He also know that you have been having bad time with meditation some time now. He know you very frighten sometimes, but very happy to see that you keep up struggle. He tell me to tell you not to be afraid too much because he very close by in the mind with you at all times. He can come to you in the mind so that you not get into too much trouble. He say you must go on – not to turn back now. Not matter if sometime meditation seem very dangerous – just go on. Lung Poh and me look after you. Nothing happen to you.'

I was just about to thank Thitavedo when I began to hear music in the near distance. Mainly it was the sounds of gongs, cymbals, hand-drums and wind instruments. Thitavedo rose and went over to one of the windows facing the bot. He then beckoned to me to come over, calling out, 'Come, brother – soon there going to be an ordination. Come and see what happen.'

Looking to the right of the window I could just see the instrumentalists as they came into view down one of the paths leading to the bot. Leading them were two men in the dress of a dragon or *Naga* as it is called in Thailand, a traditional serpent with magic powers. The costume was beautifully decorated in green, yellow, red and gold. The head, an intricate piece of carving, was worked in red, gold leaf and glittering inlays of mosaic. One of the men wore the head walking upright, the other was at the other end of the snake-like body.

As the band came closer and more people gathered near the bot, the Naga began to weave a frantic and sinuous pattern in front of the advancing musicians. Then suddenly, when the creature was almost upon the watching crowds, its mouth opened and a long spurt of flame leapt forth. Most people ran helter-skelter, screaming their delight at such fun. Some, mainly young boys and youths, turned and prepared to do battle with the fire-throwing beast. They attacked with wooden swords, braving the beast's scorching breath and thrusting deeply into the unprotected sides of the now writhing Naga. It sank to the ground in mock death and its conquerors stood with one foot upon it much like the big game-hunters one sees in photographs. The Naga, however, was also apparently something of a phoenix, for with a great belch of smoke and fire it drove off its tormentors and again continued on its way at the head of the procession.

Then followed an elderly couple – the mother and father of the young man who was to be ordained. The man was carrying a metal begging bowl and a large decorated fan, the woman a set of yellow robes.

After them came a group of beautiful young Thai women, all in native dress, coloured sarong wrapped around the waist, little white blouse and coloured shoulder-cloth. As they moved forward they danced as only Thai girls can. With slow, even tread they moved gracefully forward on their bare feet, their beautifully proportioned bodies swaying like fresh flowers in a gentle breeze. As they moved, their hands told the story of the dance. Hands and fingers which could bend backwards or forwards with equal ease wove an intricate pattern through the hot air of the afternoon. Around them – moving more quickly – came another group of younger girls strewing lotus petals and jasmine flowers all around, until even I in my room could smell the perfume of the jasmine.

These young women were closely followed by four men carrying a palanquin on their shoulders. Seated in it was a young man perhaps twenty-one years of age, dressed in the apparel of a Thai chieftain, decked with rich jewels, with rings on his fingers and a gold belt round his waist. His head and eyebrows were shaved clean of all hair. In his hands – raised in salutation – was clasped a bunch of flowers. Following him were various groups of his relations and friends.

Having arrived at the pagoda compound the young Thai dismounted from his litter and stood waiting for the procession to begin its march round the pagoda. All his friends and family took this as an opportunity to come and adjust his dress to make quite sure that he was presentable. Others came and talked with him – some, I am sure, pulled his leg about the things which he would be leaving behind after his ordination.

Again the band struck up and the whole gathering proceeded to march slowly three times round the pagoda, the young man by now looking very serious. Everyone else was extremely happy, dancing and skipping on their way, laughing and cheering loudly as each of the circuits was completed. An extra loud and long outburst of cheering told me that the procession had arrived for the third and final time at the eastern door and that by this time its central figure would be kneeling before the sima or boundary stone asking permission to enter.

Thitavedo explained to me that the whole celebration had its symbolic side. Apparently all young men in Thailand who are to be ordained arrive dressed richly as chieftains. Always there are large crowds of friends and relations and groups of young women and, of course, the parents. For the bhikkhu to be, this is the time of parting from all worldly things. From now on he becomes possessionless, without family or parents, without wife or girlfriends.

The celebrations in most cases begin the night before, when the whole clan gathers and feasts whilst the one to be ordained sits bow-headed listening to an old man chanting to him and the assembly the story of Life, of how he came to birth, of how fortunate he is that he is to become a bhikkhu so that he can follow the Buddha's way of life fully for as long as he likes.

My friend also explained that the season for ordinations was just beginning and that there would be large numbers of ceremonies from now until about the middle of July when the rainy season began. It was the custom in Thailand for most young men of twenty years to become bhikkhus for the period of the rains. When these were over the majority of them would leave the Order and return to lay life. Some, who were ordained now, would of course spend longer than the three months of the rains in the Order. Some few indeed would probably remain for life, but mainly they would leave once the rains were over.

Every young man in the country was expected to spend some short time in the Order, and by this custom it came about that practically every male Thai had first-hand experience of the bhikkhu life and rules, and thereby knew what standard should be kept by a bhikkhu. There were no life vows for a bhikkhu or samanera. Even in the Buddha's day such had been the case. Every man was free to apply for entry to the Order and just as free to leave at any time he thought fit.

Thitavedo then told me that in two hours' time there would be another ordination taking place and that Lung Poh wanted me to be present through the whole ceremony. It would be as well therefore if I took some rest or, if I wished, sat quietly in my room, having a smoke and drinking some coffee. I should try to keep my mind off everything to do with meditation or memorising. I must learn to discipline my mind so that it could put things down at will.

★　★　★

I spent the next few days attending ordination ceremonies for both samaneras and bhikkhus. I found that no matter how often the ceremony took place I always felt that I was the applicant. Every word the applicant uttered I found myself repeating, breaking out into a nervous sweat every time his memory failed or he made a slip of the tongue during his chanting. In all the ceremonies I attended never once did I see a sad face. Everyone present was happy. Each member of the family group involved was proud that one of their number was becoming a member of the Order, no matter for how short a time.

The bot on such occasions was vastly different from the churches of the West. Here was none of the coldness and silence, none of the tiptoed walking which people seem to adopt when entering a church in England.

In the bot the lay people sat around on the floor, filling the building to the walls. They came and entered as human beings, happy and joyous at being present at the ceremony. They paid their respects in the correct manner, removing their sandals or shoes if they had any and then, having entered the building, they would kneel and bow three times to the figure of the Buddha. They would then turn and salute in the same manner the senior bhikkhu present. Those things accomplished, they would carry on as if in their own homes, holding pleasant conversation among themselves until the ceremony commenced. In most cases they would have beside them some form of drink, such as tea, coffee or soft drinks of some kind. Mainly they would be smoking either Western-type cigarettes or the native variety, which are about as thick as one's middle finger and wrapped not in paper but in dried banana-leaf.

Some, I noticed on a number of occasions, wandered over to the platform where the bhikkhus who were officiating were seated and held conversation with them or offered them soft drinks and cigarettes. Later I was able to observe that this was quite normal behaviour. There appeared to be no barrier whatever between the bhikkhu and the layman. And at any occasion or time, children would enter the pagoda, pay their respects, maybe talk with some bhikkhu or samanera and go their way. At no time did I come across any self-consciousness among either the children or grown-ups with reference to their religion. The subject was never barred from social conversation.

The Thais, I discovered, were great conversationalists, and it was a very rare occasion if some aspect of Buddhist philosophy was not discussed at some point. I also noticed that if the conversation was on the subject of Buddhism and one of those present happened to be a bhikkhu, they would at times argue any point with him as they saw fit. No one appeared to believe a man just because he happened to wear the robe. If he couldn't quote chapter and verse in support of his case he would be bested by one of his opponents, many of whom were well-versed in their subject. Whatever the outcome of such discussion, all was taken in good part by all concerned, including the bhikkhu.

One of the great difficulties with the Westerner in his attempt to understand Buddhism is in relation to the standing of the bhikkhu. So often have I heard and seen them referred to as 'Buddhist priests'. Nothing could be further from the truth. The term 'priest' means to most Christians a man who, if he belongs to the Church of England, accepts the thirty-nine articles of faith contained in the Book of Common Prayer, and who has the capacity through his ordination to intercede with God for members of his flock. He has the power to give the sacraments of the Lord to members of his congregation or to withhold them as the official ruling body of his church dictates. He is permitted to perform marriage rites in the name of God. He may forbid burial in consecrated ground to those who, whilst their birth is the natural outcome of the coming together of a healthy male and female, did not manage things well enough to select as prospective parents those 'joined together in Holy Wedlock' according to the dictates of the dogmas of the church in question. He may also deny burial to some unfortunate who, whilst having been a regular churchgoer, a real striver after what he deemed to be good, a great believer in what his priest told him, took his own life in a moment when the problems of the world overpowered him.

Indeed the priest is a powerful man, holding the right to cast into the eternal damnation of excommunication any who do not abide to the letter by the thirty-nine articles of faith – even though he himself may well be in doubt about some of them.

The bhikkhu has none of these powers, neither is he called upon to exercise any of the offices of the priest. Neither he nor the people around him have any concept of a creating God who must be obeyed. Neither the bhikkhu nor his people have any articles of faith which must be believed. They have no official church in the sense in which the West has churches, serving their purpose in the ideal case as the House of God.

Whereas faith is an essential to the priest and his flock, the bhikkhu and his people have no such concept. The bhikkhu's purpose, if any, in relation to the lay folk is to lead a life which will eradicate ignorance from his mind so that he may come to understand the truth of things as they are. Then he will instruct anyone who should ask. Rarely does one find a bhikkhu holding forth on his way of life, or trying to drive people in the same direction. He has chosen to leave the daily life of the common people in an effort to come to terms with himself, to improve himself. That being so, the people will support him and help him wherever possible – but they do not expect him in any way to interfere with their lives. In fact he would be given pretty short shrift if he did.

Most of the misunderstandings we Westerners hold about bhikkhus and Buddhism itself come purely from ignorance. The majority of the early bilingual dictionaries which were produced in Buddhist countries were the work of sincere men who were usually Christian missionaries. Often, however, they were so blinded by the supremacy of their own creed and so convinced that all Buddhists were idolaters, with so little knowledge of the way of life and the philosophy of the people among whom they had settled, that on coming to the word 'Buddha' they translated it as 'God'. The word 'bhikkhu' they translated as 'priest', 'Nibbana' or 'Nirvana' as 'Heaven'. This was so in the histories of Burma, Thailand and to a degree, Ceylon.

Tragically, the confusion is not only confined to the West now. As each of these nations has come to learn English, so they have come to mistranslate their own terms and in some cases of modern educated youth, to misunderstand their true import.

*   *   *

I attended quite a number of ordination ceremonies in the bot at Wat Paknam during the five days before my own ordination as bhikkhu.

On the evening before Vaisakha day my friend and general guide Bhikkhu Thitavedo came to my room and said that we could have some talk so that he could try and deal with any doubts or questions I might have. He informed me that both he and Lung Poh wanted my mind to be free from problems and worries on the coming day. He also told me that Lung Poh had changed the time of the ceremony from 1 p.m. to 3 p.m.

The only real question which had occupied my mind for some time was that relating to the strange rapport which appeared to exist between myself and Lung Poh. If he were talking Thai in my presence, somehow I was sure that I understood what he said; if he were at a distance, some new understanding came through his being in my thoughts.

Many times in the past I had thought about the subject of telepathy. Whilst I in no way pooh-poohed the possibility, neither was I credulous about it, and I always became extremely cautious when listening to the fantastic claims of people that they themselves had experienced telepathic communication. On further examination of what they said, I usually found that it related to something which a trustworthy friend or their mother or brother or someone who was of course utterly reliable had told them. Never once had I come across a person who could give me a truly objective statement of what had actually happened so that one could accept the facts for study on a rational, scientific basis.

Invariably I found that as soon as I mentioned any controlled experiments with the claimant, they would shy away and hold up their hands in horror as if I had uttered sacrilege. Much as I was interested in the subject, much in fact as I would have liked to prove it to be a possibility, I could never get the people concerned to – as they put it –

lower the subject by bringing it under the scrutiny of cold reason. Telepathy, I found, could never be brought into discussion without having dragged with it the worst aspects of the ever popular and extremely credulous psychism, more properly called spiritism.

For some years I had turned away from telepathy as an avenue to be studied rationally, when I chanced to come into contact with the work of Dr Rhine of Duke University, U.S.A. I followed his experiments with great interest, covering as they did the possibility of mind controlling matter or telekinesis, telepathy, seeing at a distance or clairvoyance, and hearing beyond the normal or clairaudience. Whilst I realised that each of these attributes of mind had not been separated out in any of the experiments conducted, nonetheless they had each been seen in operation or were capable of operation during the tests involved.

For me the question of the validity of telepathy was answered by Rhine's experiments with symbol-marked cards used among a series of student teams grouped to work in pairs as senders and receivers. These experiments, minutely described by Dr Rhine in his published papers and books, together with the figures given by Dr Soal of London University on the question of probability, clinched the thing for me. The Psi factor, which covered all the attributes usually kept in the gooily sentimental jampot of spiritism, had at last succumbed to scientific test. Such things as telepathy and the rest were rational possibilities. They were not necessarily the attributes of supposedly spiritually gifted people. The Psi factor or capacity for such things was present in all types of mind, good, bad and indifferent.

I was so excited by these experiments that I was able to arrange a whole series of like tests with a hand-picked team, and found that the results were much the same as Rhine's. Whilst I found that we all succeeded better at some times than others, at no time could we be sure when things were going to be successful. Even when I had accomplished an almost endless series of tests with the cards, acting as sender myself and gaining marks far higher than those demanded by scientific standards, I still felt in something of a quandary because I found that I did not *feel* anything. I had no feeling that I was sending anything to my receiver – nor he that he was receiving anything. In fact the less we were concerned about things the better the results appeared to be.

I was in the position of having proof in my hands both through what I had read of Rhine's work and through my own experiments. It was enough proof for intellectual acceptance, and yet I felt dissatisfied. I had no personal *experience* of telepathy, although I was the possessor of stacks of proof on paper that such a phenomenon had occurred.

It was recalling this from the past that coloured to a degree my question to Thitavedo about the situation between myself and Lung Poh. The answer which I received from him would probably have saved me many hours, nay months wasted searching for answers elsewhere than where I should have looked for them. In the state that I was in then, however, I would most probably have turned away from such an answer, being quite sure that I knew better.

It is strange indeed how a basic ignorance, an unknowingness – which the Buddha claimed was at the root of our troubles – can so blind one that one does not know that one is ignorant; that the very facts, subjects, interests and studies which one strives so hard to master during life are, in many cases, nothing but the increasing growth of that same ignorance, the ignorance of things as they really are – and above all else, the utter and blind ignorance of oneself.

I turned to Thitavedo and explained to him that Lung Poh was much in my mind, that he appeared sometimes in my meditation sessions and that on occasions it would appear that he spoke to me in a manner which explained many points which previously had confused me. Was this possible, I wanted to know. Was it possible, as he himself had said, that Lung Poh could help me in mind, could contact me purely mentally, could know in fact what my thoughts were?

Thitavedo smiled for a moment, and then his face became serious. He adjusted the robe on his left shoulder, which had slipped a little while he had been listening to me, smoothed the folds, then replied, 'Brother, you always think up difficult questions to ask. Always you seem to be asking about truth – truth about this, truth about that. What you know of truth anyway? Must remember that all truth in our world only deal with things, facts, sensations, thoughts. Therefore truth only relative to these things. No time can truth be absolutely true when dealing with related things.

'Some thing may be true today and not true tomorrow, yet still be very true when it is true. Whilst not true in later circumstances, does not alter fact that it very true when true. What matter now, suppose I say Yes! Lung Poh can do like all you say. What matter suppose I say No! He can't do like this. You still not come near the truth. All you come near is what I say – just some words. Whatever I say not make it true for you.

'Suppose I go fetch lot of people and they all say Lung Poh can do like you think. Still not make it true because many people say so. Only way for you to know whether true is by your own experience. You are getting some experiences now – you must make some test and be sure for yourself. Then you might be able to say Yes! This is true for me, or this not true for me. It not matter one piece what other people say or what I say. It is truth in relation to you. What is true in your experience you must find.

'You keep on with practice – all the answers come in time that way. Just be some patient, not in hurry too fast. Big trouble with you is you always finding fault with yourself. Always kicking yourself for not knowing, for not being more clever and wise. Aversion for yourself very strong. This has driven you through many years to get much knowledge of many things but you never satisfied. You must begin to control your aversion, brother. Control it by coming to understand it. This also help to bring answers.

'Now, you very tired now – must get some rest. You have very busy day tomorrow. Keep the mind calm and concentrated. Keep the mind at peace for your becoming bhikkhu tomorrow. Goodnight, brother. I also very tired.'

Richard Randall/Kapilavaddho Bhikkhu (1968).

Kapilavaddho (left) receiving gifts after his ordination. Next to him is John Blofeld, the eminent Buddhist scholar.

Chao Khun Bhavanakosol, Maha Thera (otherwise known as Lung Poh, Great Father), Abbot of Wat Paknam, Bangkok.

Kapilavaddho in the newly established Buddhist *Vihara* (Monastery), Knightsbridge, London (1955).

Bangkok Airport, December 1955: Kapilavaddho (centre) returning to Thailand with three British samaneras (left) in training for full ordination. Third from the right is Bhikkhu Thitavedo. The samanera on the far left is now Bhikkhu Paññavaddho, the senior Western monk in Thailand.

Kapilavaddho with Christmas Humphreys, Founder President of the Buddhist Society, London (1955).

Residence of the Lord Abbott.
Wat Paknam Monastery,
Bhasicharoon,
Dhonburi,
THAILAND.

12.th.October.B.E.2498.

Dear Kapilavaddho Bhikkhu,

As you are well aware, it is the custom to demand that a Bhikkhu remain with, and under the care and instruction of a teacher for a period of five years.

Since you came here in March and received your Samanera and Bhikkhu ordinations into the Vipassana Dhura of the Maha Nikaya on the 10th. of April 2497, and the 17th. of May 2498 respectively, you have shown yourself to be of good character and well fitted for the living of the Bhikkhu life. You have applied yourself diligently to research and study of the Buddha Sasana, and whole heartedly to the study and practise of Samadhi and Vipassana.

We have therefor, the Community of Sangha and myself, decided in your special case, and in view of your knowledge and accomplishment, that you be allowed to return to your own country and people so that you may continue with your valuable work in the teaching and spreading of the Dhamma.

You have my complete authority to return to your country, to live alone and independent of a teacher. You also have my authority, and are very well qualified, to teach and instruct in the methods of Samadhi and Vipassana which you have learned whilst under my care and instruction.

My blessings go with you on all your journeyings. May all your efforts be crowned with success.

With Metta,

your teacher, friend, and Upajjarya,

พระมงคลเทพมุนี

Chao Khun Bhāvanākosol, Mahā Thera.
Lord Abbott of Wat Paknam,
Bhasicharoon, THAILAND.

Kapilavaddho enters the robe for the second time at Wat Buddhapadipa, East Sheen, Surrey, October 1967. The officiating monk is Chao Khun Sobhana Dhammasudhi, now better known as the writer and teacher Dhiravamsa.

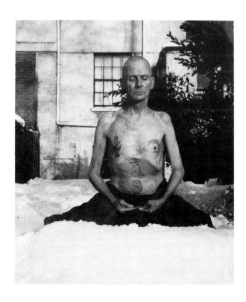

Kapilavaddho meditating in the snow!

Kapilavaddho receiving a gift from His Highness the Venerable Somdet Phra Vanarata, Vice-Patriarch of Thailand, who visited Wat Dhammapadipa, London, in October 1968.

The samanera ordination of Alan James (right) at Wat Dhammapadipa. His teacher, Kapilavaddho, is in the centre of the picture, and Chao Khun Sobhana Dhammasudhi (Dhiravamsa) is on the left. (May 1968).

9

ORDINATION AS A MONK

On the morning of Vaisakha day, the day fixed for my ordination as a bhikkhu, I arose at 4 and spent an hour and a half at meditation practice. I then cleaned my room, took a bath and robed myself ready to go to the lower floor for my first meal of the day.

When I arrived downstairs I found that Bhikkhu Thitavedo was already present. He stood in the middle of the main room absolutely beaming. Practically covering the whole floor were masses of beautifully decorated gifts, all laid out on red lacquer and gold-leafed stands.

I asked him, 'What is all this about? Who are all the gifts for?' Looking completely impish he replied in mock gravity, 'Brother, these all for you when you have become bhikkhu. You very popular with the people. Many more gifts to come yet. These you must receive from the people after ordination. But I sure that they make much trouble for you, you see.'

I told him that I did not wish to appear ungracious or churlish, but I didn't want to become rich in possessions. I thought the whole idea of the bhikkhu life was to have only eight possessions. Maybe it would be better if he told the people now that I did not want these presents, and explain why. Surely they would understand.

'You have to learn, brother,' he replied. 'The people think that there is much merit in giving to a new bhikkhu. They want to share in some little way the benefits of the life you are going to live. No, you cannot refuse their gifts which are given with such kind thought. You must accept them without worry or resentment and think of how to dispose of them afterward. In this way you will learn by experience what a burden possessions can be, for as you say, you cannot own all these extra things. There are extra allowances in small things as you know, but the less you have the better. Now forget gifts – you haven't got them yet so why worry. Now come, have some food.'

We moved into the next room to find that two tables had been laid, each with a chair standing ready. Two tables were necessary because a bhikkhu and a samanera may not eat from the same cloth or table. The samanera is in fact nothing more than a layman, and laymen and bhikkhus do not eat together. Whilst the ceremony for samaneraship is usually called an ordination, it is, in the true sense, a ceremony whereby he asks for permission to 'go forth from the lay life' (*pabbajja*) in preparation for ordination as bhikkhu, permission being granted by the one whom he asks to be his teacher.

Once we were seated, the room became alive with people. They came to each of us and presented each dish of food into our hands. Every article on the table had to be handed over. That being done, we were able to commence our meal. If it had so happened that someone had inadvertently touched one of the dishes after the handing over, it would have meant that we could take nothing out of that dish until it had been handed over again. This ruling was always strictly adhered to.

Whilst to a Westerner this process may appear to be unnecessary and hair-splitting, it served a very important purpose. Firstly, it impressed upon the one under training the rule not to take anything which had not been given. Secondly, it reminded him of the need for continual mindfulness, continual consciousness of what he was doing. Apart from this of course, all the time he would be under the close scrutiny of all the lay folk present and they would judge him accordingly.

Whilst I was waiting for Thitavedo to commence his meal – a junior never begins to eat before his senior, no matter how long it may take the senior to begin or how hungry the junior may be – I saw entering the dear old lady who had cried with joy when I had chanted for her. She came forward on her knees and offered me a bowl of bird's-nest soup. To receive this I cast a white cloth on the ground so that one of my hands was touching it. Upon the cloth she placed the bowl. I drew it towards me, picked it up and put it on the table.

This particular custom is not carried out in all Buddhist countries. In fact, I am sure that Thailand is the only one in which it is so strictly adhered to. The purpose is again to impress a rule, and expressly to help the bhikkhu. It is a rule that a bhikkhu or samanera shall not touch a woman with desire in his mind. He may not touch any part of her – her hair, limbs, hands, feet or even her clothing – if desire be in his mind. The Thai women know that even an accidental touch of a hand may set up trouble in a young bhikkhu's mind, so the custom of placing their gifts on a cloth has arisen and they are most meticulous that it is carried out.

They never come closer than just out of arm's reach of a bhikkhu. And should it so happen that the bhikkhu is walking in a crowded quarter, the women and girls move aside and remove themselves from him as much as possible as he walks his way, eyes focused on the ground in front of him. There are, of course, the coquettes amongst them, as there are with all races of women, but they get short shrift from the others if they are caught.

After breakfast I again retired to my room for more practice and a final rehearsal of the Pali for the ordination. On looking out of my windows I could see that the whole monastery area was becoming completely crowded with people, many of whom had taken up positions below the windows. Some were calling 'Tan William, Tan William' in order to attract my attention.

Everyone was very busy. Canopied shelters were being erected, loudspeakers were being hung from trees (an electricity supply of sorts had recently been laid into the area), the food shops were putting out extra stalls. Samaneras were busily flitting back and forth filling the huge water chatties in the area. Others were sweeping all the paths leading to the pagoda compound. Others were washing down the flagstones of the compound itself. Everybody busy, everybody happy, preparing for the great celebration of Vaisakha and the one ordination to take place that day.

Looking down on the people below my window again, I saw one young fellow gesticulating madly trying to attract my attention. 'Tan William,' he called in his best English, 'you seen Tan Yai? Tan Yai, where Tan Yai?' I informed him as best I could that I didn't know any Tan Yai. To which he replied laughingly, 'Very funny, you make good joke. You know him very well. Tan Yai is Phra Yai.' I told him again that I did not know any Tan Yai, neither did I know any Phra Yai. This last made the whole crowd rock with amusement.

I was completely mystified by the conversation and to tell the truth, a little exasperated. Then I noticed that Thitavedo had joined my interrogator and was himself joining in the general laughter. Looking up at me he pointed to himself and said, 'Me Tan Yai, also Phra Yai, also Phra Thitavedo. Explain later, brother.'

Thitavedo came to my room shortly afterwards and clarified the apparent mystery. The name given to him when he was ordained a bhikkhu was Thitavedo, meaning Teacher of Wisdom. Before that, when he lived in his village, he had what is called a village name. This was Yai. He had come by that name because when he was a boy he had been fat and Yai meant big or fat. Many of his villagers came to see him and still used his village name, either referring to him as Tan Yai (which meant Brother Yai) or Phra Yai (which meant Bhikkhu Yai).

Thai people, he explained, can have many names, but I would soon get used to their customs. Lung Poh for instance, on the day of his ordination as bhikkhu, was given the name Candassaro, although he was known as Chao Khun Bhavanakosol. That was a title, an office, and would be changed again if the King saw fit to grant him another title. I would find in time that the same situation would apply to myself – the people would have their own names by which they would recognise me. That was the Thai way. In all Sangha functions, however, the true bhikkhu name was always used. In the ordination this afternoon I would have to refer to Lung Poh as Candassaro Bhikkhu.

I joined with Thitavedo in the joke after that, although his last remarks about Lung Poh and the ordination caused me some little worry. I had hammered the Pali for the ordination well and truly into my mind and when the part came where I had to reply to a question as to who was my teacher I had learned to reply, 'Upajjhayo me bhante, Ayasma Chao Khun Bhavanakosol nama' – meaning, 'My teacher, venerable sir, is the Venerable Chao Khun Bhavanakosol'. This I knew would now have to be changed so that I replied, 'Upajjhayo me bhante, Ayasma Candassaro nama'. Any mistake would upset the legality of the ordination and it would have to be gone through again until every word and syllable, every act and pronunciation was correct. Left once again to myself I set about eradicating from my mind the wrong wording, repeating again and again the correct version.

At 1.30 that afternoon I was again visited by the abbot's first and second assistants. These two were completely responsible for the correctness of everything pertaining to the ordination. Both were experts on all the legal forms of Sangha business, correct wording, pronunciation, timing and acts of the various portions of the ceremony. By acting in such an office, they also would become my teachers. Their purpose was to make quite sure that I fully understood the Vinaya or legal code, the correct modes of behaviour and so forth.

They questioned me on all parts of the ceremony and asked me to chant through the whole of it so that they could correct me if necessary and advise me on any points which might be unclear to me. I went through without any mistake, even managing to get the portion on Lung Poh's name exactly right. They were quite happy with their small examination and after I had paid them the customary salutations, pouring coffee for them and offering the inevitable cigarettes, they smilingly took their leave.

At 2.15 I was visited by a young bhikkhu named Tan Kan, which was his village name and the only name by which I knew him. With him came a very young samanera whom I had never met before. They explained as best they could that Thitavedo had sent them to help me to get properly robed. For this I was extremely grateful as there was a special way of wearing the robe in the case of a samanera presenting himself for final ordination. I bathed and then handed myself over to my two attendants.

The sarong went on first as usual, being worn as a skirt to just below the centre of the calves. Next the civaram or light robe was taken by the young bhikkhu and folded from the left into layers of about six inches in width. He arranged this about me until the folds came comfortably on to my left shoulder. Then, taking the rest of the robe, he took it under my right arm and across the front of my body, and tucked it under the folded portion on my left shoulder. He then tied around my waist a length of yellow cloth, and the robing was complete. The whole process could not have taken more than five minutes. Had I been left to my own devices I am sure it would have taken hours.

The robing completed, Thitavedo came in and gave me a final inspection. When everything was to his satisfaction he dismissed my two helpers. He then took both my hands in his and said, 'Brother, I so happy today. Make me very happy that you soon be bhikkhu. Always I want a brother like you – now I got one. Never have I met a brother like you who I can understand and who understands me like you do. Sometimes maybe you think I act very cruel to you, I not tell you enough. But it better for you this way. All I want to do is help you. I will look after you all the time.

'Now soon they come for you to take you to the bot. I will leave you here. You take some coffee and quiet rest now. I go to the pagoda soon when the gong sounds and will be there as a member of Sangha so as to interpret if necessary. You very fortunate as every one of the twenty-five bhikkhus in Sangha for ordination is vipassana bhikkhu. Every one of them very advanced in the meditation, all have very clear and pure minds. This should be great help to you. When you come to bot, I see you then.'

Such thought and kindness was indeed rare even among those whom one usually called one's friends. Yet here I was with a man of another race whom I had known but for a short time, a man with whom I had closer contact than anyone I had ever met in my life – other than, of course, Lung Poh. Yes, indeed I was fortunate, I told myself, to have the opportunities now before me, to have the teachers who had undertaken my instruction and to have as friend, guide, nurse, brother and companion *par excellence* Thitavedo, who despite his seniority had just undertaken to look after me and protect me as a brother. An undertaking which was no idle boast, as time was to prove.

At 2.45 the gong sounded, calling the bhikkhus who were to officiate at the ceremony. I made my way to the lower room to be met by my Thai friends and supporters, who were to accompany me on the procession round the pagoda.

Looking out from the compound of the house I could see the figure of the Naga, the traditional fire-breathing serpent, prancing and circling around in a sinuous dance ready to take its place at the head of the procession. Standing quietly waiting in an orderly fashion were some two hundred upasikas. Each of these nuns, her head newly-shaven, was wearing a fresh and spotless white robe, and many of them bore gifts in their hands. Behind them again came some hundreds of lay folk – friends, supporters, newspaper men, sightseers.

Waiting for me immediately in front of the house were several young fellows each carrying a gigantic ceremonial parasol, under one of which I would walk on my journey to the bot. The rest would cover my personal supporters and their gifts.

My guarantor, Khun Sudhon, came forward attended by his son. With him were Khun Sanoh, Khun Siri and Khun Sridsi, all of whom had been so kind to me since my arrival and who had taken it upon themselves to look after me as much as possible. After some conversation with each of them, they informed me that it was time to move to the bot.

Flowers, burning joss sticks and tapers were placed in my hands, and slowly I followed in procession as the whole gathering moved off on its first journey round the bot.

It took me much longer to make the necessary three trips round the pagoda than it had on the occasion of my ceremony for becoming a samanera. The crowds were densely packed as far as the eye could see. We kept stopping and starting as the procession proper got itself mixed up with the crowd. Each time we stopped, the Naga worked like fury, blowing forth great belches of fire and smoke with which he drove back the crowd so that once again we could move slowly onward. At long last, my bare feet sore and blistered from walking on the hot flagstones of the pagoda compound, I arrived for the third and final time at the eastern entrance to the bot.

My supporters and friends forced a way through the crowd for me so that I might again kneel before the sima or boundary stone. Here I asked in Pali for permission to enter just as I had one month previously when I became a samanera.

Between myself and the entrance to the bot was now a solid mass of people. The more I tried to move forward, the more they clung round me, all apparently happy and all smiling broadly but each determined to get a good look at me. They were in a party mood and were intent upon enjoying every moment of it. Eventually some of my supporters managed to get through to me and forming a ring around me gradually began to force a passage through the happy-go-lucky crowd.

Among that group who got me through to the entrance was one whom I had never expected to see, although I knew that he was somewhere in Thailand. It was Peter Simms, an old friend of mine, who had founded the first Buddhist Society at Cambridge and had later come out to this country to lecture in English at Chulalongkorn University and at the Academy of Prasarn Mit. His greeting – 'Hullo old lad, how's it going? Bit of a shambles, isn't it, but we'll soon get you through' – was like cool clear music in my ears. The first real English voice I had heard since my arrival.

Once inside the bot I carried out the salutations to the figure of the Buddha and to the assembly of bhikkhus, as in the previous ceremony. Then mounting the platform and kneeling before the lay folk, I again received robes and begging bowl from them. I then proceeded to the abbot, Lung Poh. I knelt before him, and after the customary salutations asked his pardon for all faults and that we might share the benefits of the bhikkhu life together as pupil and teacher. I gave him the set of robes and the begging bowl, and he returned them to me. I took my leave and proceeded to the back of the pagoda. Here a junior and senior bhikkhu acting as my attendants stripped off the sweat-sodden robes I wore as a samanera and wiped my body. Other hands were massaging my leg muscles as I stood naked. The fresh sarong or body cloth was just being put round my waist when I chanced to glance up for the first time to realise that there were three film cameras whirring furiously away, recording the whole process.

Led by my attendants, I again presented myself before the abbot and, kneeling, asked him for the *Sarana*, or three refuges, then for the *Dasa Sila* or ten precepts of training. As in the previous ceremony, this was completed without a hitch in the Pali. I then again asked Lung Poh to be my teacher, to which he agreed. I requested him to instruct me in the requisites and supports of the bhikkhu's life. His reply on this occasion was much longer and more detailed than before. He then called me forward and placed the begging bowl on my back, securing it in position by a strap across my chest.

He then questioned me: '*Ayam te patto?*' 'Have you the bowl?'. To which I replied: '*Ama bhante*' 'Yes venerable sir.' This was followed by: '*Ayam sankati?*' 'Have you the outer robe?'

'*Ayam uttaro samkho?*' 'Have you the inner robe?'

'*Ayam untara vasako?*' 'Have you the body robe?' To all of which I was able to reply in the affirmative.

Seated as I was – with the left leg flat on the ground and folded inward, bringing the heel of the left foot tight against the pubic area, and the right leg turned outward and folded back from the knee, bringing the right foot on to the outside of the body level with my posterior – I was becoming more and more conscious of pain and cramp in the legs. I was just trying to think of a way of shifting position without being too obvious when Lung Poh commanded me in Thai, *'Dhammakay, na!'*

All thoughts of pain ceased, for this was the command to enter meditation, and this time to enter it up to the final level. Quickly the mind fell into the course of the meditational exercise, going through stage after stage, level after level, without the slightest difficulty.

Having arrived at the final position I heard Lung Poh's voice ask me if I could see him in the meditation, and if I could, what was he doing? I saw him quite clearly with my eyes shut tight as if he were sitting before me. I was able to tell him that he was smiling and was pointing at me with his right hand. He then instructed me to withdraw from the meditation.

After a moment I opened my eyes. I could see clearly around me everything as it had been before the meditation, but somehow I didn't feel part of it. Although I could see I didn't feel present in every aspect. I realised then that I was completely without any sense of feeling. Not even a feeling of numbness – just nothing. I glanced down at one of my hands and concentrated my whole attention upon it and gradually got it to move. Slowly feeling began to drift back into the body, but the lower area – the legs – remained as something only seen, not felt.

Lung Poh obviously knew what was going on with me. He prodded his own legs and then waved his hand intimating that there was nothing there. I nodded in agreement. I looked around at the other bhikkhus, seated in two ranks of twelve on each side of me. All of them were in meditation, each face completely composed and calm. Thitavedo was seated close to me in the right-hand rank as composed and peaceful as the rest. But on looking down again at my right leg, I found his hand resting on it reassuringly.

I brought my attention back to Lung Poh and in a loud voice he announced my new bhikkhu name. Kapilavaddho, he said, was to be my name. It was the best that he could find that fitted my character and possibilities. He also informed me that it was a new name that he had made for me specially, meaning broadly 'he who spreads and increases the Teaching'. He then instructed me to leave the platform and go to the far end of the pagoda among the lay people, there to await his assistants who would now proceed with the legal and truly Sangha business of the bhikkhu ordination ceremony of Upasampada.

Try as I might, I found it absolutely impossible to move from the spot where I was seated. The bowl on my back felt as if it weighed a ton, which I thought was rather strange as the bowl had always felt extremely light in my hands when empty. I rocked myself backwards and forwards but could not get my legs to work. Lung Poh beckoned some of my supporters who hurried on to the platform and literally carried me off. Having carried me to the far end of the building they gathered around me and proceeded to massage some semblance of life back into my legs so that I could at least stand.

I then stood with my back to the eastern wall of the bot and faced the platform with my hands held palms together in the form of salutation. This, I knew, would be a long wait. Here I would stand, waiting for the abbot's first and second assistants to leave the body of bhikkhus on the platform and come to me so that they could test and question me, then return to the assembly of bhikkhus and report.

Then began the ordination proper. The body of twenty-four bhikkhus had been elected by all the bhikkhus of Wat Paknam to act as their legally constituted representatives and thus were empowered as a Sangha – a group or committee – to act in all matters pertaining to the brotherhood. Their voice was law, and while Lung Poh was the senior and president, making their number twenty-five, he had no authority over and above them. All that he was entitled to do was to act as the mouthpiece for their decisions. The whole procedure would now follow strictly legal lines, following a pattern which has remained unchanged since the time of the Buddha.

First the assistants would inform the Sangha that I, one Kapilavaddho Samanero, had asked for admission as a bhikkhu, requesting Upasampada or higher ordination. I had asked that I be given this under the Venerable Candassaro as my teacher (or *Upajjhaya*). If this was in agreement with the views of the venerable gentlemen of the Sangha they would now depart and question the applicant as to his fitness. This being accomplished they would return and give their report. Every member of the Sangha remaining silent, showing their agreement, the assistants would come to me.

Having arrived they would then proceed to inform me that they were about to question me upon things of the utmost importance. This was a time for truth telling. Where the answer was yes, I must answer yes. Where it was no, such must be my answer. I must listen carefully now whilst they both stated the questions.

Then would come a long series, dealing first with my physical fitness and freedom from disease. Questions about my sex – was I fully male? Eunuchs, hermaphrodites and so forth were disbarred. Was I sane? Was I sub-human or animal? Was I over twenty years of age? Was I free from service to the King? Was I a criminal who had escaped from justice? Had I been freed from debts? Had my parents given permission for me to enter the Order? Had I the bowl and robes complete? What was my name? What was the name of my teacher?

All these questions would be asked. The two assistants, men of great experience and knowledge (the senior of the two known in Pali as *Kammavacarya*, the junior as *Anusavanacarya*), would chant the questions in unison. If either of them made a mistake in wording or pronunciation the other would correct him and they would commence again from the beginning.

They would then leave me again and return to the Sangha and chant in unison their report, maintaining the same precision as to word, content and pronunciation. The Sangha having agreed by their silence, the Kammavacarya would call me to come to the front of the group to make my application in person with the word *agacchati* – Come.

I would then go forward and kneel in front of the Sangha. Paying salutations first to the centre, then left, then right, I would ask, 'Venerable sirs of the Sangha, I ask for admission as bhikkhu. Allow me, venerable sirs, the higher ordination.' This I would repeat three times. Again with the silent permission of the Sangha I would approach the Kammavacarya and Anusavanacarya who would be seated one on each side of the abbot. After I had saluted them three times, they would ask the same series of questions as previously, but now asked and answered in the body of the Sangha. They would again state the truth of their findings to the Sangha and then proceed to place the motion before the assembled bhikkhus: that I be admitted to the higher ordination and accepted as one of the brotherhood; that I had answered all questions to their satisfaction and to the satisfaction of the Sangha; that Lung Poh had agreed and would act as my teacher. The motion having been correctly put, they would repeat it word for word three times.

If all the bhikkhus remained silent and no voice was raised against the motion, they would close by saying, 'Venerable sirs of the Sangha, you have heard the motion that Kapilavaddho be admitted to the Order under the Venerable Candassaro. Three times you have heard it stated without dissent. You have remained silent. By your silence we understand that you agree with the motion. Upasampada, the higher ordination, is granted to Kapilavaddho, the Venerable Candassaro acting as Upajjhaya – preceptor and teacher. This is a Sangha Kamma, an act of the Sangha.'

And so it was. The whole ceremony went through without a hitch. Every word, sound and act was carried out strictly according to the legal code of bhikkhus, the Vinaya. As the final words were uttered by the assistants, the whole group of bhikkhus gathered round me so that I was completely encircled, literally taken into their midst. All had their hands raised in salutation. From every face shone a smile of welcome and understanding. Each and every one of them had been through the emotional stress of this ceremony, and they well knew what it meant to a man.

I raised my own hands in salutation, pressing the thumbs deep into my eyes to dam the tears which were threatening to burst forth and flood down my cheeks. With an effort I controlled myself as the whole assembly began a chant of welcome and thanksgiving. At last, I thought, I have accomplished the thing I set out to do.

And during those moments, encircled in the body of the Sangha, my mind went back to the people in England who had helped me to attain just this moment. My mother who, on the morning of my departure, said with a smile on her dear old face, 'Bless you, son, on your way. Don't turn back. Carry it through to the end.' I thought of the family who had freed me that I might go my chosen way, of the friends in many parts of the country who by their kindness and help had made my passage possible. I thought of my new Thai friends, my supporters, the bhikkhus, Lung Poh and Thitavedo. And in those moments I realised with utter clarity that no man accomplishes anything alone.

The ceremony completed, I had to move to the body of the pagoda where a table and chair had been specially arranged for me. Here I sat and received gifts, or *Dana* as it is called. People from all parts of the country came and paid their respects and presented gifts. Representatives of various government departments of Thailand, of the American Embassy, of the Chinese in Thailand. Finally came representatives of England, not officials, these, but friends: Peter Simms; John Blofeld, who had done such great work in translating Buddhist literature from the Chinese; Brain-Hartnell, Professor of English at Chula University; and finally, Royston Mason. These last settled around me as a happy guard of honour whilst the rest of this generous gathering filed past. Finally, the last gift was received and I was literally led to my own house. Here I was told by Thitavedo that I would be allowed half an hour's rest and then I must go and deliver my lecture.

With a sigh I slumped into a chair and enjoyed a glass of coffee and a smoke. Thitavedo was hovering around me like a protecting angel, eventually managing to get everyone out of the room so that we were left alone. He informed me that the ceremony had lasted three and a half hours, and that it had probably been the biggest ordination ceremony in Thailand, with ten thousand people present on monastery ground, many of whom would stay the night.

In my lecture, he said, I must tell the people all about myself and why I wanted to be a bhikkhu. I told him that I found it difficult at this moment to talk about myself and would far rather say nothing at all. He was very sorry, he knew that I was tired, but it was traditional that a new bhikkhu gave a talk. In my case it was even more important as my name had been spread all over Thailand and everybody wanted to hear about me, to hear me talk. He also informed me of another arrangement of which I had known nothing: the talk was to be broadcast over Thai Radio. I was to speak one sentence at a time and he would interpret so that everyone got the sense of the talk as it went along. The talk would also be recorded so that a typescript of it could be printed and published.

When he had finished his instructions and had patted me on the back reassuringly, he smiled and said, 'Trouble with you, brother, you talk too much. Must get some rest. Back soon.' With that he dashed off to the lower floor and left me to myself.

Five minutes later he was back, with a cheery 'Come, brother – can't make lazy here all night. Many people wait to hear what you say'. He led me off to the front of the pagoda where a vast mass of people had gathered to listen to my talk.

I talked for an hour and a half, with another three-quarters of an hour taken up in answering questions. From what I gathered afterwards everyone was extremely interested in what I had to say. I just gave as sincere a picture as possible of the kind of life which I had led, the things which I had studied and the things in my experience which had driven me at long last to take this step.

It was during the preparation of this talk that I first came to realise the surprising depth of knowledge which Thitavedo possessed regarding Western philosophical terminology. We naturally had quite a deal of discussion as to the content of the talk, and when I showed my surprise at his knowledge he just smiled and then reeled off a massive list of Western philosophical literature which he had read. I also learned that he was conversant with Sanskrit, Urdu, Sinhala, Chinese, Pali and of course English.

The talk being over, I again returned to my room, walking back through the masses of people who were now waiting for the beginning of the Vaisakha celebrations. After half an hour's rest Thitavedo informed me that I should now get ready to attend the rest of the bhikkhus down in the pagoda compound as they were about to begin the celebration with Lung Poh at their head. With Thitavedo leading I made my way down to the entrance of the compound, there to be met by a large number of bhikkhus who were awaiting my arrival.

Night had fallen and the sky, spangled with stars so large that they looked like the most costly of jewels, was a deep velvety blue. Through the deep silhouette of trees against the night sky, across a small stream lay the pagoda – white and glistening, giving a sense of utter stillness and peace and yet of being vibrantly alive.

Just outside the compound everyone taking part had been marshalled. At a given signal the procession headed into the compound and began its triple journey slowly round the pagoda. At the head was my teacher the abbot, Chao Khun Bhavanakosol, strong and confident in spite of his eighty-two summers. His face, undoubtedly the finest that it had been my privilege to see, was radiantly happy.

Following him were some four hundred bhikkhus and two hundred samaneras, each carrying in their hands flowers, lighted tapers and burning joss sticks. It was in this group, just behind the abbot, that Thitavedo and myself walked. The scene in the compound was a blaze of colour. The brilliant yellows and, in some cases, browns of the bhikkhus' robes were in sharp contrast to the shimmering whiteness of the dress worn by the thousands of lay people. All that could be heard was the soft tread of thousands of bare feet. The air was filled with a myriad dancing fireflies and was pungent with the rich perfume of burning joss sticks.

The abbot halted the procession a moment and pointed to the sky above. There, poised in all her glory, full and radiant, resplendent in the jewel-encrusted velvet night sky, was the Vaisakha Moon. I became aware that the whole group of bhikkhus and samaneras was concentrating for a moment on the import of that moon. Each face was calm and at peace.

Slowly, against the stillness rose a sound from the vast gathering of white-robed lay people. It rippled and swelled across the compound, and faded away like the sighing of the wind in trees. It was as if the people had sighed as they joined in the intensity of the moment.

The procession moved forward again and having completed three circuits of the pagoda, the abbot and bhikkhus entered, followed by as many of the people as could find room. The abbot then gave a long talk on the Dhamma, or teaching of the Buddha. He explained to all that the best way of celebrating such a night was to practise the Way which had been taught by Gotama.

The people remained throughout the whole night whilst relays of bhikkhus kept up a continuous chanting of the Suttas, the Discourses of the Buddha.

★   ★   ★

Later that night Lung Poh came to my room with Thitavedo. He talked with me about the day and my feelings now that I was a bhikkhu. He showed no signs of tiredness after his own long day and appeared to be concerned only with my welfare. He talked much on the teaching and its understanding, stressing that I must come to personal experience in myself of all that was taught.

As he was about to take his leave he put his hand on my shoulder and said, 'Kapilavaddho, remember and think about the story of Bahiya. Bahiya came to the Buddha after having travelled far to find him, and was fearful lest he should die before he could be taught by him. He eventually found the Buddha on his begging round and approaching him said, "Lord, teach me your law, your way, for I know not when you might die or I might die. Teach me."

'Twice he asked, and twice the Buddha turned him away, knowing that his mind was not yet ready to receive the teaching. And a third time did Bahiya approach the Buddha with his request. On this occasion the Buddha replied, "Thus must you learn, Bahiya. In the Seen there can only be what is seen. In the Heard there can only be what is heard. In Feeling there can only be what is felt. In Taste there can only be what is tasted. In Thought there can only be what is thought. In Knowing there can only be what is known. These things being true as I have stated, you, Bahiya, are not in them. Since you, Bahiya, are not in them, are not here, therefore you, Bahiya, are neither in this world nor the next world nor betwixt the two. Thus must you learn, Bahiya. This alone is the end of unrest and suffering."

'I want you to think about this story, Kapilavaddho. Practise the things which I have taught to you. Think of nothing else, work all the time and you also can come to understanding just as did Bahiya. I cannot give you the truth. I cannot give you understanding. I can only point the way.'

When Lung Poh and Thitavedo had left, I again looked out of my window across to the pagoda compound. It was still lit from the dancing tapers as people made their individual circuits of homage before entering the pagoda to listen for a while to the still chanting bhikkhus. Others had stretched themselves on the ground to sleep. Others still sat in groups animatedly conversing about the day's happenings. Over and above all this came the voice of a young samanera, chanting rapidly in a high-pitched tone, then faltering and going back to the beginning of the chant, only to falter again at some other verse or line as he tried to memorise the lessons given him that day by his teacher.

As I lay down on my bench I found myself swept by a feeling of intense joy. It must have been the impact of all that the day had meant to me. The new-found sense of at last *belonging*. Before I fell asleep the feeling had developed into one of certainty that I had reached some stage of equanimity. I was convinced that I had no feelings for or against anything. I told myself that I had no desire to die, neither had I any desire to live. I was satisfied with whatever was. Little knowing how short-lived such prideful and wishful thinking was going to be, I fell asleep.

10

PANIC, FEAR AND DREAD

The next morning I rose at my usual time of four-thirty. I still felt much the same as I had the night before. The sense that I had almost accomplished my task and that nothing could go wrong any more grew stronger as the morning progressed. During that time I had mainly sat and checked my feelings and thoughts – little realising, of course, that I was dealing with purely hypothetical situations – and had just metaphorically patted myself on the back for being such a good chap, when I decided to finish a glass of coffee I'd poured earlier.

I got up and reached for the glass, and then my stomach turned over and I felt as sick as a dog. On looking down into the glass I saw that one of the house lizards had drowned itself in the liquid. They always were greedy little devils and this one had tempted fate too far. He just lay there with his body all bloated and his eyes almost starting out of his head.

I sat down again and asked myself why it was that I should feel so queer, particularly as I had been so sure that I had almost conquered all my feelings, my desires and aversions. Eventually I had to admit to myself that the queasiness of my stomach had been triggered off by the sight of the dead lizard in the coffee. I had to admit also that this sight had aroused in myself violent aversion, so violent that it had made me feel sick. I argued with myself as to what harm a dead lizard could do me – the sight of the object could do me no harm, neither could the touch of it. I eventually came back to the fact that it was my own aversion that was doing me the harm. I remembered that Thitavedo had told me that one of my main troubles was that of aversion and that I must master it if I were to progress. At this point sound thinking returned, and I realised how fortunate I was that the incident had occurred and so proved to me by actual experience how much work I had still to do.

I rose from my seat again and picked up the glass, determined to overcome the feeling of nausea in my stomach. I put my finger in the

102 _Life as a Siamese Monk_

glass and fished out the dead lizard, held him in my hands and felt him while the nausea gradually died away. When it had gone completely I put the lizard down, picked up the glass, placed it next to my lips and then drank the coffee to the last dregs without even a shudder. It was whilst I had been analysing my feelings that I came to the conclusion that it was the thought of drinking the coffee without knowing that the lizard had been drowned in it that had been responsible for the aversion which had swept over me. That being so there was only one thing to do: drink it.

★   ★   ★

I ate my meal at eleven that morning, alone as usual. I had returned to my room and was in the process of sweeping it out when I became aware that _something_ large and black had made an extremely rapid entry through one of the open windows. I put down the broom and went over to investigate.

There on my bed, which was immediately below the window, was the largest black spider I had ever seen. It had a large furry body and thick hairy legs. The spider was obviously as interested in my movements as I was in its, for suddenly it took off at great speed, making straight for me. With a completely instinctive reaction I managed to move faster than I had thought possible. The spider's final jump took it past me so that it landed on the floor. From then on for quite a while I played a fantastic game of 'foot off ground' whilst the spider dashed backwards and forwards across my room in an absolute frenzy of activity, eventually landing back on the bed as it was when I had my first sight of it.

I crept quietly over to my chair and sat down to gain my breath again and to regain, if possible, some degree of calm. Lurking at the back of my mind somewhere was the knowledge that something else had also happened when the spider had made its first lightning-like entry into the room. Something else had moved. As I sat and thought about this I glanced up at the walls and immediately realised what the other movement had been. On the spider's rapid arrival every lizard in the place had just as rapidly left. Now there was not one to be seen – usually the walls and ceiling were alive with them.

Looking again at the spider on the bed I realised for the first time that he – or more probably she – was dangerous. My lizards were courageous little creatures, always ready to fight. I had never known them run away before, even in the face of rats or snakes. At the sight of my new visitor, however, they had taken off for other parts with alacrity – which meant in my reasoning that the visitor was a threat to their lives. With equal reasoning I came to the conclusion that the spider could make mine pretty uncomfortable given the chance.

I forced myself to move slowly over to the bed so that I could get a closer look at my fast-moving visitor. It sat quite still while I looked. I was able to assess its size as being only slightly smaller than my own right hand and to see its menacingly efficient mouth working below its body. The mouth was on the move all the time rather like a cow chewing cud, the difference being that the spider appeared to possess three jaws.

It was then I realised that what I had before me was some form of tarantula – not too pleasant a creature to have as a room companion. With this realisation arose fear, of which it appeared the spider was aware: it immediately made straight for me again. Again I managed to dodge and started on 'foot off ground' once more, much more rapidly than before, as the spider rushed across the floor in apparently all directions at once. On one occasion it jumped straight off a wall outwards a clear five feet, to land on the floor again and, after a mad rush, disappeared under the bed bench.

During the rest of the day I made sporadic attempts to find and drive out the spider. Whilst I felt driven to find it and somehow get it out of the room, I always caught myself during these searches hoping that I would not come across it again. I found myself to be in a complete state of tension between the desire to find and the wish not to find – the latter strengthened, no doubt, by the fact that I was barefoot and wearing a sarong, a simple loin cloth, without underclothes. Also I was under the rule not to kill or harm any living creature. Mainly, however, I was convinced that I did not wish to confront the spider again as it was more than likely that it would chase me out of the room. I took a final look under the bed and there it was.

I decided that the best plan would be to forget it as it would in all probability go away just as it had arrived. I managed to carry this out fairly successfully for a while, so much so that when Thitavedo arrived I had forgotten about the spider under the bed. Thitavedo had brought from the abbot my bhikkhu record and identification book, duly signed by the Sangha Rajas of Thailand and Lung Poh as my teacher, attesting the authenticity of both my entry into the Order as a samanera and my higher ordination as a bhikkhu. This book contained details as to parents; place and date of birth; place and date of both samanera and bhikkhu ordinations, with the names and offices of the officiating bhikkhus; and finally the name of the area where I was at present residing and a photograph of the owner of the book.

This book is carried by all bhikkhus and samaneras in Thailand, the only Buddhist country to my knowledge to have such an institution. In a country where there are large expanses of jungle and literally thousands of bhikkhus on the move, it would be quite easy for charlatans and brigands to wear the robe to serve their ends. The record book keeps such practices under control. Both the Maha Sangha – the controlling body of the Order for the whole country – and the secular authorities enforce the rule that all members of the Order must own a record book. Should a wearer of the robe not be able to produce one within a reasonable time when asked, he is immediately imprisoned as an impostor. In this manner not only are the public at large protected but also the good name of the Order.

I took the book with some pride as Thitavedo handed it over to me. He explained that there was room in it to record any status to which I might arrive, or on the other hand to record any infringement of the rules. I was always to carry the book with me and if I moved from one monastery to another it must be signed by the abbot of the monastery I was leaving. On arriving at another monastery I was to hand the book immediately to the abbot so that he might examine it.

He then turned to me and said, 'How you feel now that you are proper bhikkhu, brother? Much better now that you are bhikkhu like me. We can get more closely by like as bhikkhus. With bhikkhu and samanera sometimes things very difficult owing to rules. Now we both under Vinaya, have same rules for both of us.'

I was able to tell him that I was indeed happy at the thought that at long last I was a bhikkhu and that I was fortunate indeed to have him as friend, guide, nurse and brother to advise me in my new form of life.

It was whilst I was saying this that memories of the spider returned. I immediately took the opportunity of telling my friend about the visitor, giving him a detailed explanation of what it was like and asking him if the creature was dangerous. I also told him how quickly my ideas as to my advancement had been shattered by both the incident of the lizard and the entry of the spider.

At the latter he laughed and said, 'Brother, you just like me when I begin bhikkhu life. Very quickly something going wrong with the mind and head swell up to big size. Think I am very great man as good as the Buddha himself. Even think my foot hardly touch the ground as I walk, I walk so high. Then Lung Poh come along and make me very angry and then I know I not what I thought I was because the Buddha not get angry any time. Not to worry. Mostly of us get like this at the beginning. Only can learn by mistakes. You learning very fast.'

He then turned to the subject of the spider: 'Spider not hurt you. This one have never heard of to bite. All things in Thailand not bite, mostly they very gentle. Not to worry about him if still in the room. Just go to sleep and he will not trouble you. Maybe better now if we have some coffee and then go sleep, time very late.'

When Thitavedo had retired I applied myself with renewed vigour to the various aspects of meditation which I had to carry out on retiring. Having completed everything required of me I laid myself down on the low bed and lay there for some time tossing and turning. It was an extremely hot night and sweat was pouring off me, a fact that seemed to make me the centre of attraction for masses of mosquitoes. After a while I gave up the struggle to get myself comfortable and rose. I took everything off except my sarong and wiped down my body with a towel. Feeling a great deal better and quite sure that I could now settle down to sleep I again lay down and after a very short time must have fallen asleep.

I was awakened by the feeling that something had run across my legs and bounded rapidly off the bed. I turned on the light just in time to see the spider crawl to the underside of the bed. All the previous fear and repugnance returned to me, and it took some considerable time before I could convince myself that the spider was probably harmless as Thitavedo had said, and that the best thing for me to do was to get back to bed. So I once more lay down and, strangely enough, quickly fell asleep again.

Again I was awakened with the sickening knowledge that the spider had crawled under my sarong and was between my legs. How I got off the bed I do not remember. All I knew was that as far as I was concerned the spider was getting much too personal. As my feet hit the floor the spider fell out from under the sarong and landed with a thud on the floor. Switching on the light again I saw him – or was it her? – once more crawling to the underside of the bed-boards.

After that I gave up thoughts of sleep for a while. I sat down in the small chair and smoked. After a time my experiences with the spider began to take a humorous turn in my mind. I even began to think as a joke that the spider's name was Flossie and that she had apparently taken such a fancy to both my bed and myself that I couldn't really blame her for her attentions. For all my joking, however, I decided that I would let Flossie have the bed for the rest of the night – I would sleep in the chair. So off with the light and to sleep again, I told myself.

I sat so for half an hour or more and became increasingly worried by thoughts that I was letting my fear of the spider get the better of me. I began to detest myself for a coward and cursed myself for holding such high-falutin' ideas as I had done on the night of the ordination. If I was to gain anything from this new life, I must force myself to face situations, to deal with things as they arose. To recognise fear and then deal with it. With such thinking came to mind the words used by the

Buddha in one of his great discourses, words which dealt with fear and dread and the way in which he dealt with them himself:

Then, brahmin, I thought: 'Suppose now that on those nights that are notable and well marked, the fifteenth and eighth of the lunar month – suppose I spend them in shrines of forest, park, or trees, fearsome and hair-raising as they are, making such shrines my lodging for the night, that I might behold for myself the panic, fear and dread of it all.'

So, brahmin, when the next time came round I did so. As I stayed there, a deer maybe came up to me, or a peacock threw down a twig, or else a breeze stirred a heap of fallen leaves. Then thought I: 'Here it is! Here comes that panic, fear and dread!' Then, brahmin, there came to me this thought: 'Why do I remain thus in constant fear and apprehension? Let me bend down to my will that panic, fear and dread, just as I am and just as it came to be.' So as I was walking to and fro that panic, fear and dread came upon me. Then I neither stood still nor sat nor lay down, but just walking up and down I bent to my will that panic, fear and dread.

Again, as I was standing still, it came upon me. But I neither walked up and down, nor sat, nor lay, but just standing bent it down to my will. And yet again, as I was sitting it came upon me. But I neither stood up nor walked up and down nor lay down, but just sitting as I was, I bent it to my will. Then as I lay it came upon me, but I sat not up nor stood up nor walked up and down but just lying as I was, I bent that panic, fear and dread to my will.

I thought over these words as they continued to run through my memory. I thought of the gigantic struggles through which Gotama the man must have passed. How each and every aspect of his teaching had come about through his personal experience. How he had personally tested and experienced every known method of austerity then in vogue in India. Of his living in burial grounds, himself in such a state that he was taken for one of the dead. I thought of the great risks which he took when he put to the test the theory that the way to spiritual growth was through starvation, going to such lengths that at one time he was taking only one grain of rice a day. At the point of death he had had the courage to turn away, knowing that this was not the way to that for which he searched.

For probably the first time, thinking on these things, I realised that this way of life which I had chosen, which the Buddha had laid down, was one that had to be walked utterly alone. No matter how many teachers one had, what they taught had to be lived out and worked out in one's own experience. If I were to succeed, I must go the way alone.

Thankful that I had remembered the words of the founder of the brotherhood to which I belonged and determined to be worthy to follow in such footsteps, I again laid my body down on the bed which I knew was shared with the spider and, with a meditation repetition running through my mind, I fell asleep.

How long I had been asleep I had no way of knowing, but suddenly I was awakened by the most agonising and excruciating pain in my left leg, just above the ankle. I bounded off the bed and turned on the light. My leg was throbbing fit to burst and the pain seemed to cover the leg from foot to knee. I looked down at the swollen mass that had been an ankle and saw a small puncture on the inside, just above the ankle joint.

Without further ado I grasped my girdle and wound it rapidly around the leg at about the middle of the calf and with a piece of stick twisted it tightly into a tourniquet. Then taking an open razor I cut across the puncture in the leg. On second thoughts I cut out the piece of flesh that contained the puncture. I then pressed and massaged the leg downwards to the ankle continuously until the wound was bleeding freely. Eventually, after a titanic struggle, I managed to get my lips to the wound and sucked furiously in my endeavours to draw out the poison.

Gradually the intensity of the pain subsided. Rather cautiously I loosened the tourniquet and waited to find out if there were any signs that the swelling or pain would progress beyond the knee. They remained in the lower leg, so I gave the wound another short session of forced bleeding and finally bound it with a handkerchief.

For what remained of the night I sat in the chair and did some serious thinking. In a matter of a day and part of a night I had learned two sharp lessons – lessons which were to stand me in good stead at a later date. I remember thinking to myself, 'So you were the one who was so certain of the fact that you were not concerned with the question as to whether you lived or died. You had no thoughts for or against anything. You were the one who had arrived at a state of equanimity. You were the one who had no fears left. Yet here you've been, fearing something for most of the night, and on being bitten by a spider you make frantic efforts to remove as much poison from your system as possible. Why? Surely to make every effort to save your life which you thought was in danger. That was what you feared – not the spider as such, but the threat to the life you so glibly thought you were not concerned about.'

So the thinking went on during that night. Every one of my actions was analysed and with each remembrance of them I realised that many had not been consciously carried out but had been purely automatic, instinctive.

As the first light of dawn streaked the eastern sky I sat in my chair a happier man, a richer man for the night's experiences. I realised in the dawn light that I had gained a little more knowledge about myself, about my character. I knew just a little more of that something I called *myself.* I had gained some knowledge of a subliminal side to character, a side that could fear, that could fight for life, no matter what the consciously-willed side of the character might say. This newly-discovered aspect appeared to have a will of its own. I realised that the experiences with the lizard and the coffee and the spider's bite had given me the key for which I had searched, the key to myself and the key to my understanding of what it was that the Buddha had taught.

I realised that what the Buddha had taught was a method whereby one could end the suffering or unrest of life, an unrest which is present to a degree in all people. The method taught not of putting the objective world to rights. It offered no rewards to the man who thought he would go out into the world to save sinners. Neither did it offer any form of vicarious salvation for the man who had been good just for such a reward. Gotama had taught a method whereby a man could come to know himself. Could come to understand where the suffering and unrest arose and where the causes for such states could be found. It was a method of self-help.

I began to understand more fully Lung Poh's insistence that the method or path must be practised fully as a whole-time occupation. In no other way could the teaching of Gotama be tested. In no other way could one know whether it were indeed true. Belief in the teaching's truth or faith in its efficacy had no place.

As the time approached for my first meal I realised that I could literally sit in my room for the rest of my life, becoming interested in less and less and repeating suttas by the hour. That by this method I might even gain some sort of smooth grey neutrality which I might take to be peace and equanimity. But all it could be, I knew, was a mental dullness, a state of sloth and torpor which I would hide behind rather than face the task before me.

My experiences of the night and the day before had given me the key. If I wanted to find the answers to my own unrest, to my crass fears, my moments of anguish, I must look within. To do this I must come to understand what it was that felt things, liked and disliked things. That saw, smelled and tasted things. I must find that something which thought it thought the things which it thought. I knew that I had the key to the problems so often in my mind. Where had I come from? What was the purpose of life? Where would I go after this life? Again some words of the Buddha from one of the suttas came to mind:

I do not say that without reaching the world's end an end of woe cannot be made – for you can end it here and now. For, my friend, in this very body, six feet in length, with its sense impressions and its thoughts and ideas, I do declare to you, are the world, and the origin of the world, and the ceasing of the world, and likewise that way that leadeth to the ceasing thereof.

With such thoughts in mind and with a growing determination to apply myself more vigorously to the training which I had undertaken, I walked to the lower floor to partake of the first meal of the day. I did not even see who it was that handed over the food – it must have been one of the local people – for I was much too absorbed with my own thoughts. Even my injured ankle had been forgotten.

The eating of that meal brought a new facet into the training I was undergoing. Being so absorbed in thought I did not even realise that I had started eating. When I did become aware of it, aware of the fact that a good half of the meal had been consumed without my having even tasted it I asked myself the question, Who was it that had eaten it? From then onwards I paid strict attention to every process that went to make up the strange phenomenon called eating.

Why was I eating, I asked myself – quickly to decide that it was because I felt hungry. Who was it then who had eaten when I had been so absorbed in thought? There was no feeling of hunger then. I had to fall back on the fact that habit had done the eating, habit which had grown strong through consciously repeated instigations through the years. When I said that I ate because I felt hungry I knew that it wasn't strictly true. All that I could say in truth was that there was a feeling of being empty. Feeling or sensation, I discovered, covered most of the activities of the something I called *me*. All the sensations which I was able to unravel from each other that morning had nothing in common. Each arose in relation to a different stimulant or datum. I well remember the tangle in which I got myself over the discovery that what I saw on the plate with my eyes was not that which I tasted when it moved to my mouth.

How long my investigations would have gone on that morning I know not, for I was aroused from my absorption by the arrival of Thitavedo and a companion. I arose from the meal immediately and paid the salutations due to senior from junior.

Thitavedo looked me over and then pointing at my left foot said, 'Brother, you got fat foot. How come? You been getting angry and kicking wall?' I told him that I had often felt like kicking walls in my exasperation since I had been at Wat Paknam but hadn't done so yet. I then explained that I had been bitten by the spider.

On hearing this, Thitavedo's companion showed much concern and intimated with rapid gesticulations and a torrent of words to Thitavedo that they should look at the leg. It was then that Thitavedo introduced his companion to me: it was his uncle who was cultivating a patch of ground in the jungle some six miles away.

Once in my room Uncle made me lie down on the bed and uncovered the injured leg. When he saw it in all its glory he hissed in a deep breath and shook his head and turned again to Thitavedo with a flood of words. Through Thitavedo I gathered that Uncle wanted to know what kind of spider it was that had bitten me. This I again explained to my friend and he relayed it to Uncle, after which Uncle had a lot more to say to Thitavedo.

My friend began to look very worried. He turned to me and said, 'Brother, I very sorry. I not know when you explain to me about spider that it can bite. I wanted you just to have good sleep and not worry and maybe I think that spider not bite you anyway, so not to worry. Now Uncle tell me that this spider very dangerous. We must find it and put it out of your room.'

I told him not to worry about the incident – the spider might not have bitten me anyway. What had happened, I presumed, was that I had kicked it with my left leg whilst I was asleep and quite naturally it had reacted by biting. In any case, I had learned a lot from the experience.

Uncle – who I later learned had made quite a name for himself as a local native doctor, dealing with herbal remedies and attending to the various bites from snake, spider and scorpion among the jungle people – gave my leg a thorough examination, prodding and squeezing it all the while. He then wanted to know if there was any pain in the upper leg or groin. On being told that there was not, he asked me what I had done when I discovered the bite. When I had explained to him the whole of my operations of the night before he laughed delightedly and through Thitavedo told me that I had acted very fast and very wisely. Cutting, bleeding and sucking the wound was the only possible thing to do. He then massaged the leg downwards for about half an hour until the wound bled again. Apparently satisfied, he bathed the leg and after a few more words with Thitavedo he left.

I then told my friend about my experiences of the day and night before, and then about my thoughts and experiences at my first meal. I told him that I was sure that I now understood what had to be done and that I wanted to apply myself solely to this task. If it could be arranged I would like to spend all my time undisturbed in my room. I wanted to see no one.

To all this he replied, 'This very great pity, brother. Some people have arranged that they come see you this afternoon. Can't stop them now because I have said "Yes, can come". Also must ask Lung Poh before you shut self away. Not to worry, brother, everything coming all right. If Lung Poh think it time for you to shut away for long time he will allow and then I make all arrangements.'

I thanked him for his understanding and efforts on my behalf and he left, no doubt to go to Lung Poh and tell him what I wanted to do. Within an hour he was back. He informed me that Lung Poh would come and see me that evening.

Thitavedo then went to the door of my room and called two of the boys, who entered carrying a large cardboard box and a flat piece of cardboard which acted as a lid. Both these lads – who were grinning from ear to ear – proceeded to clear my room methodically. Out went the bed, chair and small table, the few odd books and the robe I was not wearing. They then searched through the empty room and found my friend the spider in one of the corners. The boys let out a whoop and for a while the place was a pandemonium of flying feet and dashing figures as we all made the attempt to trap the spider in the box. Eventually one of the boys, throwing himself through the air like a rugger player making a touch-down, managed to get the box over the top of the spider whilst the other slid the cardboard lid underneath. They then ceremoniously carried the box with its dynamic contents out into the open ground of the compound and set it free.

★ ★ ★

I spent most of the afternoon meeting the people whom Thitavedo had arranged for me to see and talk with. In the early evening I again returned to my room to await the arrival of Lung Poh. I must have fallen asleep, for I was awakened by a touch on my shoulder and a voice saying, 'Tan William'.

I looked up to find Lung Poh standing by my side accompanied by Thitavedo. Lung Poh was smiling but Thitavedo was looking at me very sternly. It gradually dawned upon me that I was sitting in only my sarong, which was of course not the way for a junior bhikkhu to meet his superior. I rose from my chair immediately and robed myself in the civaram or large robe and paid respects in the proper manner to both Lung Poh and my friend. With that accomplished, the smile returned to Thitavedo's face once more.

I explained to Lung Poh what it was that I wanted to do, that I wanted to be left alone so that I might carry out undisturbed meditational practice. He appeared to be very pleased that my desires lay in this direction and said immediately that he would make all the necessary arrangements so that I might carry out my plan.

He was on the point of leaving, when I began to tell him of my experiences during the early morning meal. Strive as I might, I explained to him, I could find no such thing as *myself* in the normally accepted sense. All that I could find was some feeling or other, some percept, some concept – but never myself. Which, it appeared to me, was quite in keeping with the Buddha's teaching that all things are selfless, have no permanent abiding entity, are *anatta*, soulless. Was this correct, I asked. And if it were, what was the use of the concept of rebirth or *jati* that the Buddha had taught? After all, did he not teach that all things, all beings, were born and died and were born again in an endless round of rebirths known as samsara – the realm of coming to be, the realm of suffering and unrest? If there was no self, I wanted to know, what was reborn from life to life? Surely the two concepts denied each other, cancelled each other out.

Lung Poh replied that my findings and experiences at the meal time had been very good and in fact had been very good *satipatthana* – application of mindfulness or awareness. He reminded me that the one way – the only way, in fact, the Buddha had said – that could lead to understanding of his teaching and the release thereby entailed was by satipatthana, was by mindfulness as to the body, the feelings, the mind and the objects of mind.

But to help me solve my problem he wanted me to continue with the original meditation exercise he had given me. Upon this I was to gain the initial concentration and then I was to apply myself to remembering back through thoughts and feelings through each day, each month, each year, even back to the time of my birth. To go through the birth process and beyond to the life before, and so on ad infinitum. I was not to worry, but I must give up all my questioning. If I would practise as he instructed, the truth would come to me. All the questions about the various anomalies in the teaching would fall into perspective. I would come to vipassana or insight into the truth. I was just to keep at the practice, and at all other times practise satipatthana or mindfulness as to everything I did. This he knew I would not find difficult as the process had already started.

He told me also that he had put me completely in the care of Thitavedo, who would occasionally take a look at me to see that I was quite safe and that I did not go too long without food. I must remember that if Thitavedo interfered at any time it would be for my own good. Also, I must always be prepared for calls upon my time with reference to the Vinaya or Rules of Discipline. Under Vinaya as a bhikkhu I would normally have to go to the pagoda once every fortnight for *Patimokkha*, the hearing of the recitation of the Vinaya rules and the confession of faults if any. In my case this could be carried out by Thitavedo as my senior. All that was necessary was that I make an utterance to the effect that I was pure as to the carrying out of the rules. This would mean that I need only attend the full ceremony once a month.

Lung Poh stressed most forcibly the necessity for my following the general direction which the meditation practice might take. I was to stop the mind wandering from the task in hand. If, however, it appeared to me that Lung Poh had – during meditation – instructed me on a particular course of action, I was to follow that instruction. In this way he knew that I would find the answer to another one of my questions. I would also find out who my teacher was and where he or it resided.

Always I was to remember that I was a vipassana bhikkhu – a meditation bhikkhu. I had been ordained as that, had chosen the vipassana dhura – the burden of meditation – and as such belonged to the group known as *aranya vasi* – the jungle dwellers.

Whilst at the moment I lived in a house, he could remember the spot years ago when he had first come to Wat Paknam, when the area was jungle. Where my house now stood there had once grown a large tree. It was under this tree that he had lived and meditated by the hour. There were only five other bhikkhus living there at the time, and they lived their lives in much the same way. He knew, he said, from experience that this particular spot was very good for meditation. That fact combined with my aptitude should help toward a successful outcome to my experiment of long-term withdrawal.

When he had finished talking I knelt before him and thanked him for his advice and help. Then, having bowed my head three times to the ground in salutation, I was on the point of rising when he placed a hand on my shoulder and said, 'Don't give up, Tan William. Don't stop practice until you have found the answers you seek. *Sukhi hotu* – be happy.'

With Lung Poh's departure began for me four months of intense practice. Four months of seeing no one except occasionally Thitavedo. Four months with nothing to read or study, just left alone to myself. Four months during which date, day, time or month ceased for me to have any meaning.

11

MEDITATION EXPERIENCES

On the tenth day after my ordination as bhikkhu, acting in strict accordance with Vinaya rules, I had to confess to the ownership of much more in the way of property than I was entitled to. All these things had been presented to me as gifts from various people and groups after the ordination ceremony. Thitavedo was the bhikkhu who had been appointed by the Sangha to officiate at my confession.

I still had my eight original allowances – the three robes, begging bowl, razor, needle and cotton, drinking cup and girdle. I now possessed in excess: seventeen sets of robes, hundreds of toothbrushes and tubes of toothpaste, five tea sets made from the most exquisite china, fourteen umbrellas and parasols, three clocks, three beautiful cloisonné teapots, six large vacuum ice-jars and a dozen large-sized ordinary vacuum flasks.

Each item I had to confess to owning separately, and when I had finished and Bhikkhu Thitavedo had ascertained that my original three robes were marked correctly and that I was wearing them, he informed me that I would have to forfeit all the goods over and above my original eight articles. I was of course delighted at the news and handed over everything to him with great speed, only too happy to get rid of the stuff. I was completely taken by surprise, however, when he turned to me and handed the lot back again. I remonstrated with him, asking why he should give the goods back when I had confessed to their ownership and complied with the Vinaya rules in forfeiting them.

He laughingly explained that he had told me on the day of the ordination that these gifts would become a burden to me. The reason that the Sangha had handed back the extras after I had forfeited them was so that I learned the burden of possessions. Every ten days from now I would have to waste time confessing to ownership over and above my allowance, forfeiting the items and then having them returned to me until such time as I had managed to give them away to some deserving cases. There were many poor bhikkhus and samaneras who had very little support and were walking about in robes which were literally just hanging together, they were so old. The best thing for me to do was to get rid of my possessions by giving them away quickly. But I had to be sure that the need was great before handing anything over.

Throughout that day I wandered round the area watching bhikkhus and samaneras come and go, visiting every hut and living space. In this way I not only managed to get rid of my surplus but was able to see with my own eyes the conditions under which many of my brothers lived and were indeed happy to live. Many of the huts were built on stilts over stagnant, stinking water. None of them had such a thing as a raised bench, bed or chair. Few if any had the luxury of a thermos flask in which to keep something to drink. As I walked round I realised that most of my brothers lived in this fashion, but on not one face did I see any discontent. Each and every one to whom I gave some gift was just thankful in a wonderfully gracious manner.

The only one who showed any pride at all was a young samanera of about eleven years of age. He was wearing a robe so torn and holed that it was a wonder that it managed to cover him at all. On receiving a new robe from me he was as proud as most boys would have been with a new suit. He strutted back and forth as proud as a peacock, somehow managing to fold the large robe (my robes being made specially large as I was so much bigger than the average Thai) so that it appeared to fit him. From what I could gather he was very proud to wear a fully grown bhikkhu's robe, particularly as it had belonged to me. I saw him many times later and he was still proudly wearing the robe. In fact he was still wearing it when I eventually left Thailand.

The bhikkhu Tan Kan, the one who had helped me with robing for the final ordination, had asked Thitavedo if he might come and live with us so that he could look after me as well – a fine gesture as he was a bhikkhu much senior to myself. It was Tan Kan's being on hand all the time which allowed me to have my food put outside my room, and so I did not have to go through the process of receiving it each morning from lay supporters. Tan Kan received food for me. (One bhikkhu may receive for another, though this doesn't apply with samaneras.) In this way I was able to continue undisturbed with meditation, taking the food from outside the door or not as the case might be.

★   ★   ★

I spent all day, from early morning till late at night – if progress was good often continuing through the night as well – at the practices which Lung Poh had given me. My first aim was to be able to gain as high a degree of concentration as possible, a process similar to that of auto-hypnosis. Here, however, there was nothing involuntary or out of control. The object chosen for exercise was chosen in what, for want of better terms, must be called normal consciousness. My sole aim for a while was to gain complete and utter absorption of consciousness, to maintain the mind the whole time on the pinpoint of light which I could see in the mind's eye. The true goal at which I aimed was to attain such a degree of inner concentration that I could stop, and not be disturbed by, any of the senses.

Little by little I managed, for fleeting moments at first, to attain complete concentration. Such moments were, however, lamentably short-lived at the beginning. I came to realise that as soon as any idea had crossed my concentrated mind, I had in fact jumped away from the object upon which I was supposedly concentrating and was now thinking of something else.

Eventually I managed to keep the mind concentrated on the point of light for as long as I wished and could advert to it at will. Once I had mastered this, I found that I began to get control of feeling. I could maintain for a while a state where I could see, hear, smell and taste, but yet – at will – not feel. I began to notice other things as well. The heart beat more steadily and slowly, breathing became calmer, at times almost not taking place at all. During my experiments along these lines I learned that if I wanted to control feeling – such as pain in the legs or an ache of some kind – all that I had to do was to turn the mind to the pinpoint of light which, through persistent practice, had nearly become its normal resting place.

I remember one occasion when I decided to put the matter to the test as best I knew how: I was able to push two large pins through my cheeks without any sense of pain. I found also that I could do the same with my hands or for that matter any other part of the body. At first I found that on withdrawing the pins blood would flow, but after some experimentation I saw that if I conditioned the mind beforehand by stating to myself that there would be no pain or bleeding, then the whole process would occur without a drop of blood. Within half an hour or so there would not even be a mark or scar where the pins had entered the flesh.

Gradually I tried out the same process in relation to the other senses and found that the most difficult to conquer was that of hearing. However, I arrived at the point where I could stop hearing at will – or probably it would be more precise to say, I came to the point where I could cease to listen. Always the withdrawal from any sense was accomplished by the same method – the turning of the mind on to the

pinpoint of light. Eventually I managed to attain a degree of control
which allowed me to enter meditation rapidly, withdrawing the mind
or consciousness from all the senses one after another until all thought
and movement ceased for a period of six hours.

I learned much from these exercises about that which I referred to as
myself, and the utterly dependent nature of consciousness or mind. I
learned that *mind*, that nice round little something which we in the
West look upon as *mine*, was nothing of the kind. And whilst it was in
operation I could find no *me* looking upon anything as *mine*. What I did
find was that the term 'mind' as we knew it was far better replaced by
the term 'consciousness'. Also that consciousness could be divided
into six – consciousness of sight, sound, taste, touch, smell and finally
mind-consciousness, or more correctly, the area of consciousness not
directly connected with sensations but concerned with mental objects
derived from or based upon these.

Whilst the first five consciousnesses – or senses as we would know
them best: sight, sound, taste, touch and smell – were purely
automatic in operation, mind-consciousness on the other hand could
be either automatic or volitional. Mind-consciousness, I found, was
not a thing in itself as such but more of an event. Mind was an event
which had no self-rightness or mineness or absolute existence as such.
It was a phenomenal event which came to pass on the meeting together
of a number of dependent and related mental concomitants, many of
which were dependent upon the sensory impressions, or ideas based
upon them, and desires for or aversions from them.

Rapidly I began to discover that whilst I could accept certain of the
sensory perceptions and thoughts, to others I was violently averse. It
was not until I tried to bring myself to the state whereby I could
perceive either kind of sensory stimulation and thought with equal
interest or indifference as the case might be, that I realised how strong
and deep-rooted were these desires and aversions.

At first I tried to crush by sheer will-power both desires and
aversions and for a while fell into the trap of thinking that I had
succeeded – until one day my mind became flooded with thoughts of
sheer sensuality. These were accompanied by violent aversion, both
for the thoughts and the 'myself' who was thinking them, as I
supposed. Thoughts of women, their beauty, desirability or otherwise, are an absolute menace to a bhikkhu under training and I
suppose it was in an attempt to protect the mind from the unrest which
would ensue that I felt violent aversion for such thoughts. Aversion
was not strictly correct. It was more an intense mixture of both desire
and aversion. A rapid fluctuation of consciousness from one to the

other, bringing with it a complete state of unrest and a whole series of recriminations as to the rightness and wrongness of such feelings.

For days I fought these thoughts and feelings, these desires for all the things that woman meant. The mind became filled with visions of desirability with limpid eyes and breasts and thighs and lips beseeching in their searching. The more I struggled, the worse things became. The more I tried to crush such thoughts and visions, the more prolific did they become.

After many days I became aware of a sense of almost complete exhaustion accompanied by extreme fear, a state of almost uncontrolled hysteria. I felt as if I were on the borderlines of sanity. I realised that the situation must be resolved, some way of dealing with it must be found, or I would have to give up the bhikkhu life or go off my head in the process.

I turned the mind back to the past and found in so doing that woman had played a very large part in it. I had always liked women and what they stood for, had spent many years photographing them, glamorising them in portraiture for stage and screen. Displaying them clothed in the latest fashions for magazines and papers, naked and unadorned for the fashionable photographic salons. And when I wasn't photographing them, I was either sculpting or painting them. I had never denied my liking for them either to myself or to my friends and acquaintances, but until now I had never realised the depth of my own sensuality or my desire for them. I realised as well that it was due to this interest in them in the past and all the experiences I had had with them that the mind was now able to produce its visions of desirability.

After many hours of thought I came to the conclusion that force was not the way to combat such desires. The thing to do – if possible – was not to take any interest in them, either by disliking or desiring them. To go with the tide without any recriminations as to the rightness or wrongness of the situation.

From that decision onwards some semblance of peace returned to my mind. Gradually the visions, thoughts and desires receded. And later when they sometimes came into mind as is their natural way, there was no longer any disturbance in body or mind. They were no longer resented or desired. They came and went and caused not a ripple in their going.

I spent days of deep meditation on this aspect and came to the conclusion that it was this *not-fighting* kind of fighting, this *going with the stream* kind of mental awareness, an awareness of just paying mere attention to any mental object without becoming involved, which would lead to eventual success. What I had now to do was to attain the same awareness, the same mere attention, to all the senses and all the thoughts and objects of the mind.

During the whole painful period through which I had just gone I appeared to have lost all contact with my mental image of Lung Poh. Now I found in meditation that his image had returned, and with it more sense of certainty. It was standing there again and saying, 'Yes, Tan William, that is the way. Go that way – you will learn much.'

I did not pick on any particular sense to apply mere attention to. I was quite content to keep going until one sense or another aroused interest. It so happened that sight was the first to interest me, and that was purely because I asked myself what it was precisely I was seeing when I said 'I am seeing'.

★   ★   ★

Many days went past before I had any success in finding the answer to my question on seeing. Time after time I felt sure that success was close at hand, but as soon as the feeling of certainty welled up in me the mind became too excited and I found myself looking for definite things, searching along predetermined lines, along lines which had been thought out previously.

Suddenly one day I partook of a completely new experience: I experienced the phenomenon of sight in an entirely new way. Not in any way as one seeing a fantasy or hallucination, or the aberration of a mind on the borderlines of sanity – all which, by now, I knew quite well – but an experience of seeing which left me with a feeling of utter certainty as to the truth of that which I experienced.

I cannot with Aldous Huxley say 'I was seeing what Adam had seen on the morning of his creation – the miracle, moment by moment, of naked existence' (*sic*). I have never been Adam to my knowledge and have no way of knowing what his experiences were. Only he can know his, and I mine. Neither can I for one moment conceive the notion that the experiences were in the same realm as those of Meister Eckhart, William Blake, Plotinus or, for that matter, the whole historical list of religious mystics. My experiences stood as true to me, and it was neither necessary nor desirable to synthesise them with those of others in an attempt to strengthen them. It was truth of experience to me which was the important thing.

The experience came about quite naturally, without even the slightest excitement, or knowledge, during it, that I was seeing any different way. It was the sudden flood of thought after the event which appraised me of the fact. At the time I was casually looking at my left hand, when suddenly it stood out vividly – or rather that portion I was seeing did. The colour of the flesh was clear and translucent – never had I seen such purity of colour before. The hand had lost all sense of solidity, as is usually supplied by the habit of the mind with the normal act of seeing. Here, all that was presented to the eye was colour, its lights and darks and pastel shades giving planes of depth to the portion of the hand cognised and, withal, a sense of pulsating activity in the colours seen.

At the moment of this strange new experience there was no sense of the object seen being 'out there', in the manner of being 'out there in the world'. Or, for that matter, of being 'in here' in the sense of being 'in my mind'. The event just *was*. It was neither here nor there. Neither was there any thought of it being mine or that it was *I* that saw or experienced it.

Having had such an experience I spent days on the quest of it again and eventually arrived at a state of reasonable proficiency whereby I could *see* any object in like manner more or less at will. I say 'object' but from my experience I cannot truthfully say that. The 'object-concept' complex experience only arose after the eye had scanned innumerable times the *something* supposedly *out there*. It was these minute separate experiences of colour-data, searched out (I might almost say felt out) by the eye, which gave the impression of pulsating life to the whole experience. I repeatedly applied myself to all manner of visual data with similar results each time.

More and more I began to realise the importance of Lung Poh's insistence upon mental discipline and training. It had been purely by bringing the mind to a state whereby it could approach any sensation or cogitation with equal unbiased attention – literally, mere attention, a state where the mind does not add to or detract from that experienced, through either desire or aversion – which had brought to me the possibility of such a great series of experiences.

I began to realise after *seeing* in this new manner that the 'object' of sight was purely a matter of colour. Of itself it was neither pleasant nor unpleasant, desirable nor undesirable, harmful nor harmless. It could not even be touched. It had neither heat nor cold, roughness, smoothness, nor hardness. For a moment my whole world nearly collapsed when I understood fully for the first time that in truth I could not touch that which I saw. I began to realise that my world was of my own making, although at first this was but a very dim glimmering of the truth of such thoughts.

After having gained some success at the practice of this new *immediate seeing*, I spent a week reviewing my position and reconnoitring the situation. I had, I knew, gained much. I realised fully – or so I thought then – what impermanence meant. I knew that I could never experience the same thing twice. Although I fell into the trap of thinking I was doing just that when I recalled what I called each seeing experience, I was somewhat shattered when I realised that in fact I was experiencing a *new event* based upon a past experience, that the new experience – which I took to be the original – whilst based upon a past experience, was *new*. Not only that: it could be warped by faulty memory, emotional stress, desire or aversion.

Certainly these new experiences brought me to some understanding of the changing nature of things. No matter how I tried, my hand was never the same hand for two seconds together, neither was my chair the same chair. Some change had taken place even whilst I gazed at it. It appeared to me that everything seen was seen but once. It was ever changing, becoming something other. Try as I might I could not refute the logic of 'Any change in a thing is a change of thing, therefore not the same thing'.

My chair looked to me to be the same chair whenever I looked at it, but I realised now that the only sameness about it was the term 'chair' and the ever-present mental concept which accompanied it. The only order or reality which existed in 'chair', 'my hand', 'table', 'lizard', 'bird' was obviously supplied by the mind. They went on with a sense of continuous existence and yet I learned that they had not a *real* existence. There was no ideal chair or hand existing somewhere out there: they only existed in mind. The only *real* I could find was in the data presented in the act of sight before the mind had added its terms and concepts.

I looked at my hand again and then at the chair, saw them with the beauty and revelation of *immediate seeing* and laughed hilariously to myself at the thought, 'You cannot sit on this chair which you see, neither can you touch it with the hand you see. To do that requires something entirely other, an entirely new experience, an entirely new set of data for a different sense to appreciate and with which the mind would no doubt play its tricks.'

I next applied myself to the sensation of touch, or the sensation arising when the body, or any part of it, comes into contact or impact with something apparently other than itself, and the other innumerable instances when part of the body comes into contact with another part of the body – such as one's hand rubbing the nose and so forth.

At first I found that 'feeling' better described the sensation of touch. At my first attempts, the sensation was always accompanied by pleasantness or unpleasantness. And if on occasions, as sometimes did happen, the mind wandered off on to an object of sight or sound, there was no reaction at all in the sense that any sensation of touch arose from the object I was supposedly touching.

Eventually, after many failures and threats to myself to give the whole thing up, I became successful in coming to *feel* in a new way just as I had done with seeing. I managed to arrive at the state whereby I could appreciate the bare facts of the sensation without added emotional complications such as pleasure and displeasure.

I experimented with a large number of surfaces – the surfaces of a leaf, a lizard, table, chair (of different woods), paper, food of various kinds, liquids, clothing, parts of my own body, a dead rat and a dead snake. In every case all that I was ever aware of was the degree of heat or cold, roughness or smoothness, hardness or softness. All my experiments I carried out with the eyes shut as I found it better to be able to approach the sensation without giving the mind a chance to complicate the situation. Even in this way, however, I often ran into quite a lot of trouble and occasional scares.

I remember on one occasion I was feeling a surface and had first registered the fact that my immediate reaction was one of coolness, giving place rapidly to softness and followed by a slight roughness. I was then overtaken by intense panic. The surface in my hand had moved of its own volition and my mind had immediately supplied the information that I was holding the dead snake but that it had only been sleeping. I opened my hand and dropped the object of my experiment, only to find that it was but one of my larger and most friendly lizards. The dead snake was still very dead with the rest of the junk in the box I kept for the purpose. Time and again I found the mind bursting in upon the experiments with false information, information certainly not contained in the experience of *immediate seeing.*

Again, as I had with seeing, I learned that there was nothing pleasant or unpleasant, desirable or undesirable, in the thing touched. At the stage of *immediate feeling* all that was present was the mere data representing heat, cold, hard, soft, rough, smooth – presented individually and never jointly. The emotional liking or disliking aspect of the sense of touch, I found, was added by my mind. A mind which I had discovered reacted largely by a habit or series of habits based upon and continually strengthened by my general character.

Touch, I found, was a vast field to explore. There was a domain of things *out there* which I could feel. I could again prod and touch my own body. Again I could pay attention to the feelings I had inside my body. What was the difference, I asked myself, between the something I felt *out there*, the feeling I had who felt it, and the feeling I said I felt when feeling a feeling inside my body?

For days I remained convinced that in true fact I could never know what the thing *out there* felt like – all that I was really accomplishing was feeling myself. If I touched anything, I told myself, it was not the thing which I was becoming aware of but a sensation at the ends of my fingers. Therefore all that I had accomplished after days of hard work was that I was feeling me and could never know the something *out there*. I spent hours in mental turmoil, feeling at times that my mind could stand very little more without breaking under the strain. This was added to, no doubt, by an outbreak of self-aversion; for it looked as if I would have to accept a philosophical view I had always argued about: Subjective Idealism.

However, I weathered this new storm and applying myself to my exercises again, managed to bring my mind back to some semblance of harmony. And then, one late afternoon, the perfect experience took place again. During that experience the sensation of touch was neither of something *out there*, nor did it take place *in here*. The thing to be touched and the touching thing were two entirely different phenomena, the sensation of their impact entirely another again. Through the experience I was continually aware of change, transience, impermanence. The very fact of finger coming into contact with an external object required movement – which is another aspect of change – to bring about the contact. On contact being made rapid changes began to take place both in the thing touched and the touching thing – for how else could any sensation arise?

I found it to be the same story with those feelings which took place inside my body: the feeling of flesh areas coming into contact with each other internally, the feeling of muscular contraction or pain in a joint or intestines. At first, in dealing with these internal feelings, they were located anatomically. But as the attention became more and more concentrated the true experience came, and I knew that even these feelings or sensations, which I would have at one time maintained to be my own, at the moment of true experience had no place *out there* or *in here:* they just *were*. Neither time nor space nor location had any place in the experience.

On more general lines, of course, I found that feeling made up so much of that something I referred to as *me*. Hunger and thirst and their satisfaction were but feeling. I could not tell a position of my body without the sensation of feeling. My very sense of balance was automatically registered by the sensation derived from water flowing over hair-like nerves in canals behind the ears. Walking or moving my limbs was known most certainly through feeling – sitting, standing or lying down were the same.

In fact, the more I advanced with these experiments on feeling or the sensation of touch, the less could I find of *myself*, the *me* of me. Most of the actions which had supposedly been *mine* in the past were now known to be mainly but the reactions of an amoebic psycho-physical organism whose main purpose appeared to be that of appeasing sensation. It was driven to satisfy those sensations for which it had desire and to try to eradicate or remove itself from those which it desired not.

Such thoughts as 'I am hungry' lost all sense. There was but a feeling, a sensation, which had to be stopped. Even the eating of the food with which the sensation of hunger was stopped was in the main but another sensation to be enjoyed for as long as possible before the final moment of alleviation. I found no one there acting as the *enjoyer* in the sense *I am enjoying;* no one perceiving the percept other than perception itself. Even the monster 'craving' which enjoyed appeared to be a two-headed monster. It desired to have on the one hand and not to have on the other, leading to a complex eroticism which it called enjoying itself.

I found that the same findings held good when I turned my attention to the senses of taste and hearing. Taste was a mixture of both touch and taste. Food was found either to have the attributes of hardness, softness, smoothness, roughness, as well as degrees of heat and cold – which was the sense of touch in operation; or as having sweetness, sourness, bitterness, saltiness.

Having come this far I decided to apply myself to a strict period of satipatthana – meaning literally 'the setting up of mindfulness'. Whilst what I had been doing in relation to the senses was in fact part of mindfulness, I now wished to apply it fully.

When I began my training under Lung Poh, he had explained that his system of meditation was a mixed system. It comprised both samatha and vipassana exercises. The former were designed to develop calm and deep concentration, leading to the attainment of the jhana or trances. Vipassana on the other hand was a series of exercises designed to bring insight through experience into the realities of existence. It was satipatthana – continual mindfulness – which could bring final understanding. In reference to satipatthana, Gotama said:

The one way, bhikkhus, leading to the purification of beings, the passing beyond grief and woe, the gaining of true insight, to Nibbana, is the setting up of mindfulness, wherein a bhikkhu is mindful as to body, feelings, state of mind and the contents of mind.

The whole system of satipatthana exercises was supposed to be maintained at all times. The mind had to be kept at the task of being attentive, mindful of everything that was going on. The mind was to keep its task of watching, of being aware. At no time was it supposed to charge off fancy-free on its own desires. Mindfulness should be maintained from knowing the first waking thought or sensation in the morning right through the day unbroken until the last thought or sensation before sleep.

I applied myself to the task every day, day after day. Everything I did had to be slowed down. Every step I took and every sensation dependent upon that step had to be known. Every time the mind wandered away from its task, I would retrace my steps to the point where I had lost concentration and commence again. Gradually, as I mastered the technique, the process of mindfulness became more or less automatic. And the type of mental state that had arisen during my experience of *immediate seeing* and the rest became more or less general.

I managed to maintain a situation where there was never any tension or feeling of struggle. I just learned to take things as they came and to be fully aware all the time. The more I practised the more I learned about myself – my body, feelings, state of mind and its contents.

12

PAST LIVES

As the days wore on I fell more and more into the study, the awareness, of state of mind and contents of mind. Here I found precisely what I had found in relation to the body, senses and feelings: that there was always a state of change, nothing ever remained the same from one moment to another. No permanence could I find in all these spheres.

Here in the mind, however, things were even more rapidly changing. New state followed old with bewildering speed. Old contents, concepts, names, ideas, desires, aversions, visions of people and places were driven out as others, avidly eager to hold the stage, took their places. It was watching these mental states which I think was the most wearing and shattering thing in the whole of my experiences.

The world appeared to me now to be peopled not with human beings, animals, trees, birds and so forth but with mere sensory and mental phenomena, none of which had entity or soul. They came and went with fantastic speed and in their going I knew that they could never come again. I was overwhelmed with a sense of utter loneliness. Not one of these could I talk with or enjoy: they were empty and vacuous.

Yet, I thought to myself, I was all right, I still had something, a me-ness about me, a something that went on through all this apparently nonsensical world. What, I asked myself, was the use of all this striving, all this effort, if all it was going to bring me was a sense of utter emptiness, a world void of reality, a world of complete and utter change, without permanence or certainty anywhere? Where in all this was to be found anything to be reborn? Had not Gotama himself said that all beings are reborn again and again? Yet here I was, unable to find anything in the way of an inhabiting entity in any of the people and things I saw around me. I hadn't even been able to find the 'I' of myself as yet, although I was certain that I had one. This feeling of certainty that I had a *me* surely must be true – otherwise where did such conviction and certainty come from? I must find myself, I must know if rebirth is true, I told myself. I must know where I have come from and where I am going.

With such questioning as a basis, with the unbearableness of the situation as a driving force, I turned the mind back upon itself, applying it to every preceding thought and sensation, every event and situation backwards through the day. Each succeeding day, instead of going forward to new experience, the mind was turned to remembering everything of days gone by. Wherever I left off at night I picked up again the next morning and continued on my backward way.

Memory sharpened to a terrific degree under this discipline. I was soon remembering things of my extremely early childhood, pushing myself well beyond that and coming to an area of experience which was almost entirely sensational. Violent and frightening flashes of shapeless colour gave way finally to utter darkness, a feeling of tearing constriction on my body and a ghastly sensation of drowning as I tried to breathe, each breath taking in liquid through my nostrils and filling my lungs, knowing that I must breathe but unable, until I felt I must die as all sensation left me.

And yet to say that all sensation left me is not strictly true. There was a knowledge of agonising expectancy, a searching, a violent striving for something I knew not what. Next I became aware of a gurgling sensation in my throat followed by pain in my heart. A feeling of age descended upon me, a sense of being spent and without strength, giving way rapidly to a certainty that 'I' was alive.

What a different *alive* and *I* it was. My whole body and mind felt different. I had often spoken of being old, but never like this. This was *really* being old. I opened my eyes and found myself looking out on to a small bamboo-built hut, a hut that reeked, I knew, of myself, reeked as only the lonely aged can reek. A few pots and pans, some strings of dried fish hanging from the dust-laden walls and a small bag of rice comprised the contents of the hut – my only worldly possessions, quite obviously. Of human occupants, other than myself, the hut was completely empty. I fell to weeping at my loneliness. To die like this without friends was terrible. To have no family, no friends at this moment was surely the most terrible thing that could happen to a person. Why had it happened to me, I wailed to myself. Had I not been generous to everyone?

I looked down at my body and found the reason for it feeling different. It was a woman's body, an old woman's body. A body thin and scrawny, the skin like dried and wrinkled parchment hanging in dry folds about the aged bones. The breasts hung down as thin and lifeless as a snake's skin after being sloughed. The hands, as they felt the thighs, like gnarled talons, each bone and tendon standing out clear and stark against the intertwining blue-black tracery of veins. The thighs, now a travesty of that which I dimly knew they had once been, were so thin that the femora showed through, as did the knee joints and the hips. And the pelvic bones and pubic area pointed out of the near-dead flesh like some unholy joke against the beauty of womanhood.

My mind grasped at the past, threw back to younger days. To days when this old body was something beautiful and desired by all. As a young woman I was driven by desire. As soon as desire had been satiated by one man, the desire arose for another. I grew to a position of power and wealth. A woman desired by all the men in the district yet possessed by none. A woman feared and detested by the local women.

As I went backwards and forwards through that life-experience I realised that the driving force in my life was that of sensuality. An overpowering desire for the male and yet withal a detestation of myself for dependence upon them. I lived completely without any sense of ethics, all my actions being carried out purely to best serve my own ends. I lied as only a woman can lie, even at times convincing myself that it was truth I told.

I discovered that in my early childhood I had an elder brother and a younger sister both of whom had died by the time I was seventeen, the brother from snake-bite and the sister from malaria. My mother, who died when I was sixteen and a half, was a dear and gentle woman in whom I took not much interest. She, with her womanly instincts, saw me obviously as a potential danger not only to her own marital happiness with my father who idolised me, but also to my brother who hung around me like a lover most of the time.

As my age increased I found that my physical charms began to fade and that men were less easy to get. Gradually I found that instead of being pursued, I was now forced to blatantly pursue men, eventually having to offer presents for their favours. Until I had at last arrived at the point of death, with nothing further to give, and a body that could arouse desire not even in the most bestial.

I retraced my steps again through that life, again went through the process of birth and death. Again I found myself in the past as a woman – not so old this time, and still beautiful in a way. Driven by the same desires, however, and dying finally from a knife thrust from my husband who had at long last found me out in my lies and affairs.

Back through this new experience I went, and instead of going through the process of birth, became conscious of excruciating pain in the area of the head, followed by a return to a previous life-experience: being stoned to death by villagers. Again I was a woman, still with the

same urges, carrying on the business of marriage-broker and abortion-
ist. My machinations had cost the life of both child and mother, the
mother in this case being the best loved wife of the local village
chieftain. My penalty was death by stoning.

After this experience the mind took on its search for the past of itself
with relish, going back to supposed life after life. Lives as both men
and women, old and young, rich and poor. Each life always driven by
some desire or another. Sometimes the desire for power and riches, at
others the desire for knowledge or supremacy in the field of learning.
Sometimes, when poor, just driven by the desire for the next meal. But
always driven by desire, even if only the desire to live.

As far as I can remember all these lives took place in Asia with the
exception of one in medieval Germany. At no time was I a famous
figure in the historical sense – never once was I an Egyptian princess or
the right-hand man or woman of some renowned magician. In these
experiences I reacted again to all the sensations and situations which it
is possible for the human being to undergo.

Quite suddenly the process stopped. I had my answer. Or at least I
had an answer or answers which were satisfactory to me. I knew for a
certainty that going back into supposed past lives would never bring
me to the beginning, the starting point of the something I called *me*. I
had learned that the very nature of consciousness was to remain
conscious, to grasp at anything that consciousness may remain. In this
way there could be no beginning, just an endless coming to be of
sensations and situations which had existed before – for surely the very
consciousness of oneself was but a memory of the past.

Was I not after all but a collection of memories from a past mainly
constructed upon sense data and ideas and desires based upon them?
Was not that which I called *my life* nothing but a record of a continually
changing consciousness in search of sensation or ideas?

Suddenly the thought sprang to mind: 'You silly little man, you
never *were* born in the absolute sense. "You" is but a convenient term
to describe a particular event in the relations between mental and
physical concomitants, each of which is as transient as the event itself.
You have no past, neither have you a future in the absolute sense. The
past which appears to be so much *you* is so because it has been
rationalised by the mind. The very logic of life is but of the past. The
past is the only logical thing in life: the future is quite random.

'Again the very sensations and situations on which you based your
supposed life, the events on which you base your logical existence, are
but particularisations. They are picked out from a mass of probable
events which took place in that supposed past.

'No, little man! You were never born, you had no beginning. The *youness* of you is but a relative thing among all other things which are themselves but relative. The very authenticity of *you* has a validity only in reference to other things, people, events, which were contiguous in the experience which you claim as *yours.*'

*   *   *

With these thoughts and ideas flooding my mind I knew that at long last I was beginning to understand the teaching of Buddhism. The anomalies which appeared to exist in the teaching faded away. I could understand now how it was that Gotama could on the one hand teach that all beings were born according to their just deserts; that each human and animal consciousness was born and reborn according to their *kamma*, rising higher or lower as the case might be in the evolutionary scale with each new birth. And how on the other hand he could teach that all things, all beings, were transitory, were anatta – without permanent abiding entity such as soul or self. And yet again, that there was a state beyond the world, a state of freedom from suffering and unrest called Nibbana (or Nirvana in Sanskrit). I knew also that this very Nibbana was not a state in relative opposition to that of the sensible world, but a state beyond all relationships. It was absolute, indefinable, nothing could enter or leave it.

In those hours immediately following the 'silly little man' thoughts, many things fell into their true perspective. I suppose for a long time during my mental tussles in meditation I had been experiencing things much as a schizophrenic would (that is, of course, providing the various psychological papers published on the subject are true). For quite long periods I had viewed things and experiences with a feeling of awful truth – when I began to realise that all the things which I experienced were but a matter of sense data. Nothing that I could see, hear, smell, taste or touch had any abiding entity.

Even the visions of my mind which turned these sensory data into things which people the world – such as men, women, children, animals and the rest – were apparently empty phenomena. I was attacked at such times with a sense of appalling loneliness: here 'I' was, the only real thing in this world of meaninglessness. At other times I was overpowered by feelings of exultation due to the fact that 'I' was the one who created all these empty automatic somethings, could make them do as I wished.

My trouble was that I saw things as they truly were, but had not learned to place the constituents of the something I called 'myself' into the world of my experience and treat them the same as the rest. Once *that* had been accomplished, the dichotomy ceased. I then knew that the questions – 'Where have I come from? Where am I going? Who am I? Do I have a permanent soul?' – were but wrong questions. They could not be answered without definition. And even when defined the answers could at best only be true in a relative sense dependent upon the definition.

I now knew – and with the knowing touched for the first time in my life peace and tranquillity – that the whole of sensible existence had no first beginning, that all things in the world and all things in that which observed it were dependently originated. Everything which existed came to be but momentarily dependent upon past causes and present supporting circumstances. No *thing* was a thing in its own right. It was a *thing* only dependent upon a past something which was now non-existent and upon present things in its environment against which it could be related and verified and so, by its very 'otherness', be given the name and *thingness* of its existence.

The very basis of my knowledge of the sensible world was dependent upon differences between things. The validity of the sensible world was utterly dependent upon the impermanence of the phenomena, the momentariness of things apparently permanent, the momentariness of its constituent parts. The words I used to describe this world only had validity in so far as they were used in opposition. If I tried to explain the meaning of one word I had perforce to use another, in some mysterious way hoping to get my meaning across.

I could see myself now as an observer of the world and knew that any emotional change in me changed my view of the sensible things in my world or environment. Conversely, any change in the environment brought change in me.

Such thoughts to me were a joy. I had to the best of my understanding and satisfaction found the teaching of the Buddha to be true. Nothing of me had been annihilated in the process, for how can that be destroyed which one has never possessed? All that had happened was that I had lost a concept, a concept of *myself* or *soul* as permanent in opposition to a changing world. A concept which was itself but ignorance or blindness to the truth. I was part of my world and my world was part of me. We co-existed interdependently. My world and myself were at peace. There could be nothing wrong with that world unless I made it so.

For some days further I contemplated these new thoughts and discoveries, for a while wondering at my stupidity in not being able to learn from the books precisely what they had meant. I had known the thing intellectually as I thought but knew now that the experience of the truth of existence according to Buddhism is something so utterly different from the intellectualisation of the experience in the books, those books which when read and studied in the West give rise to such heated arguments as to the meaning contained in the words.

Experts in Oriental languages, aided by grammarians and philologists, attempt to prove their pet views on the subject by purely intellectual means, referring to stems, cases, contexts and roots, leaving themselves and others floundering in bewilderment at the intricacy of their many inventions. Others, reading one paperback on the subject, begin to hold forth as experts, no doubt basing their right to knowledge of the subject on their ignorance of their professed Christianity for which they argue so forcibly.

Still others, at university level, usually holding a chair in comparative religion, hold forth in pedantic terms on Indian religion and Buddhism in particular. Their main claim to knowledge may be that they spent some time as missionaries in the East, where they were mainly occupied with shutting their eyes to the wisdom around them while trying to cram their dry-as-dust churchiological way of life into the spiritually well-fed minds of the natives.

Again others, the elite of the argumenters, the self-styled Buddhists of the West, know – with an awe-ful knowing – the meaning of the words. After all, they claim, if anyone should know it should be us: we *are* Buddhists. And when they are pressed, where in the main does their supposed knowledge come from? From nothing other than more printed words. The words of Madame Blavatsky, who apparently got the Truth from some hidden Master in Mysterious Tibet. Or from Leadbeater, who was even able to draw the residence of the so-called Master – although he had never visited him other than in the astral, he claimed.

They all – even the Theosophically-tainted Buddhists – argue among themselves upon words in books. Books written by people who have read books written by people on the subject. They are but doing what I myself did, for it is far easier to hold opinions and argue than to strive for and gain one small portion of the actual experience of Truth.

The question as to the validity of the experiences of previous lives which I had undergone did not worry me at all. I realised that every succeeding moment of consciousness, being different from that which had just gone, was in fact a new consciousness. If anything was born again and again it was surely consciousness.

Again, consciousness – no matter if it be made to comply with all that we in the West call 'mind', or simply made to refer to consciousness of sensation – could only exist in relationship with and in dependence upon physical form – body or mass. Whilst consciousness was not in itself physical, it operated dependent upon the physical. Even if I thought to escape this dependency – as indeed I had – in realms of thought far removed from the physical, all that happened was that the body appeared to remain very quiet and calm, but all the time the heart was pumping blood sugar and oxygen to the brain cells, which must have been ticking away merrily in their efforts to maintain a basis for such high-blown consciousness.

To me, the experiences were a matter of what the mind had grasped at from its hidden contents during meditation. Having picked out the incidents and characters which it did and made them its own, they became *mine* in much the same manner as if I had gone into a store and bought goods which I called *mine*. The main purpose of the experiences had been served in that I had obtained the opportunity, in a relatively short time, of a much-stretched time-span, giving me a better perspective of life in general.

The odd thing was that the experiences themselves were to me experiences of past lives and happenings which took place in the present. I went into them in much the same way as one goes into the experiences of day-to-day life, with a sense of going forward, not back into the past. The only difference which I could find between these and ordinary day-to-day experiences was that where in ordinary daily routine and thinking about the future there would be an air of expectancy or trepidation, and always an uncertainty about that which life may hold for one, here in these present experiences of past lives – or fantasies, call them what one will – there was an air of foreknowledge, a knowing of what was going to happen. And, as I first thought, worse still, a knowledge that one could not dodge what was there in the past experience.

I imagine that the process through which I had put myself was something like that observed during some of the experiments in regressive analysis used by some experimental psychologists. The mind, being turned back upon itself, produces its pattern, shows the contents of its character. The main difference is that most regressive experiments have been carried out either with hypnosis or drugs combined with suggestion, much as Huxley obtained his experiences through the use of mescalin. In my own case there were no drugs used, and the auto-hypnotic state which must have obtained during the experiences was self-produced by a disciplined and gradual growth in the strength of concentration.

Of one thing I am certain: no amount of drugs, either ancient or modern, can take the place of a long period of mental and physical discipline as an aid to the understanding of Buddhist teaching. Whilst Huxley talks about mescalin bringing much the same physiological changes as would be brought about by Buddhist monks who chant suttas by the hour and thereby bring about chemical changes in brain-cells which give rise to spiritual experiences, as far as my own experience goes this is far from the facts.

Whilst there are many Buddhist monks who chant suttas by the hour, their reason for so doing has nothing to do with meditation as such, or for that matter, the gaining of spiritual experiences. The chanting bhikkhu or monk – and there are many thousands of them in Buddhist countries – is rarely if ever a meditation bhikkhu. Invariably they are scholars – literally walking books – who spend all their time memorising the books of the teaching and teaching others to do likewise. It has been claimed that if all the written collections of the Pali Canon were destroyed overnight, they could be reproduced from the memories of these *banakas* or repeaters. The others who go to make up the number of chanters are those who are experts in ceremonial: they know all the propitious chants for all occasions.

I doubt even the use of a word such as 'spiritual' in relation to the experiences gained by a vipassana bhikkhu (meditation monk). It is not visions of other worlds or the attainment of godlike experiences for which he is searching and training himself. He is only really concerned with *this* life, and concerned more specifically with where it takes place – in his own mind and body. If he were questioned as I have been questioned – and indeed questioned myself – as to what his spiritual experiences were, what was the realm of the gods like and so forth, he would undoubtedly reply: 'How do you come to know about other worlds when you know nothing about this one yet? First I try to know and understand myself and my world. I have no time to worry about other worlds – a man's lifetime is very short.'

Certainly, many of us in the meditation group had, to say the least, odd experiences. Fantasy ran rife at times; at others, one's very sanity could be held in question. Invariably these states were brought under control, and the one who had experienced them had made gains in the right direction.

The various experiences which we had gave us all an amazing insight into the content of our own characters. Under the discipline and training given by Lung Poh the essential character of the trainee stood out stark and clear. However simply and honestly a man may have come into the Order and stated his reasons for becoming a vipassana bhikkhu, honestly believing his stated reasons to be the truth, once under instruction and discipline it was not long before the hidden side of the character showed itself.

★　★　★

Four months and one week had elapsed since my ordination as bhikkhu and my self-chosen retirement into seclusion. During that time I had not been conscious of seeing anyone. At times I remembered seeing feet and then hands offering me a bowl of food. I spoke to no one during that period.

It was at the end of the seventeenth week of seclusion that I received a visit from Lung Poh and Thitavedo. I was disturbed by a loud banging on my door, to which I promptly replied that whoever it was could go away as I was seeing absolutely no one. This brought even louder bangings, and with them the voice of Thitavedo commanding me in the name of Lung Poh to come out.

'Brother,' he shouted, 'Lung Poh here to see you. Must come out now. Must obey Lung Poh. Come out, brother!'

It was not until I heard the deep tones of Lung Poh's 'Tan William', however, that I opened the door of my room and walked out into the main hall of that upper floor, to be met by the kindly smiling faces of my two stalwart guardians. For such they had been, as I later learned.

13

THREE KINDS
OF TRUTH

It was only during my talk with Lung Poh and Thitavedo that evening
that I gathered any idea as to the time of my withdrawal. Time had
flown so fast that I had lost count of both days and nights. Four months
and one week, they told me, I had been locked away in my room. This
made – excluding the time it had taken for my two ordinations – just
over six months in which I had been completely withdrawn from my
fellow men, without conversation or reading matter, my whole time
taken up with the system of meditation which Lung Poh had given me.

I had some difficulty at first in speaking. Being much more interested
in listening, my attempts were monosyllabic. Gradually, however,
Lung Poh and Thitavedo drew me out. I gathered from Thitavedo that
he had looked in on me more or less every two days, just to see how I
was progressing and that my health was good. Lung Poh, I learned,
also came to look at me at various times. Both of them took pains not to
disturb me in my meditation.

Lung Poh looked at me fixedly for a long time as I sat and enjoyed a
glass of coffee and a cigarette – the first cigarette I remembered
smoking for many weeks. He just sat and looked, with a smile of utter
tenderness on his face, and I felt quite happy for him to do just that. I
felt so absolutely at peace with everything, quite sure that Lung Poh
and Thitavedo somehow knew how I felt and what I had been through.
And so it was, for Lung Poh said, 'So! Now, Tan William, you know all
the answers to your questions, it would seem. You tried no doubt all
the things which I told you to do. What do you think of previous lives?
Were they yours?'

I replied that in the conventional sense they could be called mine.
My mind had in fact chosen them as such. Whilst I had no way of
proving to other people that such was the case, they were as valid as a
memory from twenty years back would be. On the other hand I had to

say that there was no such thing as '*my* past lives'. The whole of experience, everything in the sensible world, the things of the mind – thoughts, ideas, concepts, desires, aversions and ideals – I had found to be a matter of dependent origination. I could find no one cause for any sensation, thought or idea. Even the idea of 'myself' I found to be dependently originated. Always I had to refer to the past to find 'myself'. But never had I found 'myself' in the permanent sense.

I told him that I now saw truth in three ways. Firstly there was conventional truth, in which I could refer to a man existing whom I called George. George I had known for many years and he was still the same George. This was a world of truth where men were men, trees were trees, and mountains were mountains. A world of truth inherently accepted, in the conventional usage of language.

On the other hand, I could see things through the eye of a second aspect of truth, a truth whereby things could be seen from a more scientific standpoint. All material things could be analysed into their finest constituents. None of the *things* of conventional truth were things here. Here, the terms man, tree, mountain, table, chair, etc, had no validity. *Things* disappeared and in their place were small – minutely small – particles of matter which, with the aid of mind, came together to constitute the things of the sense world, and just as rapidly dissolved, to partake in the coming to be of something other.

Finally, there was, as I understood it, a third truth. A truth which was without beginning, without end. Through this truth I could understand that conventional truth was purely that which was relatively true within the meaning of words in ordinary language. The second or more scientific truth, whilst at first appearing to be a final or absolute truth, was itself just as relative as the first, but dealing with different terms and, in those terms, with minute particles of matter.

I could see no reason for calling a halt to analysis of these particles which the books had mentioned, for surely these very particles could be analysed again and again into smaller and smaller particles. After all, were not the very particles into which material was analysed but the work of the mind again? From the point of view of logic and comparison I could not see much difference between the mind coining such things from material as man, tree and mountain, or atoms, molecules and *dhammas*, as they are called in Buddhism.

The third truth was to me absolute, without relationship. It had nothing to do with Dependent Origination, not having been originated. It was a realm or truth of 'no-thingness' as opposed to the truth of 'thingness'. Yet at the same time it did not attain its validity or truth by reference to its opposite.

It was to me what was meant – in one way – by the term Nibbana. It was and could be an experience, and yet it could be said that no one experienced it in the sense meant by '*I* experienced it'. For during the experience itself there was but the experience and no dichotomy of experience and experiencer. Only later in conventional language could I refer to such experience, but never as *mine*. Had there been *mineness* in the experience there would have been *thingness*.

I felt sure that this third truth was *the* truth, that this was *vijja* (knowledge) in the Buddhist sense as opposed to *avijja* (ignorance). Through this truth I could now see that all my questions were out of place and had no meaning in the ultimate sense. The whole world of experience was, it appeared, made by mind. And even the mind itself was but one of the relationships of the many-faceted experiences or events which took place in that mental world, that world of relativity.

★ ★ ★

When I had finished my long answer to his question I looked up at Lung Poh and found him to be smiling happily. 'This is very good,' he said. 'You have learned much and understand the teaching of Gotama very well now. But why do you find that there are three aspects of truth when the books only refer to two? None of the Abhidhamma books [books of analysis and philosophy] state any more than two aspects of truth – that is, of course, in relation to truth as such. The books refer to there being *sammuti sacca* (conventional truth) and *paramattha sacca* (ultimate truth). Why do you find a necessity for a third?'

I replied that I found this to be necessary because of my own experiences and reasoning. Again, I felt that my third truth was implied in the earlier books although not specifically stated. In the *Abhidhammattha Sangaha* (Compendium of Philosophy), an early commentarial work, both the conventional and ultimate truths are stated, and then comes reference to Nibbana as an existent state and truth. And whereas the first two truths gain their validity by opposition and relationship, the third, Nibbana, stands away from these by being completely without attributes. That being so, it could not be discussed or explained. Later scholars in some of the different schools of Mahayana had attempted to discuss this final truth, although without much success. In fact the more they had tried to explain it, the more attributes they found for it, the further did they get from the truth. In any case, it did not matter much what the books said. I was prepared to stand by my own experience.

'That is very good,' said Lung Poh. 'Your studies have been very deep and your knowledge of the books is sound. But more important, your meditation has been most searching. What you have gained in understanding is yours and cannot be taken away from you. Arguments as to opinion in these matters are of no importance. A man who knows by experience as you now know does not have to enter into argument, for only the unsure try to win arguments.

'Now I am going to tell you that I have watched you very closely since you have been here and I am very happy with what you have done and the tenacity with which you have applied yourself to your self-chosen task. I must tell you that your meditation training is now at an end. You must now meet the people.

'There have been many requests for you to give lectures in various parts of the country as well as in Bangkok. I do not wish you to refuse these requests, for you can teach my people many things about the teaching of Gotama Buddha. You can say things in a way which I cannot use. People will listen to you, I am sure, because they have followed your progress with great interest. With Thitavedo acting as interpreter you should be able to give a very instructive series of lectures. Some of those to whom you talk will understand English, but with the help of Thitavedo's understanding of both your language and your personal style, and with his understanding of your philosophical terms, I am sure that everyone present will benefit. The first of your talks has been arranged to take place in three days' time at the famous Wat Sampya in Bangkok.'

I was quite disturbed to hear Lung Poh say this. I had not the slightest wish to leave the peaceful state of my daily life and would have much preferred to go off and live quietly in a jungle hut somewhere in the north.

I told Lung Poh of my views on the matter, stressed to him that I had not come to Thailand to teach, that I had come to learn. But he was not to be moved.

He explained to me that I had come to him with an excellent knowledge of the traditional books of Buddhism both in Pali and English. This had saved a deal of time both for him and myself, and I had been able to spend all my time at meditation. Had I come to him without any sound knowledge of the subject, much time would have had to be spent in my learning by heart the whole of the Vinaya or Rules of Discipline, and the whole of the Abhidhammattha Sangaha, these being the two absolute requirements for one who would become a vipassana (meditation) bhikkhu. As it happened I came knowing these and much more besides. I knew the intellectual side of the teaching very well but required the discipline and experience of meditation.

It was the fact that I had made, as he was quite well aware, great gains through meditational experience, had been able to prove many of the statements in the teaching itself, plus the fact that I had years of experience as a lecturer, which had made him decide that I must now go out and share what I had with the people. The great thing was to share what one had. He did not want me to go forth and thrust things down people's throats. But if there were requests from the people for me to talk or lecture on the teaching, I must in all fairness comply. After all, the people gave Dana – gifts of food and support. I also must give to them Dana, Dhamma Dana – the gift of the teaching.

After Lung Poh's explanation I could not refuse his request, particularly when I remembered that his own life was completely one of service to the people. So I decided to try to emulate his example, with the knowledge that if I accomplished only half of what he had done in his lifetime I would not be doing too badly.

I rose from my seat and knelt before him. I thanked him for all that he had made possible for me and promised him in return that I would carry out any instructions he might wish to give as to my work. I bowed before him three times. Having patted my shoulder and spoken a few rapid words to Thitavedo, Lung Poh departed for his own house, leaving Thitavedo with me.

Thitavedo was the first to break the silence which ensued. 'Lung Poh very proud about you. All time he talk about Tan William. You very fortunate he want you to lecture. It shows all the people how much he think of you. Now you must prepare for talk at Wat Sampya. What are you going to talk about?'

I told him that I would talk upon traditional methods of meditation in Buddhism, and that I would refer both to the books and some of the commentaries, and also to my own experience.

This Thitavedo thought to be a very good subject, and he left me to my own devices, stating that he would call and see me several times a day from now on as there must be many things which I wished to discuss with him.

How right he was. I felt somewhat diffident about lecturing to these people. These Thais were a free people, who never in their history had been overrun by a European power, who had developed in their own way and at their own speed. They had been grounded in Buddhist ways of life for many centuries. Their country boasted nineteen thousand pagodas and some million bhikkhus and samaneras. Lecturing to them was a task which I approached with growing apprehension. Coming from an entirely different background, from a civilisation where success – usually spelt money – was the most important thing, how could I talk to these people on a subject which was an integral part of their civilisation?

I discussed my difficulties with Thitavedo on one of his visits. He just laughed and said, 'Brother, you worry too much. People the same all over the world – so busy with living and making success, not have much time for philosophy, religion or ethics. Thailand is Buddhist country, England is Christian country. Nearly whole population in England would say they are Christian if asked. Same in Thailand: everybody say they are Buddhist. Yet how many people in England understand Christ's teaching and really practise it? Very few, I bet you my life. Same in Thailand: everybody Buddhist but not really understand.

'Most of the customs you will see carried out by the people are not Buddhist customs but Hindu customs. Just like as in England most of the ceremonies and customs not Christian customs but really come from the old pagan cults which were in the country long before Christianity came. Christian missionaries come here and call us pagans, which we are and proud of it. They forget that England and Europe have never been truly Christianised and are as pagan as ever they were.

'Not to worry, brother. You can teach my people much and you will find that they are very willing to learn. Many sincere people will come and listen to you, you will see. Everybody speak with you now that you not Phra Farang [European bhikkhu] but Phra Thai [Thai bhikkhu]. They look upon you as one of themselves and they seem to think that you understand them and their ways.

'So I say again, "Stop worrying and give a good talk at Wat Sampya". This is going to be big occasion, maybe the biggest talk in Bangkok for many years. The whole talk is to be broadcast through Thai National Radio as a live broadcast. All other programmes will be stopped until your talk is finished. Also instructions have gone out from Sangha headquarters that bhikkhus may ask you questions after you have finished your talk. This is most unusual as bhikkhus do not usually ask another bhikkhu questions in public. But Lung Poh thinks your knowledge is good enough so that anywhere you go in the country now everyone, including bhikkhus, will be allowed to ask questions of you.'

14

A RADIO BROADCAST

The day of my lecture at Wat Sampya was an extremely busy one. Throughout the morning I had been inundated with visitors, all of whom apparently were going to be present at my talk.

I had just finished my midday and last meal when several more visitors arrived bearing gifts of cigarettes and coffee. Among them was Khun Sankhavasi, Vice-President of the Royal Thai Buddhist Association in Bangkok, and several of his friends. We had just started a conversation – Sankhavasi speaking excellent English – when Lung Poh entered the room accompanied by his two assistants. Everyone present rose and greeted them in the customary manner.

When all were settled again Khun Sankhavasi informed me that a rather special visitor had arrived in Bangkok that day. His name was Robert Samek, and he was senior lecturer in Commercial Law at Melbourne University, Australia. He had come to Thailand, breaking his journey to Chicago where he was taking up a fellowship at the University, especially to learn something about Buddhism at first hand. Could I help? And would I be prepared to meet him that night for some conversation on the subject?

It was at this point that Lung Poh aired his views. He said that it had been decided by the Sangha that I was the best person for Samek to meet, but that it would not be possible for me to see him that evening as I was already extremely busy and had a long lecture to give at Wat Sampya. It would be best if Khun Sankhavasi could bring Samek to my residence at 9.30 the next morning so that we could all have some talk as to his requirements. To this Sankhavasi agreed, and after the usual formalities he and his friends left – en route, they told me, for Wat Sampya to hear my lecture.

After my visitors had gone I just had enough time to have a rapid bath before a car arrived at 2 p.m. to take Thitavedo and myself to Bangkok.

We left my house and made our way through the pagoda compound and along the paths to the high-domed bridge over the river, followed the whole way by some two hundred white-robed nuns and many local inhabitants. On arrival at the other side of the river I found a mass of cars and buses awaiting us. Many of the vehicles were packed tight with yellow-robed figures of bhikkhus and samaneras. Others were filled with children, men and women – even the very old appeared to be making the journey. Over the whole scene there was an air of festivity, as when supporters gather to follow their favourite football team to some important match. Only in this case it appeared that the whole of the population of Wat Paknam was making the journey to Wat Sampya in Bangkok to listen to an English bhikkhu talking in public for the first time in the history of their country.

From the smiles I saw on their faces, from the respect shown by boys and men as they bowed their heads to touch my feet, and as the women, keeping their distance, bowed in salutation, I realised that to them I was one of themselves. I was theirs, a Thai bhikkhu, and they were proud of me. As I stepped into the waiting car I only hoped that they would have cause to be proud of me after the lecture had been completed. More than ever I began to realise in the few moments before we drove away that I loved these people. I was completely at home with them, more at home in fact than I had ever been in the whole of my lifetime. And not knowing what the future holds – as is the case with all men – I determined that I would spend the rest of my life in this land among these happy, kind and tolerant people.

On arrival at Wat Sampya we were met by the abbot and senior bhikkhus of the monastery and then led to a vast Dhamma Sala or Teaching Hall. The place was packed to capacity, the hall a blaze of colour. Half the seats were taken up by yellow-robed bhikkhus, and many of these, I learned, were Great Elders who had travelled from all over the country.

The abbot led us to a table, and once we were all seated refreshments were supplied. At this point one of the radio technicians requested that I go to the platform to try the microphone – sadly enough microphones and loudspeakers appear to be almost as prolific as mosquitoes in Thailand. Once on the platform, the necessary tests having been made, I was able to have a good look round. The hall was completely open, each side leading out into a vast compound. I had thought it to be packed to capacity, but that huge compound was even more so. Every available space was taken up for as far as the eye could see.

On my return to the table Thitavedo gave me coffee and a cigarette and told me to enjoy them as I would soon have to begin my talk. It would be a long time before I was able to get more refreshment. He explained that when I had finished I was to deal with questions for as long as I liked or whilst there were still questions being asked. The broadcast would continue the whole time, and the talk and questions and answers would also be recorded on tape. Even Wat Paknam had a supporter there who would record the talk so that it would prove useful in the future.

I began speaking that afternoon at 3 and sat down again, having answered the final question, at 7. I spoke small portions of the lecture which Thitavedo immediately interpreted. This was the best way, I decided, to hold the interest of the audience and to maintain the sense fresh in people's minds.

The questions came fast and furious. Some of them, being completely political, I refused to answer as was my right as a bhikkhu – traditionally a bhikkhu has nothing to do with politics. In the majority of cases the questions were excellent. Many of them, coming from the bhikkhus present, went very deeply into the subject. Others came from extremely knowledgeable people.

The only question I received which roused me in any way was one that I was asked by a young American journalist. He, as is quite usual, was trying to score a point off the Thais rather than to ask a constructive question.

'If Buddhism is such a wonderful thing,' he wanted to know, 'when are the Thais going to give up drinking, going to cinemas, smoking opium and generally acting in a decadent manner far worse than the West?'

As he was asking the question I watched Thitavedo and as many of the audience as I could. Thitavedo turned his head to me and winked roguishly. Over his face spread a smile of utter simplicity – a smile which appeared to imply that what he had just heard was a string of compliments rather than a series of insults to his nation as a whole. The rest of the audience – after Thitavedo had translated the question – remained calm and smiling, but with an air of subdued expectancy.

I turned to my young questioner and replied: 'Sir, do you mind if I ask you a few questions before I attempt to answer yours? The answers which you may give will, I am sure, help us to arrive at understanding.'

'Sure,' he replied. 'Shoot – go ahead, brother.'

'How long,' I enquired, 'have you been in Bangkok?'

'Just two months.'

'Have you managed to get out of Bangkok yet?'

'No sirree, I've been far too busy.'

'Would you agree then that the only thing which you know about the Thais and Thailand is based upon the little you may know about Bangkok? And would you not further agree that Bangkok is much like any other international city? Are not the inhabitants of these cities usually of many nationalities, and are not the habits and customs of these cities but a hotch-potch collection of the supposedly civilised and social habits of all international cities, rather than the true habits and customs of the race and country in question? Would it for instance be sensible or correct to judge the American nation purely on the goings-on in Chicago?

'Now my final questions. When are you going to find time to tear yourself away from the bars, clubs and cinemas of Bangkok? When are you going to get out into the country so that you can meet the Thai in his own environment? When are you going to send home an article based upon your true experience of the country, rather than doing what so many of your fellows do when they hash up a slick article based upon nothing but hearsay, with the aid of many a glass of whisky to help the imagination?'

My questioner smiled ruefully, ran his fingers through his cropped hair, hitched his camera case up on his shoulder and said, 'You got me, brother. Should have kept my big mouth shut. What you have said is true in the main and I guess if I had taken the trouble to think I would never have made such damnfool statements. Sorry, brother – no harm done, I hope?'

I had made my point and was happy with the result as was everyone else in the audience, particularly when I called the young American over to the platform and we shook hands in a perfectly friendly way. Altogether a successful day.

As I prepared to leave the hall, people swarmed round me, congratulating me on the talk. Some said that it was too difficult to understand and asked if they might visit me at Wat Paknam to ask further questions. During most of the time I noticed that the young American stayed close by my side. Eventually I was rescued from the throng by a group of my friends – Thitavedo had dashed off and gathered them together – to whom I immediately introduced my American questioner.

This was a good thing for him and them, because he received invitations into their homes and through their connections was able to visit many parts of the country in the months to come. He became quite a friend of mine and later when he began to bring his articles along for me to read, I found a vast improvement in the factuality and balance of his reporting. For his part, he was instrumental in my meeting a number of visiting Americans and having long discussions with quite a number of American anthropologists who for some mysterious reason appeared to be swarming over Thailand.

★ ★ ★

At 9 the following morning my house had become a hive of industry. All the rooms of the ground floor had been thoroughly cleaned and further chairs had been brought in. To my surprise I saw that a tape recorder with two microphones had been wired up and was ready for use. The compound had been swept and rush and bamboo matting had been spread over the hard granite chips which I had asked for on my arrival so that I might toughen my then tender feet.

I had just greeted the arrival of Lung Poh and his assistants when Khun Sankhavasi appeared accompanied by quite a large number of friends. This group included most of the officers of the Thai Buddhist Association and Khun Amnvey Athaithan and Khun Theam Chanakul, both of whom were officers of the Thai-Chinese Buddhist Association. I was delighted to find representatives of both Associations present because in England – and, I suppose, in the West generally – it was more or less thought that Buddhism was split into two opposing schools: Theravada on the one hand and Mahayana on the other. This supposed split was much advertised in England, some people going so far as to give lectures which attempted to heal this tragic breach. With the coming together of this morning's gathering I could see at once what I had always thought: there was no such thing as a breach, for the Thais were Theravada Buddhists and the Chinese were Mahayana. The differences were only a matter of geography and language.

Sankhavasi left, saying that he was going to meet our guest, who should have arrived at the other side of the bridge by now. On his return to the main room of the house he was accompanied by a tall, slim, fair-haired young man whom he introduced as Robert Samek.

Samek was obviously a little nervous at being thrust among so many yellow-robed figures – quite a large number of bhikkhus had gathered. I understood from him that he had only been in Bangkok for two days and that the oppressive heat, the unfamiliar food, the persistent attention of hordes of mosquitoes and a fear of malaria were making him feel considerably off-colour.

Very quickly my friends saw what was required to bring comfort to poor Samek. They brought cooling lotions which they rubbed on his arms, face and legs, and a black-looking drink – which I knew quite well by now – to settle his stomach. These, together with cool drinks and an easy-going conversation, soon made him feel better. Before long he changed into the bright-minded fellow I knew he must be behind all his discomfort, and very quickly he became 'Bob' to everyone present.

Samek informed me that he had graduated from Cambridge and had gone out to Australia to take up a senior lectureship in Commercial Law at Melbourne. He was now on his way by easy stages to Chicago, where he was to take up a fellowship for about a year. He had come to Bangkok especially to find out as much about Buddhism as possible. He was not a Buddhist, but was extremely interested in the teaching and had read a number of books on the subject. Some of the ideas he could accept, but there were many that he did not agree with and others which he could not understand. Could I give him two or three hours of my time and explain Buddhism to him?

I told him that I was prepared to give as much time as he required but that quite frankly two or three hours would produce nothing but confusion. It would be far better if he could remain with me for forty-eight hours. I assured him that we could make him quite comfortable. Bob was delighted and jumped at the offer. It was at this point that Lung Poh – speaking through Thitavedo – stressed the fact that he wanted the conversations recorded on tape so that they could be heard at leisure by anyone who so wished. He hoped that Bob would agree to this, and of course he did, without any reservations.

Bob had a number of questions to which he wanted answers. He had read as widely as possible on the subject but knew no Pali or Sanskrit, nor had he had the good fortune to find first-class translations from accepted sources. He knew all the popular ideas, and was quite well-versed in the general statements of Buddhism.

Naturally I questioned him on his knowledge, trying to search for a beginning for our discussions. He told me that he knew that the teaching of the Buddha was based upon the Four Truths: the Truth of suffering, the Truth of the cause of suffering, the Truth of the cessation of suffering, and the Truth of the path which leads to the cessation of suffering. He also understood that this last was in fact also known as the Eightfold Path, consisting of Right Understanding, Right Thought, Right Speech, Right Action, Right Living, Right Effort, Right Mindfulness and Right Concentration.

He told me that he had heard of *kamma* (*karma* in Sanskrit) and rebirth and had a number of ideas as to what these terms might mean. He knew also that the Buddha was supposed to have taught that everything was impermanent and changing and that all things were anatta, or without a self or soul.

It appeared to him that there was some confusion in general views on Buddhism. Some people seemed to think that it was a religion of compassion, tolerance and loving-kindness. Others said that it was purely a negative and nihilistic philosophy. During his reading on the subject he had also seen much mention of the two great schools of

Buddhism, Mahayana and Theravada. From what he had been able to gather there were great differences between these schools. Did that mean that their basic teaching was different?

I decided to make the starting point of our discussions the question of the two schools. Whatever differences there were between Mahayana and Theravada, I explained, were largely due to geography, language and local custom. The term Mahayana was generally used when referring to Buddhism in northern countries of the East, such as China, Tibet, Japan. This great school had also spread in early days to Vietnam, Burma and Thailand, although these had quickly turned to Theravada. The Theravada countries today were Thailand, Burma, Cambodia, Laos and Ceylon.

The basic teaching was the same in both schools. Both operated around the Four Truths and the Eightfold Path. It was upon these basic teachings that all Buddhist thought revolved.

In Bangkok there were both Mahayana and Theravada monasteries and pagodas. The Chinese, when they began to come to Thailand, had brought their own customs and rituals with their Buddhism. The monks of the two schools were very good friends. In fact I had had personal experience of sitting through a ceremony with monks from both Theravada and Mahayana.

The rules for the Mahayana monks were slightly different – in the majority of cases a little less austere. I told Bob what one of my Chinese friends, a Mahayana monk and a great scholar and calligrapher, had said during a lengthy discussion of ours. We had been sitting in a Chinese pagoda during a part of a service where there was much beating of gongs and tap boxes and repetition of suttas, all of which was overlaid with a thick pall of smoke from burning punk or incense sticks. This experience was something of a surprise to me as I had been used to the much quieter affairs of my own Theravada pagoda. I must have raised an interrogative eyebrow, for my friend turned to me with a smile and informed me that I was not to be bothered by the noise – this was Mahayana custom. And then he said, 'You see, my friend, how strange it is. Your people have Theravada and my people have Mahayana. These are their Buddhism. But you and I, we have neither of these for we have the same Dhamma [teaching].' With that Bob was satisfied.

I next dealt with his point about negativism and nihilism in the teaching. I explained that the best way in which to view the Four Truths of Buddhism was as if they were the pronouncement of a medical practitioner. Such a person would, on being called upon to treat a patient, first diagnose the ailment, then find its cause, bring about a cure and place on record the method used.

Gotama had done precisely that. He found through his experience of
life that there was much suffering in the world. There was illness,
bereavement, old age, disease, pain, unhappiness. All these he
referred to as *dukkha* – suffering or unrest. He said that this state in
some degree was always with man. Hence the First Truth, that of
suffering. Here he states the disease. In the next Truth he states the
cause, the Truth of the cause of suffering. This he says is craving –
thirst or desire in its many forms. Next he sees that suffering can cease
– the cure. Finally he brings out the method by which the cure may be
brought about – the Fourth Truth, the path which leads to the cessation
of suffering or the Eightfold Path.

On this basis the teaching could not in any circumstance be called
negative for it offered man complete release from unrest and suffering
– not a temporary state of health as if gained from a palliative, but a
complete cure.

On the charge of nihilism I explained that it was mostly failure to
understand the true import of the first two Truths – of suffering and its
cause – which had led to so many misinterpretations. Gotama had laid
great stress on these two Truths. It was in explaining them that he
propounded his law of *Paticca Samuppada*, or Dependent Origination.
This law was the basis of all the picturesque 'Wheels of Life' which
were illustrated in books about Tibet.

Gotama had so often stated to his bhikkhus: 'He who understands
the Dhamma understands Dependent Origination. He who understands Dependent Origination understands the Dhamma.' This law
was the basis of all Buddhist philosophy. It was the very keystone of
Buddhism, whether Mahayana or Theravada.

Samek said that he had heard of this law and had often seen
illustrations of the Wheels of Life which I had mentioned but had never
understood them. He therefore asked me to explain Dependent
Origination more fully.

I told him that it taught the conditionality and dependency of all
phenomena, mental or physical. The doctrine of anatta or imper-
sonality, selflessness or soullessness of all phenomena had been
arrived at by analytical methods, methods by which man and existence
had been reduced to impersonal insubstantial ultimates. Dependent
Origination on the other hand operated upon a synthetical basis,
showing the dependency, conditionality and relationships of these
ultimates of existence. It explained, in fact, the conditional and
dependent nature of the stream of mental and physical phenomena of
existence normally referred to in conventional language as soul, man,
ego, animal and so on.

Dependent Origination was organised into twelve 'links' or steps:

1. There is ignorance.
2. Through ignorance, good and bad actions, both bodily and mental, are conditioned. Good and bad actions mean essentially the volitions of mind – kamma or karma in fact. The Buddha stated: 'Bhikkhus, I say that kamma is volition.'
3. Conditioned by past good and bad volitions is consciousness (*viññana*), meaning all that can be meant by mind.
4. Conditioned by consciousness are corporeality and mentality. Corporeality means the four elements of materiality – extension (solidity), cohesion (liquid), temperature (heat), motion. Mentality means feeling, perception, mental formations (volitions past and present which will condition the future) and all associated ideas in mind. And consciousness covers the five consciousnesses of sense as well as mind.
5. Conditioned by corporeality and mentality are the six bases of sense: sight, sound, smell, taste, touch and mind.
6. Conditioned by the six bases of sense are the impressions – that is, impressions from the five senses and mind, the impact between sense and data or mind and mental object.
7. Conditioned by the impressions is feeling: pleasant, painful and indifferent.
8. Conditioned by feeling is craving: craving for pleasant feelings, craving not to have unpleasant feelings.
9. Conditioned by craving is clinging, an intensified craving: clinging to erroneous opinions, sensuality, ideas of a permanent self, rites and rituals.
10. Conditioned by clinging is becoming. Becoming here means the good and bad volitions dependent upon the past which condition a future state.
11. Conditioned by becoming is rebirth – strictly speaking, the Pali term means birth. This is the birth or rebirth of mentality and corporeality.
12. Conditioned by birth is old age and death.

I explained that numbers (1) and (2) refer to the past, (3)-(10) to the present conditioned by that past, (11) and (12) to the future conditioned by that present.

This system, I explained to Samek, was the method used by Gotama to explain the Dependent Origination of suffering. It could be viewed in two ways:

a. That through ignorance of the Four Truths and all that they entailed in a past life, kamma or volitions had arisen which had brought about the birth of consciousness and all its associated mental and physical attributes in the process of procreation. As life went on, driven by craving, the process would be repeated again and again, birth giving rise to death and death giving rise to birth.

b. That through ignorance of the past moment came the uprising of present consciousness and its supporting physical constituents. The volitions (kamma) of that present would condition the future momentary death and birth of a new consciousness.

The whole theory spoke of momentarily existing phenomena, both mental and physical, which came to be and passed away, each present momentary existence being conditioned by and related to a past, itself being related to and conditioning a future. The theory taught that no *thing* was a thing of itself but only in relationship and dependency. Whilst we might use the conventional term man for all the mental and physical phenomena, in the strict sense there were only the momentary conditioned and conditioning mental and physical phenomena. It taught of continual change, of nothing ever being the same thing for any two moments.

Samek found this somewhat hard going and said so, for which I did not blame him, the whole system being extremely involved. He began to grasp the import of the system when I demonstrated to him the question of touch.

Touch, I explained, which appeared to be such a personal matter and a thing which existed of itself, had no existence other than in dependence upon and relation to other things. Firstly there had to be some objective data for touch to arise. Secondly there had to be some physical sense which could come into contact with the objective data. Thirdly there had to be some mental aspect which could evaluate the sensation as pleasant, painful or neutral, desirable or undesirable.

For a while Samek was still confused, mainly because of the conventional use of terms. A man, he said, was the same man no matter if one met him today or tomorrow. Everybody would know him as the same old Joe Bloggs, for instance. I agreed that for all general purposes that would be true, but that in the ultimate sense it could not be maintained. There was a Buddhist axiom that any change *in* a thing is a change *of* thing. And while we might call Joe Bloggs the same man on two different occasions, it was not strictly true, as Joe Bloggs was older or younger as the case might be. Joe Bloggs was just a convenient term – much as electron is a convenient term for a nuclear phenomenon which is constantly changing and becoming something other, although we still persist in calling it an electron.

I stressed the point with Samek that the theory of Dependent Origination was well worthy of deep study. In fact it demanded such study, being a very deep subject. It was a theory which was completely on all fours with modern scientific views of the universe, and covered in its orbit the questions of time, space and relativity.

Samek and I discussed this theory at great length and I am happy to say that he finally grasped its import. However, the conversations and arguments which we had on so subtle a philosophical theory, running almost parallel with advanced modern scientific views, would have no place here.

★ ★ ★

At the end of his two days' stay at Wat Paknam I took Bob all round the area of the monastery, showing him the various places in which bhikkhus lived and their general conditions. It was his first experience of such lives and conditions. I am sure that his respect for the bhikkhu grew on account of his visit. Of his thankfulness for his stay and his experiences at Wat Paknam I am convinced, because he tried so hard to convey his feelings to both Thitavedo and myself before his early morning departure. But Bob was nothing if not thorough, for the very next day the following article appeared in the Bangkok Press:

THE STANDARD

Bangkok, Thailand. August 7th, 1954.

Mr Robert A Samek, a senior lecturer in Commercial Law at Melbourne University, who is stopping in Bangkok to study Buddhist philosophy, is on his way via Rangoon and London to take up a teaching fellowship in Chicago.

He was deeply impressed by discussions with Bhikkhu Kapilavaddho.

Mr Samek said: 'I want to record my sincere thanks to the Buddhist Association which has helped me to make my visit to Bangkok truly memorable. It gave me the opportunity of seeing the unique temples and monuments and of meeting many of its distinguished sons who have always received me with courtesy and real friendliness. This in itself would be ample reward, but the Buddhist Association has also been instrumental in bringing about in me a far greater understanding of the doctrine of the Buddha and of what is widely known as the Eastern approach to life than I had thought myself capable of heretofore.

'For my progress in that direction I wish to express my particular gratitude to a European, Bhikkhu Kapilavaddho, who by his deep knowledge, patience, lucidity and honesty of purpose has succeeded in revealing to me some of the footsteps of the Buddha. I would also like to thank the abbot of Wat Paknam and Bhikkhu Thitavedo for their kind hospitality.'

15

TEMPLES AND SNAKES

After the visit of Robert Samek, my life became very busy. Lung Poh had apparently decided that I should be taken round to the various pagodas in Bangkok to meet as many Thai people as possible. He obviously wanted me to gain as much experience of the country and people and their customs as I could. A number of my friends and supporters made it their immediate responsibility to take me to all the famous places and to meet, as far as possible, all the famous people.

Early one morning three of them – Khun Sanoh, Khun Siri and Khun Suang – arrived at my house and informed me that they wished to take me to visit various pagodas in Bangkok. They had obtained Lung Poh's permission to take me out, and would I please get ready to leave immediately as we had a fairly busy day ahead of us.

I made myself ready and we set off for Bangkok by car. Our first stop was the world famous Wat Phra Keo – the Temple of the Emerald Buddha. The pagoda area itself was situated within the Royal Palace, which probably accounted for the steel-helmeted and armed guards on duty at the main entrance. Once inside the walls of the palace grounds I was able to look at the fabulous scene. Never before had I witnessed a scene so breath-taking in its fantastic and fairy-tale quality.

Spread out before me was a flight of imposing stone steps which rose to a platform some twenty feet above ground level. As I climbed upwards I marvelled at the intricacy, the fineness of the workmanship in the stone balustrades. On the platform itself were the pagoda buildings, each housing a figure of the Buddha, all of them vying with each other in my mind as to which was the most beautiful. Buildings of white, red, gold and green. Buildings with intricately carved teak doors, with slim golden spires striking upwards in the blazing sun, as if striving to outreach each other into the infinite blue space of the sky above. Buildings decorated with mosaics of glass and richly-coloured porcelain, sparkling like jewels in the sun.

Between the buildings were stone *cetiyas* or reliquaries, some very small and others massive in comparison, each with its spire or *prang* reaching upward into the sky with the rest. One of these, as large as an English suburban house in area, was a blaze of gold with a spire topped by a golden parasol reaching a hundred feet up. The main part of the structure was covered by thousands of inch-square golden mosaics, each of which had cost – so I was told – the equivalent of one shilling and six pence in English money. The parasol topping the spire was constructed of fourteen carat gold.

As I walked toward the main building, the pagoda of the Emerald Buddha, a slight breeze rustled the tiny silver and gold bells which hung from the eaves of each building, filling the air with a gentle tinkling music, a music which appeared to originate in the very sky itself, giving the whole area an atmosphere of remoteness and peacefulness.

The pagoda itself was built in the form of a cross, with entrances at the cardinal points. From the centre of the roof rose the tallest spire in the area. We entered by the eastern door, a massive double door made of teak, every inch of it carved with traditional designs and inlaid with mother-of-pearl. Inside the air was pleasantly cool and softly lit. At the far western end rose a highly decorated and intricately carved shrine. Rich red lacquer and gold leaf were in profusion. The shrine rose tier upon tier up into the high roof, every tier decorated with flowers, silver and gold and rich silks and brocades.

On the topmost tier, beautifully lit, stood the Emerald Buddha, a figure some two feet tall and carved from almost priceless green jade. The headpiece and flame of wisdom above – a style common to all Thai Buddha figures – was of solid gold. Below, arranged tier on tier, were other Buddha figures of various colours of jade. The main figure, the green Buddha (the Thai term *kheo* also means green), stood out like a major star among these lesser but beautiful images.

Its exact history is lost in the past, but it is an object of veneration and power to South-East Asia. Cambodia, Burma and Thailand fought for possession of this priceless treasure, this bringer of luck and power. Eventually it settled, and now brings its blessings to this, the pagoda of Wat Phra Kheo. Such is the veneration which the whole nation holds for the green Buddha that at the beginning of each season of the year, each of the four quarters, a new gold headpiece is made and fitted to the figure, the old being placed in a glass case for safekeeping.

As I watched, people came and went silently on bare feet, bowing three times in salutation and reverence to the exquisite figure of the Buddha above them. I could not help but contrast the strange unpredictableness of man, who on the one hand (if he were Western) would complain that the figure was not emerald but only jade; and on the other (if he were Thai) would venerate the figure irrespective of its monetary value as if it were indeed the Buddha himself. But as for Gotama Siddhattha, the man who had become the Buddha, had he not said:

Yet not thus is the Tathagata truly honoured, revered, respected, worshipped and deferred to. Whosoever, Ananda, be he brother or sister, lay-brother or -sister – whosoever dwells in fulfilment of the law or teaching, both in its greater and lesser duties – whosoever walks uprightly in accordance with the teaching – he it is that truly honours, reveres, respects, worships and defers to the Tathagata in the perfection of worship.

These were the words of a man, a man among men, who had taught against the efficacy of rite and ritual, who had taught and beseeched his followers not to worship him but simply to carry out what he had taught, with the potent promise that if they did so they could obtain what he had done.

As I sat and watched the people come and go in the calm and peaceful atmosphere of Wat Phra Kheo, I could not help but think of the perversity of man. Man who would work and slave to produce such a place of beauty, a place of treasure beyond price, in worship and veneration. Man who was so confused in his mind that he could think that by raising these breath-taking pagodas and by worshipping his own creations of what he thought the founder of his faith was like, he could bring about the release from unrest and suffering which, Gotama had taught, could only be attained by individual effort and insight.

My visit to Wat Phra Kheo was an experience of joy – joy in the striving of my fellow men in their efforts to climb ever upwards, creating in those efforts a beauty almost beyond this mundane world, creating from material dross such edifices that the mind was enabled to soar to heights beyond normal experience. And yet the very creators of such beauty were bogged down with their own creations, wandering ever farther from that which had been taught with such compassion and understanding, into the rites and ritual, magic, fortune-telling and sheer animism which they had made for themselves from the teaching of Siddhattha Gotama.

As we were leaving the main gate, I was dragged back to the present-day world by the clanking of the ammunition-belts and the booted tread of the armed and helmeted guards, one of whom had stopped rather forcibly a European who was wearing his shirt with his sleeves rolled up to the elbow. The guard had him gripped strongly by the arm, much to the consternation of the European. It was explained to him that his behaviour in wearing his sleeves rolled up was an insult to the Buddha. Dutifully, full of apologies, he rolled them down and buttoned his cuffs, and was then allowed to enter this fairy-tale land of men's creation.

As he went I saw others entering the gate, both Thais and Europeans, all showing arms and elbows but with short-sleeved shirts which could not be rolled down. The guards ignored them and they went their way in peace. Again I wondered what Gotama would have thought of such goings-on, and realised that he would probably have been far less concerned than I, saying in fact that these were but people, that people were much the same throughout history and that one should view their actions with compassion and tolerance.

★ ★ ★

The next day my friends called for me again and took me on a visit to another famous pagoda – Wat Benjamabopitr, known as the Marble Pagoda, on the outskirts of Bangkok. The whole edifice had been constructed from Carrara marble shipped especially from Italy and had been built by Italian craftsmen to traditional Thai design. The one jarring note was that it was windowed with stained glass, being unique in this respect throughout the whole of Thailand. Thai pagodas are never glazed owing to the intense heat, the open window-space being only shuttered against the rains.

The whole of the pagoda compound was paved with highly polished marble, giving the effect, in the heat, of being a shallow ornamented lake. The pagoda itself, built in traditional style, had entrances at the four compass points and stood out stark, cool and remote in its odd beauty against the background of the open sky.

Within the compound walls were gathered together probably the finest collection of Buddha figures to be seen anywhere in the world, ranging in history from the early fourth century of the Christian era up until modern times. And demonstrating the influence of early Hindu civilisation on the culture of Thailand, the whole of the epic story of the Mahabharata was painted around the entire compound wall. I spent hours viewing these murals and marvelling at their craftsmanship, particularly when I realised they had been painted by a team and not by one man. So strong is the tradition of this style of Thai painting that one can detect absolutely no difference where one artist has left off a scene and another has taken over.

My friends and I spent most of the day wandering round the area of Wat Benjamabopitr, seeing things of rare beauty and value in this quite modern pagoda – none of the pagodas of Bangkok date from much before the eighteen hundreds. I was able to talk with many of the bhikkhus who lived in the compound and eventually was fortunate to have a meeting with the Sangha Nayaka, who, next to the Sangha Raja, was the most influential bhikkhu in the country. He lived in a small house at the far end of the compound, which was where I met him. He was an extremely able and learned man, and acting as he did as virtual Prime Minister for the brotherhood, he led an extremely busy life. He still found time, however, to talk with me for over an hour.

He recalled that he had been one of those Maha Theras or Great Elders who had been present at a function held at Wat Paknam in my honour after my bhikkhu ordination. He had apparently followed my career with great interest and was well posted with news about my doings at Wat Paknam. He said that Lung Poh had visited him often and told him how I had stuck to meditation practice. That interview was one of many I had with this charming and learned man who became a great personal friend during my stay in Thailand.

As we left the Marble Pagoda, walking along the wide marble-paved path, out again into the world of cars, people, loudspeakers and Coca-Cola signs, I looked back and saw wandering across the path a pi-dog, a type of which there are hundreds of thousands in Thailand. This poor creature was a mass of mange, not having a hair on its body, its carcase covered with open sores. Since its whole body was a mass of irritation, at every other step it would stop and scratch to ease its suffering, and then howl at the greater pain created by the scratching. People and bhikkhus came and went along the path but not one interfered with the dog, no one tried to drive it away. Everything and everybody was entitled to enter the pagoda and who was to say that a poor lowly dog should be disbarred.

This could never have happened in England. Someone would have come forward, some group or society would have stepped in, and with great beating of chests and loud protestations as to the sinfulness of letting dogs suffer in this manner, they would have collected the animal and destroyed it, under the pretext that it put it out of its suffering.

The Thais, however, and for that matter all Buddhists, have other views. Everything wants to go on living. Everything values its life. It should therefore be allowed to live out that life to its end without interference. Do unto others as you would wish done unto you. You value your life, they would say, so take not the life of another even if it be a dog.

All of which left me wondering what we Westerners mean when we say that we are putting something out of its suffering. Are we not in fact putting it out of *our* suffering, just destroying it because we cannot stand our own thoughts? Are we not just suffering from an intense aversion to some object of sight which we must at all costs remove from our view so that our artificial view of life is not marred? Is it not in truth the same urge which drives us on the one hand to destroy all things which we for convenience call pests, and on the other to put to sleep our dearly beloved pets and so 'end their suffering'? Is it not the same aim which drives us to both forms of action – the aim to maintain some peace of mind within ourselves, even at the cost of other living things; to sustain some security in life, no matter how many lies or how much irrational thinking has been the basis of such security? Even our hypocritical phrase 'putting to sleep' we use as a sop to conscience, rather than face the truth that we are killing.

I am not implying that the Thais never kill. Of course they do: they are human beings first and, ideally, Buddhists next. But they do not lie to themselves when they do so. There are people employed as butchers, fishmongers, hunters and the like – suppliers of food. Even these, forced by livelihood to kill, will make every effort to maintain two days a week wherein they undertake the Buddhist precept not to kill. There are occasions where a mother may feel her child's life is threatened by a snake. Often she will kill under such stress, but there is always a genuine sense of remorse that she has been driven to such action.

I have on the other hand observed a situation where a Thai, on passing a butcher's, has seen that some animal is about to be killed, and has walked up and stopped the killing by the simple process of buying the animal from the butcher, leading it off and turning it loose in some pagoda and monastery compound.

The monasteries and pagoda areas are sanctuaries for all kinds of life. Here everything is safe from harm so far as human beings are concerned. In these places all forms of animal and insect life are prolific. Snakes, scorpions, rats and lizards go about their lives unmolested in these areas and no one would think of deliberately killing any of them. Rarely indeed does one ever hear that a bhikkhu has been bitten, or died from a bite of one of these creatures.

I can remember a particular occasion at Wat Paknam when a party of us – Thitavedo, myself and three other bhikkhus – were making our way home from my house to another part of the monastery. We were walking along a footpath when we came to an intersection where our path crossed another. Suddenly we all stopped in our tracks. There in front of us, crossing our path, was some five feet of glistening black snake. It was moving quite fast until it came level with us and then it slowed down, moving its head back and forth in a wide arc as if to survey us.

I looked at the rest of the party and on not one face could I see anything of fear or aversion. They just stood there calmly watching the snake, who was but a matter of twenty-four inches from their bare feet.

I broke the silence by saying jocularly to the snake, 'Come along, old chap. Hurry up – we want to get along.' At that precise moment the snake decided to move on in its original direction and within a matter of moments it had disappeared up the path.

An excited buzz of conversation broke out between Thitavedo and the other bhikkhus, all of them gesticulating excitedly and pointing in my direction. Thitavedo by now was hardly able to contain himself through amusement. He turned to me and laughingly explained that the others had thought I must have a very strong *mantra* or magic with snakes to make it move away so fast. He had explained to them what it was that I'd said, and that in fact the snake had moved under its own volition, not from any command of mine. I joined in the joke with them, and remarked that obviously the snake must have been an Englishman in some previous birth, for how else could it have understood my command? The story of the English-speaking snake went the rounds of Wat Paknam for a considerable time after that incident.

I had a number of similar experiences with bhikkhus and the local wild life. Never once did I see fear in a bhikkhu on any of these occasions. The main reason, I think, was that all of them were meditation bhikkhus and had spent some time on their own in the jungle, even as I had myself. One hears many stories of the supposed power of bhikkhus over animals, and their power to remain free from harm. From my own experience and observation I would say that the apparent powers can be traced rather to a physiological process than to any occult magical sources.

Most forms of wild life react strongly to the sense of smell. The odour from a frightened man is entirely different from that of a man who is calm and without fear. The odour of a fearful man, even to my nose, is more acrid and acid. It is the effect of this scent change which I am sure brings about vindictiveness in the animal, a vindictiveness which is but a form of protection against something which it has instinctively learned to distrust.

I remember an occasion when I was sitting in the deep jungles of northern Thailand, watching a coiled cobra in some brush at the foot of a tree. I knew quite well that it had observed me, but it went quietly on with its business, occasionally darting out its tongue and lapping up some ant or insect which came its way. Through the trees came a jungle-dog – slightly larger than the pi or scavenger variety which one sees around the villages and towns. He spotted me and skirted round for quite a time, eventually gaining enough courage to come and have a sniff at me. I remained perfectly still and he passed on to the next tree trunk to continue his sniffing.

The cobra had also seen the approach of the dog but had not moved its position. The dog in its wanderings drew close to the cobra, though completely unaware of its presence. The cobra still remained coiled and in no way ready to strike. Suddenly, when about two feet from it, the dog saw the cobra. The dog's whole attitude changed. His hair stood on end. The whole body stiffened. The lips drew back from the teeth, the mouth fell open and sweat drooled from his lolling tongue. An object of fear, trembling and panicky threat and action.

Almost simultaneously, the cobra reared up, spreading its hood. This was too much for the dog. He jumped back a pace and bolted, howling as he went. The cobra settled back to its quiet pastime of lapping up the odd ant which passed its way. I am sure that the reason for the cobra's defensive attitude was a reaction to the acrid smell from the sweat of that dog's tongue, a dog who was in panic and fear and liable to do anything.

★   ★   ★

During the next few weeks I visited all the famous pagodas in Bangkok, each and every one of them unique. Some in idyllic settings; others, rising from sheer squalor, surrounded by commerce and almost choked, it would seem, by the hovels and human hordes which clustered around them. But always the golden spire thrust upward into the free sky above.

I visited both Thai and Chinese pagodas, both Theravada and Mahayana. Here the people would come to pay their respects and in some cases, I suspect, to pray to the Buddha. They would bring flowers, joss sticks and a candle, all of which they would place on the shrine in front of them. Then some of them would move away and for a small fee try their luck on a fortune-telling wheel or have their fortunes told by bamboo sticks. Some, to make quite sure that the fortune would be correct, would bring the box of bamboo sticks with them to a place in front of the Buddha figure and bow many times to the figure before throwing the sticks.

The larger proportion of the pagodas did not have these devices, rightly leaving the people to find such help elsewhere. I found the devices much more prevalent in the Chinese districts or where Chinese influence had been felt. The Chinese or Mahayana type of Buddhism had moved much more toward some idea of vicarious salvation than had Theravada, and this no doubt accounted for the fact that there was much more belief, to my view, in magic and occult intervention in the Chinese pagodas. Whatever one's views might be, however, one could not but respect the utter sincerity with which the congregations of both Thai and Chinese pagodas carried out the religious offices, and the utter tolerance with which they viewed each other's practices. For as they would say, 'We have different customs but the same teaching.'

16

MAGICAL FEATS

My friends decided that it was time I met some of the people who claimed to have extraordinary powers or *iddhi* as they are called in Buddhism. They said they had heard of a Chinese monk who had the power to talk with the dead. Of a layman who was famed for his power to protect people against being cut or killed by a knife or shot dead by a bullet. Of a bhikkhu who apparently had the power of turning rice grains into prawns.

They asked me what I thought of such things and I told them that to the best of my knowledge such things had nothing to do with the teaching of Gotama Buddha. In fact he had taught against such displays. I agreed, however, to their offer to meet such people, assuring them that I was certain there was a reasonable explanation for any peculiar powers.

First we went off to the north-east of Bangkok to a Chinese pagoda, where the Chinese bhikkhu resided. After I had been introduced to him I told him that I had heard of his powers and would like to see him demonstrate them. He told me that his fame had come about through an incident when one of his bhikkhus had died.

Apparently he had been sitting beside the bhikkhu when death took place, and he had a strong feeling that the dead one wished to tell him something. At that moment, he noticed that what appeared to be rays of light reached from his own hands to those of the corpse. Somewhat shaken, he asked the dead one what it was he wanted. He was instructed that the body of the bhikkhu was to be arranged so that it sat upright in a cross-legged posture. In this position, he was informed, it would not decompose for a long time, and it was to be kept and shown to the people as a mark of the power of the Buddha's teaching.

He then brought out a number of photographs of himself seated beside the cross-legged body of the dead bhikkhu, showing distinctly the white lines running between his own hands and those of the body. I had seen much of photography, having been a photographer myself, and this reminded me very much of the so-called spirit photographs which were the vogue of spiritualism at one time in England, most of which were fakes. I could not accept the photograph as proof but held my counsel. I again made my request that the bhikkhu demonstrate his powers. He refused, but said that I could see the body in question, stressing that it had been dead for four years – a fact which I later verified.

The body turned out to be, as he had said, very well-preserved. It was sitting upright with the legs completely crossed in the meditation posture, the hands folded in the lap. It was slightly shrunken of course, the skin hanging tightly around the bones, a deep brown in colour. I felt the skin of the arms, face and stomach and found it leathery and oily.

I came to the conclusion that its state of preservation was largely due to some peculiarity of climate rather than some strange power possessed by the departed owner of the body. Change had taken place in the body and the final break-up and decomposition was bound to occur, no matter how long it might take.

I stressed these points to the bhikkhu, saying as Gotama himself had said: 'All things are transient, all things must come to an end, nothing remains the same for two moments.' He smiled and agreed but asked me if it were not wonderful that it had lasted so long. I told him that I could see nothing wonderful in such a situation and that there was a reasonable explanation for the phenomenon. We agreed to differ but remained on very good terms.

After our discussion we were all served with China tea and cigarettes. During the conversation which ensued it turned out that the bhikkhu had also heard of the layman who could protect one from knife-thrust and bullet. From what he said this man was famous for miles around and his nightly gatherings were always full. The bhikkhu said that he knew the man well and would like very much to accompany us on our visit. My friends agreed and in the evening we all set off by car for the other side of Bangkok.

We eventually arrived at a two-storeyed teak house on the outskirts of the city. We were met by the owner, a slim man in middle age, white-robed. He had a thin intelligent face and forceful brown eyes. He was very proud to meet me, he informed me, as he had heard so much about my stay at Wat Paknam. He was very proud that I should come to see him perform the application of his powers on all who wished.

The usual greeting successfully accomplished, he escorted us to the upper floor, which spread across the whole area of the house, making a large hall now packed with people. He seated us on the floor close to a cushion against the far wall at one end of the room. Having seen that we were comfortable, he seated himself on the cushion facing his audience. He then poured water from a large jug into a glass as he intoned in Pali and Sanskrit. He then blew loudly over the heads of the audience, who by this time were completely enraptured by the proceedings.

From the back of the assembly a man arose and made his way to the man of power, seating himself cross-legged in front of him. He paid some money to an attendant seated close by and then, turning to the man of power, placed his hands in his. The white-robed figure of our host tensed as he took the hands. My friends explained to me that the man who had come to the front wanted to be protected from injury by knives.

By this time most of the assembly had their eyes closed, including the applicant for protection. As I watched our strange host I saw that whilst his eyes had narrowed to slits he could still see and was in fact watching me very closely. He then began to tremble throughout his body, and gradually, as if imparted through the hands, the body of the applicant began to tremble likewise. Our host then talked to the applicant in a low undertone and blew repeatedly on his forehead. He picked up a number of large knives in turn and demonstrated their keenness.

Taking one of these, he held the applicant's bare arm in the other hand and began to cut at the arm as if he were slicing a loaf of bread. When he had finished there was no sign of blood or injury on the arm. He then applied razor blades to various parts of his subject's body without any apparent injury. All the time he kept me under very close surveillance. I was sure that he was aware that I knew how such things were accomplished.

With each new applicant for protection – and there were very many that night – he gave me the knives to test, and at my request he let me feel the temperature and pulse beats of a number of the applicants.

It was when it was announced by one of the attendants that all those who had been treated that night could never be killed or injured by a knife that my conjecture became certainty. He was at that moment watching me closely. I picked up a wicked-looking knife and felt its edge with my thumb. Enquiringly, I looked directly at him and then at the last applicant, and made the minutest thrusting action with the point in the direction of the man. No one else witnessed the interplay between us, but a slight smile spread over my host's face and almost imperceptibly his head shook. He was to that extent an honest man, for his action had informed me, as I well knew, that he had no power to impart to anyone that would protect them from a direct knife-thrust with the point.

His whole performance had been extraordinarily well staged, but all the things he accomplished that night could be accounted for by hypnosis and trickery – dangerous trickery no doubt but trickery nonetheless. Later, when the audience had left, I had the opportunity of talking with him off the record and of reproducing on my own flesh some of his effects, both by trick and auto-hypnosis. We parted on extremely friendly terms and he thanked me for not stealing his thunder during the evening's performance – a thing I would never have done. A power is a power, and power is a matter of know-how, and if that becomes common property the magic is gone and the power no longer exists in men's minds.

The belief in magical powers is fairly widespread in Thailand, which is perfectly natural in a country still largely jungle, a country of remote villages and abundant wildlife. The villager, bitten by the snake, has no other recourse than to go to the village medicine-man. Quite often all the treatment he will receive will be that the medicine-man will utter a few chants and then, wetting his finger with spittle, draw a line round the affected limb above the bite, chanting all the time and impressing on the patient that the poison will not go beyond this point. The remarkable thing is that very often such treatment is perfectly successful. There are failures, but in the main it works.

Medicine-men who are snake-experts abound in the country. Generally speaking they are men of great courage and intelligence with an amazing power and control over all types of snake. They certainly appear to have no fear of them. And they invariably use the same treatment on themselves if bitten as they would on any villager who might come to them.

I was present when one of these experts was called to the compound of a house whose occupant was being troubled by a cobra. The snake-man moved round the compound until he had found a snake hole. The hole itself had the circumference of a man's upper arm and was situated close to a small ant-hill. He made quite certain that the cobra was not in the house or foraging anywhere in the grounds, sniffing all the time like a dog searching for a scent. This sight confirmed my own observation that snakes have their own peculiar odour, although one requires a very fine sense of smell to be aware of it.

Then approaching the hole again, he thrust his right arm deep into it. I watched him flinch slightly several times. He then slowly withdrew his arm from the hole. His hand, bleeding from a number of wounds where he had been bitten, was holding a large cobra tightly behind the head. Placing the snake in a bag and tying the top, he wetted his left index finger with spittle and made a complete circle above the elbow of his right arm. He then sat in a typical meditation posture and began to chant in a mixture of Thai and Pali. Gradually his body took on the appearance of catalepsy. He remained like this for about ten minutes. Then, rising to his feet, he collected the bag with the cobra, took his leave and went his way. I saw him again the next day, apparently none the worse for his experience.

I made a number of enquiries to find out how such men get their training. All that I could gather was that each snake-expert had several pupils to whom he gradually imparted his skill and knowledge. They were sworn to secrecy so far as laymen were concerned, only being allowed to discuss their calling with their own kind. I imagine that part of their training took the form of taking increasing doses of snake poison into the system both by mouth and through skin puncture so that the body built up a certain resistance. They must undoubtedly have spent most of their time with snakes, studying their habits and ways. They were all experts – those I observed – at making a snake strike at some object before tackling it by hand; in this way the snake lost some of its paralysing venom. All of them had the power of hypnosis well developed, whether applied to snakes or other animals, and they could hypnotise themselves into self-induced catalepsy.

I have often heard Europeans laugh at what they call the superstitious beliefs in magic which exist in such countries as Thailand. Personally, I have never found them as laughable as the credulous magic-mongering which occupies the time of supposedly highly intelligent people in the backwoods of London's Earl's Court and Mayfair, or the remote fastnesses of St John's Wood and Hampstead.

★   ★   ★

Several of the Thai newspapermen had become my friends and I had been copy for most of them at some time or other during my stay at Wat Paknam. One morning a group of them came to me and told me that they had arranged that the bhikkhu who was supposed to be able to change rice grains into prawns would demonstrate his powers. Much to their delight he had agreed to the presence of a few scientists and medical men, and he had raised no objection to the whole procedure being photographed and reported. The demonstration was to take place that afternoon at a monastery on the northern outskirts of Bangkok.

They told me that they would be very happy to take me along so that I could see the whole thing for myself, and they would be pleased to have my views after the demonstration. I said that I was very sceptical about such things and I could not see how prawns could grow from rice grains. If such a thing were possible, it would be just as possible to produce kittens from chickens' eggs. Nonetheless I would be pleased to accompany them as I would very much like to see how the trick was done.

When we arrived at the monastery we were shown into a large open-sided meeting hall. The place was crowded with people, both men and women. In the centre of the room was a slightly raised platform upon which were seated five bhikkhus. Before them was a small low table on which stood a large glass bowl and a glass pitcher of water.

I was seated close to the edge of the platform in a position reserved for myself and some dozen or more other bhikkhus. One of the bhikkhus on the platform rose, came forward to the low table and sat himself down in front of it, cross-legged. He was a slimly built man of probably forty years of age. His features were refined, his bone structure excellent. As he sat there he looked the perfect picture of calm. The most striking thing about him was his eyes, oblique brown eyes like those of most Thais, but they seemed to have a lightish blue ring encircling the coloured portion, making them appear lit from behind.

I looked around the hall and saw that everyone had settled back into a silent and attentive expectancy. Several cameramen had moved into position. Two laymen, one carrying a large magnifying glass and the other with a stethoscope dangling from his pocket, represented the scientific observers.

Complete silence was called for. The bhikkhu poured some fresh water into the bowl and placed on the table some rice grains, which a number of us examined. When we were all satisfied he folded his hands in his lap and commenced a low chant in Thai and Pali. His chant completed, he gathered a few grains of rice and dropped them into the bowl of water. He then sat motionless again, quickly withdrawing himself into what I knew was an extremely concentrated state of mind. This was the moment we had been waiting for, the moment when he would exert all his mental and magical power to bring about the change from rice to prawns.

I watched the glass bowl closely to see that no one added anything further or in any way approached the table. For fifteen minutes I watched and waited but nothing happened. The rice grains were still rice grains.

The bhikkhu opened his eyes and announced to the assembly that he had failed. He was sorry, but something was wrong. He then called the other four bhikkhus to him and remained in conversation with them for a few minutes.

He then said that he would try again, but he must request that all women leave the hall. There was a protest from some of the women at this but it was explained to them that if any of them were menstruating or pregnant that would interfere. He thought it better that they all leave rather than put a few through the indignity of leaving knowing that all knew their condition. These explanations were received by all present in good part and with much laughter from most of the women. Quickly they all left the hall.

The bhikkhu commenced his preparations again. Again I watched the grains of rice drop into the bowl and the bhikkhu attain his highly concentrated state. Never once did his hands go near the bowl again until the demonstration was over. No one else approached the bowl, I am sure.

I fixed my attention on the grains in the bowl, waiting. Waiting and watching. And then, in the bowl, I saw the semi-transparent shape of a young prawn. The rice grains were gone. Camera bulbs flashed as the newsmen worked feverishly to record the amazing event.

Suddenly the bhikkhu opened his eyes, stretched out his right hand to the bowl and dropped some white powder on to the surface of the water. The prawn faded away before my eyes, leaving only the grains of rice once more.

It was the most astounding performance I had ever witnessed. Not so much the apparent physical changing from rice to prawn – a circumstance which I still say is utterly impossible in the physical sense, but the demonstration of this man's extraordinary power of suggestion over a large gathering of people. It was a power so strong and well-developed that he had been able to project an image intensely enough for us all to see. I do not know of anyone who did not witness the change.

The next day my friends visited me again, bringing with them a series of photographs which had been taken the previous afternoon. All of them showed the prawn in the bowl quite clearly. On seeing these I was somewhat taken aback, as it appeared that my own theory of suggestion and projection was destroyed by this photographic evidence.

The newsmen were quite fair. They stated that all the photographers had not been successful. Some of their plates had shown only the rice grains in the bowl, others an indeterminate blur. In no case could they guarantee that the actual photograph showing the prawn had been taken at the exact moment when the apparent change from rice to prawn took place. Frankly, they said, they were at a loss to explain the phenomenon, just as I was myself. They had thought of sleight of hand on someone's part, but had no evidence of it. They agreed with my theory of the matter as the only possible rational explanation.

There we had to leave the matter. The newspapers were full of the story the next day and I was happy to see that they had all given a completely factual report of the proceedings, leaving their readers to come to any conclusion they desired on the evidence. I still do not know how the prawn got into the photographs.

I learned from my newspaper friends that the bhikkhu in question had first joined the Order when he was twenty years old and had remained there for ten years, during which time he gained great proficiency in meditation, taking the line of the trances or jhana rather than vipassana or insight. He developed a number of the powers or iddhi, such as clairvoyance, clairaudience and, to a degree, telekinesis. It was the latter, the control of material things by mind, which appealed to him most.

He then left the Order and returned to lay life, taking to himself a wife in the process. Some three years later the wife died and he immediately returned to the Order, being again ordained and commencing as a novice.

These powers of mind are quite common in Buddhist tradition. The very processes and disciplines through which a meditation monk goes during his training are almost bound to bring them to the surface. Gotama himself spoke of them, and he and most of his senior monks were quite accustomed to them.

However, Gotama always stated that the powers alone could not bring freedom and understanding to a man. They could become an impediment, and for that reason a man should go beyond such things and not become enmeshed in them. And to stress how strongly he felt about their misuse, he made a rule – which is still valid in the Vinaya today – that any bhikkhu who was guilty of displaying his powers before the lay public was at fault. Such things, he said, were not good for the people as it made them look for magical answers to their problems, whereas the only real way to solutions was that which he had taught: the way of the Four Truths and the Eightfold Path.

* * *

A few days after this incident I was taken to visit the one remaining pagoda which I had not seen in Bangkok – the famous Wat Bodhi as it is popularly known, although its proper name is Wat Jetubon.

This pagoda is unique in that it set out originally to be a university where people could come to gather knowledge on all subjects, including science and medicine. The abbot, the Venerable Dhammatiloka, was a great personal friend of mine. On our arrival he met us personally and spent considerable time showing us round the monastery and its various buildings.

The place was a treasure-house to me. One building I entered had been used at one time as a school of anatomy and physiology, the walls being covered with tiled illustrations of the human frame dissected into its various parts. Here, I gathered from the abbot, bhikkhus once taught the mysteries of the body to any who wished to study. These early instructors had become experts through their practice of meditation, arriving at their knowledge through complete and one-pointed mindfulness regarding their own bodies. By introspection they came to some understanding of the inner structure and contents of the body. Whilst many of the illustrations were crude by modern standards and some of the organs were of a peculiar shape, their general content was well up to modern ideas.

Most of the buildings showed quite markedly the effects of Hindu, Chinese and Thai traditions. They blended so well that many with eyes less accustomed to the various styles would have accepted them as of one tradition. It was somewhat strange to find in this Buddhist monastery a large emblem of Siva the Hindu god, depicted as he so often is by a large stone-cut representation of the phallus.

In one of the many large halls I found depicted an ancient system of massage stemming directly from Ayurvedic traditions, with sculptured bronze figures showing the system being applied to the human form. It was a system far removed from what I had known as massage. It dealt with pressures on arteries and nerve-endings and the stretching of tendons. The illustrations interested me immensely. I asked the abbot if there were any people practising the system today. He told me that there were many experts in it, one of whom he knew quite well, a man who had been a bhikkhu at Wat Paknam but who had retired from the bhikkhu life.

I had not been in too good a state of health recently, suffering intense pain in my limbs and joints and having continual trouble with my ankles, which were sometimes very swollen. I mentioned this to the abbot and he said that he would arrange for the massage expert to call on me and see if he could help.

Some days after my visit to Wat Bodhi I was visited by the ex-bhikkhu. I recognised him immediately, for I had been present at his disrobing ceremony. I told him of my troubles, that I was finding it more and more difficult to sit with my legs crossed in the traditional manner, and that I was suffering continual pain in my body.

He explained to me that his system was based upon a fundamental theory of the constitution of matter, from both the Buddhist and Hindu standpoints. All matter, as I knew well from the Buddhist point of view, was said to be composed of *pathavi* (earth), *apo* (water), *tejo* (fire) and *vayo* (air). These divisions were common also to Hindus, and for that matter, the early Greeks. Gotama had refined the theory and made it much more scientific, in that these four divisions were expressed as observable attributes of matter. *Pathavi* was not just earth but meant that a material object had extension or occupied space, there having the attributes of hardness or softness or resistibility in a variety of degrees. *Apo* became cohesion, *tejo* became temperature, and *vayo* became change or movement, or it could refer to chemical changes in the body.

The whole purpose of the system, he said, was to bring about a state of ideal balance between these four attributes of the material body. To do this meant applying pressure on arteries, nerves, joints and tendons and temporarily increasing or decreasing the blood flow to various parts of the body as required. He also informed me in passing that the method had been used in ancient times to bring people to the experience of dying, and he himself could bring about that state and then bring life back.

I asked him if his theory would have any effect upon myself if put into practice. On his confident assertion that it would I allowed him to practise his odd therapy upon my body – not so much because I thought that it might give me relief but because I wanted to experience the system at first hand. In some ways it reminded me of some of the more hidden Zen or Japanese methods used in the training of a monk to bring him to understanding through shock.

For some days I placed myself entirely in his hands and suffered agonies as my limbs were stretched and twisted and tendons extended to what I thought must be breaking point. His thumbs and fingers seemed to find every nerve, sending shocks of pain through my limbs. Gradually the swelling of the ankles subsided and I found it easier to sit in the cross-legged position.

He then applied himself to the circulatory system. First he thrust his hand deep into my body about three inches above the umbilicus, increasing the pressure until his fingers were pressing heavily into the aorta. With this I felt the blood flow into the upper part of the body, accompanied by loss of feeling in the legs. With the release of the pressure the blood flowed back to the lower portion of the body, bringing with it a feeling of warmth and well-being.

He applied circulation-control to all parts of the body, using the known pressure-points, the theory apparently being to build up blood-pressure behind a point of stoppage and then to suddenly release it. I learned a great deal about my body and its inner feelings from his attentions and undoubtedly I felt better – if only temporarily: those particular pains and swellings were the main reason for my eventual retirement from the Sangha.

It was on the final afternoon of his treatment, when he had his hand deeply thrust up under my ribs, pressing high into the aorta so that I felt sure my heart was beating against his fingers, that he informed me that he could stop my life and bring it back with that particular pressure. It would be quite safe – would I like to try? The pressure of his hand was having a great effect, interfering with my breathing and causing spasms of cramping pain. With sweat pouring into my eyes I nodded agreement to his experiment.

Instantly his pressure increased and my whole body writhed in an effort to escape. My lungs tried to work but could not. The muscles of the abdomen went into spasms, as did the diaphragm. The heart beat gigantically but as though fighting a losing battle. The senses of sight and hearing failed, leaving me with only an agonising feeling of struggle, the blind struggle to stay alive no matter how unbearable might be the pain of that struggle. With all my mind I wanted to let go. But something – life itself, or the desire for life, or karma, call it what one will – decreed that the struggle continue. That period up until loss of consciousness was for me the physical experience of death.

Consciousness returned, bringing with it a feeling of utter peace and well-being. I opened my eyes with a new understanding and looked up into the smiling face of the ex-bhikkhu. Gently he wiped the sweat from my body and helped me to sit upright. He then procured some coffee and a cigarette for me and bowing low three times, took his leave.

The next morning I arose and went on the begging round, feeling healthier than I had for some weeks. On arrival back at my house I seated myself and began to eat from the bowl a delightful meal of rice and curried prawns. And this time, the rice was rice and the prawns were prawns.

17

FROM MOUNTAIN PEAKS TO RUBBER FORESTS

I feel I can never adequately thank the friends who made it possible for me to see so much of the beauty which exists in and near Bangkok, and to meet both men and women of strange powers. Even one small lad of fifteen years, I remember – a samanera at Wat Maha Dhatu, who had developed his mental powers so far that he could instantly attain a state of catalepsy for any period demanded of him. This state was so deep that when I eventually found his pulse, after some difficulty, it was beating at only forty to the minute. The body was cold and fixed in its posture, giving the appearance, to cursory examination, of death. In this state, the consciousness was utterly beyond any pain or suffering, no matter what was done to the body. These things and many more I saw, and in some cases marvelled at.

It was after these visits that Lung Poh called to see me with Thitavedo. The time had come, said Lung Poh, when I must go out into the country to talk with and lecture to the people. The Sangha, or controlling body of the monastery, had arranged that I was to commence a lecture tour which would take me to the extreme north beyond Chieng Mai, right down through the country to beyond Haad Yai and Song Khla in the south, to the borders of Malaya. It would be a strenuous tour, as I would have to travel by all manner of means and at times would have to reach quite remote places.

Thitavedo would go with me, and I would also be accompanied by Khun Sanoh, Khun Siri and Khun Suang. It was these friends of mine, he explained, who had undertaken to organise and manage the whole tour. I was very happy indeed that the three musketeers – as I called them – were to be with me on the trip, as we were all such very good friends.

Lung Poh's next remarks completely surprised me. He informed me that the day after I returned from the tour I was to return to England. Here I was to lecture and teach those who desired.

I was confused and shocked by the news, for I had never entertained ideas about returning to England. I felt quite sure that it was the last thing I wanted to do. I had come to Thailand to gain some peace of mind and some understanding of myself through the teaching of the Buddha. I had gained both these, and was living a peaceful, happy life among a people I understood and who appeared to understand me, a lovable people whose utter kindness and tolerance had taught me so much. I certainly did not want to leave my way of life with these people or their country, where a man's private life was his own business and he could live it without being molested or coerced. They were a people and country in fact with whom I had felt more at home than anywhere else.

I told Lung Poh that I did not want to return, but he said that I must. Everything had been arranged, my passage already booked and paid for. He told me that he knew that I had many friends in England and that there were groups and societies of people who were trying to study and practise Buddhism. I had a duty to these and to myself, for was it not these people in England who had made it possible for me to come to Thailand? I had to return, he said, to repay my debt by way of service and instruction to them. I also owed a debt to my past, and I must return to the country of that past to test my way of life, to see if in true fact what I had learned would sustain me in any circumstance.

I remember how gentle his face was when he explained that he knew that I would have difficult times ahead of me on my return. He told me that most probably what I had done would be misunderstood, as would my purpose in returning. None of these things was I to be affected by. I was to return and teach and to show people that a man can change, and by that return to prove to myself how much I had changed since the day when I first asked him to be my teacher and had told him the whole story of my past.

I thanked Lung Poh for his patience and understanding and on his request gave him the addresses of two people in England whom he could inform of the time and place of my arrival.

★   ★   ★

Our tour was to be a long one, covering some three thousand miles or more. This naturally meant that my friends who were to manage and organise the tour would be very busy packing for themselves and their families, and arranging in advance all manner of types of transport. Fortunately Thitavedo and myself had nothing to pack or worry about concerning changes of clothing and footwear. One of the great things about the bhikkhu life is the ease with which one can move from one place to another without being cluttered up with all kinds of apparently very necessary things. All that we ever carried on a long journey were the three robes which we wore, begging bowl over one shoulder and a small handbag made of cotton or silk. In fact that was the whole of our luggage for the entire tour. We did not even wear sandals.

On the morning of our departure the compound of our house had taken on quite a festive air. Many old friends and their families, and numbers of new visitors as well, had gathered in the compound. Although we were not leaving Bangkok's main station for the north until early evening, our visitors had begun to arrive at about 5 a.m. When we left for Bangkok by car later that day there were some two hundred people still there. Once we had gone they would, I knew, spend the rest of the evening going round the monastery visiting the bhikkhus and in most cases giving them refreshments.

The Northern line station in Bangkok was one of the cleanest from which it has ever been my pleasure to travel. A large single-span roof placed high up and well-glazed gave the station an atmosphere of light and coolness. The platforms were well-washed and spotless, and not a sign of smoke or soot could be seen anywhere. This rather surprised me because I knew that the majority of Thai locomotives were wood-burning. My friends informed me that these were never allowed to come into the station. The long-distance trains were drawn out by diesel locomotives and a change-over to the larger wood-burning type made some miles out.

Our train was waiting at the platform. The carriages appeared American although they had been made in Japan, and they were large and roomy. We were escorted to the middle of the train and shown into our compartment by our three friends.

I was surprised to see that it was a private compartment for two, having two sleeping berths, wash-basin, electric fan, small table and chairs. We were taken along to the other offices in the carriage. These were the same as in all long-distance trains, with the difference that each carriage was also supplied with a large bathing room complete with shower and a huge earthenware container of water. Altogether far too luxurious for bhikkhus, I thought, but our friends had insisted. Once our two and a half days' journey commenced, however, some of the apparent luxury faded, for we often ran out of water and for most of the time the electric fan was not working, a situation which amused Thitavedo considerably.

Our journey led us through the great flat plains of Thailand's rice fields, fields in which latterly more rice has been produced than in any country in the East, including Burma. The farming methods used are ancient but still apparently the best. All ploughing takes place whilst the ground is under water, a simple wooden plough being generally used, although I did notice one or two steel-bladed models too. The water buffalo is used as motive power for the plough – huge beasts these, weighing around two tons. They have a name for being ill-tempered and dangerous, but invariably I noticed, as our train moved through the countryside, that they were driven and cared for mainly by some diminutive impish-faced boy or girl.

Wherever our train stopped – and that was quite often on the first day – either at a recognised station or out in the country to take on more wood from huge piles stacked beside the line, crowds would gather. They were mainly boys and girls with all manner of goods for sale. As soon as the train pulled in they would simultaneously shout their wares and prices in high-pitched sing-song voices, their faces eager, alert and smiling as they rushed from one end of the train to the other. All kinds of fruit were offered, as were examples of local handicrafts and coffee: black or white, hot, cold or iced, the last invariably served in an empty condensed-milk tin with the lid conveniently turned back. The usual method of drinking was to hold the tin by the lid and use it like a cup, taking care to keep the top lip away from the jagged rim. Having finished the drink, the customer threw the tin out of the window to be collected and refilled for the next person.

The mystery to me on that part of the journey was that no matter where we stopped, even if in an area which seemed to be without habitation for miles around, these groups of young salesmen would appear with goods to sell – and never once was iced coffee off the list.

We passed through the ancient capital Ayutthaya, a mass of ruins now, having been taken apart brick by brick by invading Burmans during their ancient wars with the Thais. On to Lopburi, where stand ruins of old pagodas similar in style to those of Angkor Wat in Cambodia, the only difference being in the materials used in construction. At Angkor Wat huge blocks of basalt had been used, carved into things of breath-taking beauty. Here the material had been locally produced terracotta bricks, built up and carved with the same meticulous attention. From what I could see the ruins were very well cared for and much had been done to keep them in a good state of preservation.

Travelling through the great rice-bowl of Thailand was extremely hot, so hot that both Thitavedo and I longed for the night-time when we could settle back into our bunks, leaving the windows open so that a gentle breeze would waft into our compartment to keep us pleasantly cool. Or so we imagined it would be as we talked during the heat of the day. Came the night, and with it, hordes of hungry mosquitoes. The carriage windows were protected with close wire-mesh frames, but we left these open to get as much air as possible. Whilst the train was in motion everything was fine. As soon as it stopped our compartment absolutely swarmed with mosquitoes. We spent most of the night rushing to the windows when the train stopped to raise the mesh screens, then once we were underway again, lowering the screens so that the mosquitoes were drawn out of the compartment.

By late afternoon on the second day we were in mountainous country and things generally were a little cooler. Thitavedo and I had been sitting back sipping iced coffee and talking about our times together when our friends the three musketeers rushed into the compartment to tell us that we would soon be crossing a famous bridge. I had heard about this bridge just before I left Bangkok. Part of it had been washed away by torrential rains and there appeared to be some doubt whether the train would be able to cross it.

Just as they finished talking the train chugged to a halt on the single-track line and we all looked out of the windows to find that we had been travelling along a ledge in the mountainside. Above us on the left towered the peaks, below us on the right was a sheer drop of hundreds of feet. Looking forward to the locomotive I saw the bridge, an amazing structure more like a huge wooden trestle than any bridge that I had ever seen. The whole thing was built of teak and spanned a gap of some five hundred yards. Along this the single track ran about three hundred feet above the canyon. The more I studied the bridge, the more I marvelled at the engineering skill and patience, not to mention the back-breaking labour and organising ability, of those who had first built it and those who had recently repaired it.

Whilst we were waiting the guard came through and informed us that we were the first train to use the bridge since its repair and for that reason the train would travel over slowly in two halves. We were in the front section and would go over first.

Slowly the train moved forward on to the bridge and made the crossing at about five miles an hour, the longest and most exciting five hundred yards of train travel which I have ever experienced. Once on the other side I asked Thitavedo what would have happened if the bridge had not been repaired in time for the arrival of our train. He said that the matter was quite simple: we would just have climbed and scrambled down one side of the mountain and up the other, then embarked on another train which would have been waiting on the other side.

Looking down into the cleft in the mountains which we had just crossed, and at the jagged rocks, so unscalable that even a mountain-goat could not have found foothold, I heaved a sigh of relief that the repairs had been completed in time and saved us from what I was sure would have been a nightmare trek.

★ ★ ★

At midday we arrived at Chieng Mai, the northernmost city of note and the end of the railway. Quickly we were all escorted to waiting cars and driven through the city – a city clean, spacious and airy, nestling into the surrounding mountains – to the largest pagoda and monastery, Wat Maha Phra Singh. Here we were met by a reception committee of bhikkhus headed by the abbot, Chao Khun Vimolyanamuni. After paying him the usual salutations, I was led by him to the rooms set aside for me in his own quarters. Thitavedo was housed close by.

Making this my base I travelled all over the area, visiting such towns as Chiang Rai and Chiang Saen on the extreme northern borders between Burma and Laos, Mae Kit in the north-west and Lamphun and Hambong in the south-west. I gave lectures at all these places and with stops at various village pagodas was averaging four lectures a day.

After nine days of constant travelling on journeys which more often than not entailed my being on the road by 4.30 a.m. and not returning until midnight, my friends decided that I should have a rest for a few days. They said that they knew of the ideal place, deep in the mountain teak forests. Here there was a small clearing in the forest owned by a very great friend of theirs, Khun Thira. A small bamboo hut had already been built for me away from the rest of the huts in the clearing. They informed me that they had arranged for us to make the journey the next morning, and that the party would consist simply of themselves and their wives, Khun Thira, Thitavedo and myself.

The next morning I rose early and went out into the compound of Wat Maha Phra Singh to find the whole party waiting for me. I was introduced to Thira who spoke very good English. He explained that the journey we were to undertake would be difficult because of heavy rains, which in mountain and jungle could make things even worse than normal. He was living in hope, however, that the two jeeps and the landrover in which we were to travel would get us through successfully.

We left Chieng Mai in a north-easterly direction, Khun Thira driving the leading jeep, followed by the other which was driven by Khun Sanoh and carried myself and Thitavedo, the landrover bringing up the rear.

What an experience that journey was! Picking our way firstly through thick bamboo jungle, then climbing higher, through mixed bamboo and teak jungle, catching here and there a glimpse of tiger, elephant and buffalo, all of whom viewed us with utter surprise before disappearing from view. Cautiously we nosed our way up and around mountain ledges with sheer drops on one side of anything up to a thousand feet, exhilarated by the majesty of great teak trees, jungle smells and the beauty of rainbows through the trees as mountain streams leapt out into space to fall with a sound like distant music hundreds of feet below.

And amidst all this unspoiled natural beauty came modern technology in the form of our jeeps and landrover, accomplishing the almost impossible, diving into mountain streams and forging their way through with abandon, climbing gradients surely never dreamed of by the designers. Again and again I marvelled at their stability and their capacity for gripping almost any surface presented to them.

There were times when we had to walk miles on foot while the transport made detours. It was during one of these walking sessions, when Thitavedo and I had decided to take a short rest and were leaning on our staffs, that I had my first experience of something I had read about so often in travel books and stories of jungle treks, where the author says, 'I felt that I was being watched by unseen eyes'.

We had been standing at rest for a few moments, just about time in fact for me to light a cigarette, when I had a very strong impression that we were being watched. I looked all round, at first seeing nothing other than a few large python looped lazily round the branches of some of the trees. Not even a monkey or bird could I see or hear. I knew of course that the surrounding jungle must be absolutely teeming with life, but one never heard much from it during daylight. The feeling of being watched persisted and again I searched with my eyes over a large circle from where we stood.

Suddenly I found myself gazing into two brown eyes which were looking into mine from between the leaves and undergrowth. I looked more closely and found we were surrounded by peering eyes.

I told Thitavedo of my discovery and he laughed good-naturedly. 'Brother, you getting very smart. Your senses getting very sharp. These people been here ever since we stop. Some have follow us for maybe last mile. Now you call one – they very friendly.'

Glancing over to the first pair of eyes I had seen, I pointed to them, then to my cigarette, then to myself. My face wreathed in what I considered to be the broadest and friendliest of smiles, I beckoned them to come to me. The brush parted and out stepped a brown-bodied young fellow wearing a simple sarong round the waist. Quickly others stepped out from the cover. A wonderfully strong and healthy lot they looked as they stood there, both men and women, all bare to the waist and wearing the short sarong which showed their well-muscled calves. They smiled at me, a little shyly. Eventually with Thitavedo's help – the amazing fellow appeared to know these people's dialect – I managed to get them close around me. My first gesture of friendship was to offer them a puff of my cigarette. When this was finished I gave them one each.

Thitavedo told me that they had heard that two bhikkhus were coming into the jungle, expecting of course that they would both be Thais. They had never seen a bhikkhu like me so they had followed us in the hope of learning more about me. Now they would leave as he had told them all they wanted to know.

I asked him who they were and where they came from – I had not seen any signs of a village for hours past. He told me that they were members of a small tribe or clan, typical of many who lived in the jungle.

We eventually made contact with our transport again and arrived at our destination in the early evening. The clearing – which Khun Thira referred to as his kingdom – was high up in a cleft between mountain peaks. Here out of the virgin jungle he had cleared about an acre in the form of a circle. Running through part of it was a fast-flowing mountain stream, over which he had constructed a bathing hut from bamboo, supplied with crystal-clear mountain water fed in by bamboo pipes. Lower down were lavatories supplied with abundant water again piped in through bamboo.

My greatest surprise came at the centre of the clearing. Here I found four well-constructed huts with poles outside each bearing electric light bulbs. Behind the huts the stream had been dammed to control its flow so that it could fall upon a giant bucket-type water-wheel constructed entirely from teak. This drove a dynamo through a series of wooden gear-wheels and liana belts. Khun Thira explained that it was not a very reliable system as every time there was a heavy downpour of rain the stream became a torrent which invariably wrecked the water-wheel.

My own hut was away from the clearing, just inside the jungle. It was built of bamboo, except for the four main supports which had been fashioned from young trees. The whole structure was raised above the ground with a veranda all round. I walked into the hut to find that a mosquito net had already been hung for me over a portion of the springy bamboo floor.

That evening we all sat in the centre of the clearing and talked far into the night. At last, tired and happy, I took my leave of the party and made my way to my jungle hut. Once on my own I lay back for a while watching the mosquitoes through the net. I noticed that many of them were the anopheles or malaria-carrying variety and realised the reason for Thira's insistence on my taking mephacrine tablets before I retired.

I just lay back and thought for most of the night – not in deep silence as many would assume, for the jungle is anything but quiet in the night. No, I lay back and thought to the accompaniment of a myriad insects, the chatter of monkeys, the distant trumpeting of elephant and the deep-throated grumble of a remote tiger in search of food. Amidst all these numerous sounds I felt at peace, secure.

I thought of the things which it had been my good fortune to learn and experience of the teaching of the Buddha, and of the effects of its tradition upon a people. I thought of it as a way of life, a life of tolerance, of compassion for one's fellow creatures. I thought of it as a mental therapy, a self-applied treatment whereby one could bring peace and harmony into one's individual mental world. Surely that was the only world which man could know, the only world to which he could bring peace – the world of his own concepts, his own reactions, desires and aversions.

As I lay there in the cool of the mountain night I thought again of the practice of Metta, the meditation on amity, a method of mental training so widely misunderstood, a method whereby every thought, vision, opinion, like and dislike for persons and creatures which could arise in the mind could be brought to a state of peace and equanimity, leaving a man in harmony with the world and himself.

In the early light of dawn I thought of the Buddhist way of life as one that could satisfy all that might be called spiritual strivings in man. Yet Buddhism was so different from most religions in that it had no arguments with the findings of science. It was a way based upon a rational and scientific view of life, its attributes, causes and ends. I viewed it as philosophy, a philosophy so refined in its thought as to far outdo the associationist philosophy of Aristotle, a philosophy which bridged the gaps and fell into none of the traps and antitheses of either Realism or Idealism, expounding an empirical psychology and phi-losophy of momentariness and phenomenalism.

And lastly I thought of it as a way of life which had taught me so much and brought me to terms with myself.

Although I had not slept all night and had spent my time in thought, I felt quite refreshed as I left my hut in the early-morning light and made my way to the centre of the clearing to be met by Thitavedo and the rest of the party. After we had been presented with food and drink, Thitavedo told me that at one time an old bhikkhu lived in the jungle about a mile from our present position. We would, he said, set off and see if we could find him, as he thought meeting him would be a good experience for me.

After about an hour's walking into the jungle, during which time we took many a compass-bearing, we came to a small hut built into the branches of a low tree, with a series of primitive steps leading up to it. Thitavedo called out in Thai, and in a very short time the door of the hut opened and out came an old man in tattered brown robes. As soon as he appeared, monkeys from the surrounding trees scampered toward him, clinging around his bare feet and clambering on to his shoulders. He looked down at us and smiled and called to Thitavedo by name and invited us into his home.

Once inside and seated, I gathered through Thitavedo some of the story of this charming old bhikkhu's life. He had settled in the jungle at this spot some fifteen years previously, begging his food from a jungle tribe who had a settlement some six miles distant. His only companions were the monkeys and various animals who surrounded him. When he had first arrived, he told me, he was full of fear. But gradually he had become used to the life and the animals who lived around him, so much so that a mutual trust and understanding had grown between them.

To illustrate this understanding he told me a story about a large female monkey whom he knew to be about to give birth. Each morning she and many others met him on his return from his begging round to gather food from him. One day he missed her, and glancing over to her usual resting place noticed that she was cooing and chattering to herself, rocking in her arms a small thin bundle of grey fur. Turning to his bowl he took a handful of rice and took it over to her. She held out one of her paws and took the rice, but would not let him see her new youngster. Somehow, he said, she looked weak and distraught and extremely unhappy. As she made none of the usual sounds of greeting he left her and returned to his hut.

In the early evening of that day he was disturbed by an insistent scratching at his door. He opened it to find the monkey, still clutching her babe close to her breast, waiting outside. Leaving the door open he went over and sat in a corner of the room. The monkey followed him and squatted down on the floor in front of him. She then placed her new offspring into his hands. When he looked down at the feeble morsel of life he realised the reason for her anguish. The newborn in his hands was of monstrous birth and could not live much longer. Everything about it was monkey except for the head, which had a horn about an inch long growing up from the nose.

He did what he could for the poor little creature, wrapping it in old pieces of cloth to protect it from the cold air and feeding it with water and honey from his fingertip. All the time the mother sat in front of him, rocking herself backwards and forwards and crying to herself.

Later during the night she again took the child in her arms and there it died. She looked down at it with tears streaming from her eyes and licked and fondled the little creature all over. Then leaning toward the bhikkhu she held out her arms and placed the body into his hands. Turning about she left the hut, never to be seen again.

That was the story he told me. When he had finished he went into a corner of the hut and produced a small teak box which he handed to me. When I opened it I found it contained the small dried body of a monkey, perfect in every detail except for the head which was like that of a minute rhinoceros with an inch-long horn growing from its snout.

Stories of monstrous births are not uncommon in Thailand, even in relation to human beings. The whole attitude of the people is very different from the Western approach to the subject. Quite often, I learned, in the case of a human birth of this kind, the small body was preserved and kept after death, the parents thinking that it would bring luck. The subject appears to hold no mysteries for the Thais, for they believe that consciousness is always striving to attain higher grades of physical bodies to be born into. This consciousness is born again and again in a long round of rebirths, the body attained at each birth being high or low in the evolutionary scale according to the good or bad acts of the character in previous lives. The monstrous birth is not monstrous to them in that sense, but means that some consciousness from a lower life-form has striven to attain human form but has not been quite strong enough. During my travels I had many opportunities of talking with people on this subject and that appeared to be the popular view. It is, of course, not a strictly Buddhist view, but rather a mixture of Hindu, Buddhist and remote animistic beliefs.

We bade farewell to the old jungle bhikkhu and returned to our clearing.

I remained in Thira's clearing in the jungle for four days. The climate here was delightful, the temperature being in the eighties during the day and dropping to about thirty-five degrees at night. I just sat around and soaked up the beauty of the scenery, occasionally walking through the jungle to the top of a small peak, there to sit and gaze out into the infinite distance, searching out peak after peak until the desire to search faded away and utter peace remained. To me, this small clearing in the jungle surrounded by mountain peaks, with its musically burbling streams, trickles and waterfalls of crystal-clear water, was my Shangri-la. And like Hilton's hero, having found my Shangri-la I had to leave it.

On the morning of our return to Chieng Mai I looked around at the great trees and the mountains towering above them, heard again the sound of the nearby stream. I looked and said goodbye to it all. Then, thinking how wonderful it would be if I could settle there some time in the future, I walked over to the jeep which was already started up.

At that moment Thira came up to me and raising his hands in greeting he turned and pointed to my favourite peak some thousand feet above, his face somewhat sad.

'Brother Kapilavaddho,' he said, 'we have all been very happy to have you here in our little kingdom. We would like you to live here all the time, but we know that you have much work to do and that you must go back. See your favourite spot up there? If ever you come back to Thailand, come to me and I will build you a house right on the top where you used to spend so much time. Here you can spend the rest of your life in peace and quiet and all of us here will look after you.'

I thanked him for his great kindness, thanked them all for the friendship which they had shown me, then climbed into the jeep beside Thitavedo, and we set off on our return journey.

*   *   *

Once back at my base in Chieng Mai things became hectic again, every hour of the day being organised and scheduled: rushing around the surrounding districts delivering lectures; officiating at the opening of a new pagoda; going off into the jungles to the north-east to open two new meditation retreats, each of them a clearing in the virgin jungle with separate bamboo huts dotted about among the trees; and finally, my last lecture in Chieng Mai, to an audience of six thousand. This lecture was well attended by resident missionaries from the West, mainly American, and they requested that afterwards they might send a representative body to Wat Maha Phra Singh to discuss the various points I had raised. I agreed, but although I waited far into the night they did not arrive.

With final goodbyes to Chieng Mai and its delightful people, including the King's beautiful troupe of dancing girls, I set off on my journey to the south.

We changed trains and stations at Bangkok to make our connection for the south. En route I stopped off at Nakhom Pathom, where rests the oldest pagoda in Thailand, enshrined in a fabulous golden glazed tope or reliquary rising over three hundred feet into the blue sky. From there to Sara Buri, a city famous for its Buddha Footprint Pagoda, a place of great pilgrimage where thousands thronged. On to Phet Buri with its fantastic caves, underground shrines and hill-top pagodas. All the time talking, talking, and opening more jungle retreats. This latter was a great delight to me, for with all the increase in the speed with which Western ideas and civilisation were being absorbed by the Thais, at the same time there was an increase in their interest and participation in what they called Buddha *Sasana*, the teaching of the Buddha.

I travelled to most of the towns and settlements through the south, travelling by train, car, steamer, small native boat and foot, stopping for a while at Song Khla on the south-east coast and its inland sea. From there to Haad Yai, again to live in a bamboo hut built over a swamp which ran alongside a new meditation centre which I opened.

Wherever I went I had to talk. I arrived in villages in the rubber forests of the deep south where I was not scheduled to lecture, and invariably found posters of some kind announcing my talk. In this way I travelled right down to Betong on the Thai-Malay border. Here it was decided that I have a morning's rest and I was taken to visit one of the rubber plantations.

Sitting in the jeep I noticed that the driver was armed with a .45 revolver. I asked the reason for this and he informed me with a smile that sometimes people were taken and held for ransom. As I was somewhat famous now I might be of value. He referred to the participants in this business as bandits and never once mentioned the term Communist. From what I could gather, the popular sport in the district was that of kidnapping a worthy subject and selling him back over the border. No one appeared to be particularly worried about it, taking it as a matter of course.

Then came the long journey back to Bangkok, and finally arrival at Wat Paknam on the evening prior to my departure for England.

★ ★ ★

That last evening at Wat Paknam will, I am sure, remain in my memory for all time, bringing with it thoughts of the many friends who had come to say goodbye, of a people who had treated me as one of themselves. Of Thitavedo who had cared for me so well, who always walked in front of me in the jungle in case there should be a snake or scorpion in my path who might do me harm, who had in fact on one occasion been stung by a scorpion which surely would have stung me had I been in front, and who on another had with his bare hand swept away a large scorpion from the unwary fall of my bare right foot. And finally of Lung Poh, a learned and wise man, a father indeed who, with his last words to me, said:

'Now you go back to your people, Tan William. Face whatever has to be faced. Teach what you have learned, no harm will come to you. There may be some who wish to do as you have done. If that be so, bring them back here and we will arrange to support them. You will have to work hard because you will have to gain the support of your own people, so that their passages are paid for. You will succeed, I know. I will see you again at the end of one year. Blessings and wishes go with you.'

Taking leave of such a man was the saddest moment of my life, and I had experienced many sad moments in my fast and furious years. But leave I must, as he had commanded.

The next day I was driven out to the airport at Don Muang. As I climbed aboard the plane which was to carry me to England I took a last look back and waved to the masses of yellow- and white-robed figures of bhikkhus and upasikas, hundreds of them from Wat Paknam and other monasteries, who had come to see me off.

18

RETURN TO BRITAIN

Two days later, on the 12th of November, I arrived back in England, to what had been my home – and to notoriety. I was met at London Airport by my mother and old friends of mine, the Bartletts, husband and wife, and was immediately driven to Manchester by road. I still wore the thin cotton robes which had been my dress in the high temperatures of Thailand, robes which I continued to wear without underclothing during my whole life as a bhikkhu in England.

On arrival in Manchester that evening I delivered a lecture to a gathering of the Manchester Buddhist Society. The next morning I read a report of my arrival in one of the daily papers. 'Women prostrated themselves at London Airport yesterday,' it stated, 'as a shaven-headed yellow-robed Buddhist holy man stepped from a Dutch airliner.' I suppose two does make legitimate the use of the term 'women'; it made a better story, at least, for the reporter. The word 'prostrated', however, had no right in the report at all: my dear old mother has never been known to bow the knee to anyone.

Three days later I took up residence at the London Buddhist Vihara in Knightsbridge where, owing to the return to Ceylon of the previous bhikkhu, I became the sole bhikkhu in residence.

Here I lived and worked, quickly gathering around me a band of helpers. Classes and lectures were organised for three nights each week, other nights being taken up with lectures for the Buddhist Society by arrangement with my friend of many years, Christmas Humphreys, the President.

For weeks I was the subject of newspaper articles, which by and large did much good for the work I had undertaken. Generally speaking I had very fair treatment from the Press and through their publicity received hundreds of letters from all over the country from people who were interested or were in need of help. They were instrumental also in bringing together around me a stalwart group of friends and helpers who stood by me through thick and thin. Without them none of the work which I accomplished would have been possible, for I arrived in England with nothing of monetary value.

For a year I continued to work and organise, lecturing all over the country and managing to lay the foundations of the English Sangha Trust and the English Sangha Association, the purpose of each being to support an English Sangha or brotherhood of Buddhist monks.

During this period I had three young men come to me who wished to take up the bhikkhu life. I trained them and eventually ordained them as samaneras. They were an added responsibility, as it was now my duty to see that they be allowed the opportunity of the bhikkhu or higher ordination. This meant that by some means I had to get them to Thailand.

With a feeling of urgency – brought on by the fact that I felt so utterly tired and was at times tormented with pain in my limbs – I worked even harder, increasing my lecture schedule and writing many articles. At the same time my friends started an appeal and thanks to this and money supplied by one of the young men who had entered the Order, I found that at the end of the year we had enough to pay for our party of four on their journey to Thailand.

On the 30th December 1955 I again arrived at Don Muang Airport, this time not alone but with three juniors. All my old Thai friends were there to welcome us, Thitavedo and I being delighted to see each other again.

At Wat Paknam we took up residence in my old house. After Lung Poh had interviewed my three juniors he placed them in the care of Thitavedo and myself for training and preparation for the bhikkhu ordinations. I put them under the same strict meditation practice I had undergone myself.

It was during this period that Lung Poh came to me and told me that he had recommended that I be raised to the status of Anusavanacarya. This would entail that I underwent an examination on all parts of the teaching and the legal aspects of Vinaya or Code of Discipline. The test, he said, would take place in a week's time so I must work hard, as he wanted me to act in this new capacity at the ordination of the three juniors. He informed me also that my old friend the abbot of Wat Bodhi, Chao Khun Dhammatiloka, was to act as my opposite number in the capacity of Kammavacarya.

This was indeed a great honour, for to my knowledge no English-man has ever held such office or sat for such a test. I worked hard and managed to pass, and duly officiated in my new status at the ceremony. In Thailand this itself made history. Never before had three English subjects been ordained together – in fact the only other Englishman ever to be ordained in the country had been myself.

Work and study went on apace at Wat Paknam, and the juniors became very popular with the people. They had everything which they could desire to help them including a complete library of the Pali Canon and a large number of books of reference, all from my own library which had been shipped out to us. Judging by their behaviour they were extremely happy in their new surroundings.

On requests from England I again left Thailand, returning home on the 21st of March 1956, again to take up the work of lecturing and of strengthening the Trust and Association.

* * *

On my return the Sangha Trust managed to find me a small flat in which to carry on my work. My main task now was to organise as quickly as possible, so that by the time my junior bhikkhus returned from Thailand there would be a house in which we could all live.

The Trust and its helpers worked like Trojans to help me in my task. I myself worked night and day, and I know drove my willing helpers hard, but they never complained.

During the next few months I travelled much over the country, making visits to York and to Hull to lecture at the invitation of Hull University, and to the Universities of Liverpool, Oxford and Cambridge, lecturing on my subject to undergraduate clubs.

Each of my days was taken up in seeing visitors, giving advice and instruction where possible. My mother came often to see me. She had become a Buddhist and was working hard to gain as much understanding of the teaching as possible. I noticed that she was not in the best of health, but when I taxed her with this she turned it aside with a smile, saying, 'The trouble, son, is that I'm getting old. I'm beginning to feel old.' She then went on to discuss what she would like done in the event of her death. The one thing which she appeared to want reassurance about was that I would officiate at her cremation, as she wanted her body disposed of in a Buddhist manner. I reassured her and promised that I would carry out her wishes.

There was a great rapport between Mother and myself. We understood so much about each other without the need of words. I was aware that she knew that I could not go on much longer at my present pace. She also knew that I thought my usefulness was almost at an end, and that I felt that I should move out and hand over to a younger, healthier man. On my part I knew that she was suffering more pain than enough, was certain in fact that she was suffering from cancer. These things we knew, but we never expressed them in words.

She came to see me one day and the poor old dear was looking terrible. After a lot of persuasion I managed to get her to agree to see a specialist. A week later she was in hospital for extensive tests.

Things never appeared to happen singly, for the day before she was to enter hospital I received a cable from Thailand informing me that one of my juniors was ill and should return to England.

I left for Thailand the next day. On seeing the state of affairs with the juniors I decided to bring them back home immediately. We arrived back on the sixth day after my departure, having accomplished a journey of almost a thousand miles up-country in the process. The whole rapid trip was made possible by the speed with which the Trust operated and the close cooperation between Christmas Humphreys for the Buddhist Society and Reg Howes, a stalwart friend, for the Trust, in producing funds.

Very soon after that the Trust found a house for us at Swiss Cottage and we moved into The English Sangha House, as it was named.

Now that the juniors were with me, I felt that I could safely hand on the authority and responsibility to Paññavaddho Bhikkhu, one of the juniors whom I held in high esteem. He had an excellent mind and had been scientifically trained in lay life. I was quite certain that he was ready to take on the responsibility.

My forward commitments had to be fulfilled. These included completing a book of introduction to Buddhist philosophy which was later published by the Trust, and appearing at the annual celebration of Vaisakha, or Wesak as it is called in England, and the annual Summer School for the Buddhist Society. At both these I announced publicly that these would be my final appearances. I was coming to the end of the road and I knew it. I had nothing more to teach, and doubted very much even if that which I did teach was understood.

I made it known to the Trust and the Association that I wished to return to Thailand so that I might wander off into some jungle height, there to settle. This request I could see was not popular. People wondered what they would do without me, they said.

All the time I had been teaching and lecturing I had stressed the uselessness of following a personality, trying to get my listeners to understand that it was the teaching that was important and to follow that teaching, to put it into practice. For all that, being human, they still appeared to value the personality over all else. Whenever I talked or lectured they turned up in force.

Much as I wanted to return to Thailand, no funds were forthcoming. I could see that there probably never would be for such a project. My general health appeared to be getting worse and I decided that soon I would retire from the brotherhood of bhikkhus and return to lay life to fend for myself and maybe regain my health.

The results of the tests on my mother showed extensive cancer of the stomach and she entered hospital for an operation. I visited her there many times and could not but admire her great courage and tenacity, as she strove to combat the pain and keep her mind on the meditation exercise which I had taught her.

One month later she died. Her death, for me, was a victory for a worthy warrior. She had battled with courage through all life's problems and in her last moments had died with her mind composed and at peace with herself and the world at large.

I carried out the cremation service as had been her wish. That was my last official function as a bhikkhu. On the 24th of May 1957 I retired from the brotherhood, Bhikkhu Paññavaddho officiating at my disrobing.

★ ★ ★

Now, at the end, I can only feel thankful for all the experiences which came my way and for the great help which the bhikkhu life was to me, none of which would have been possible without the help of many good friends.

I have learned much, but one thing stands out clear in my mind. That is that the teaching of the Buddha is not a matter of Theravada or Mahayana, societies, groups, associations, organisations or trusts. It is a matter for the individual himself, showing him a way, a way which each man must walk firmly for himself, with full responsibility, on his own two feet.

I have my way and I have my memories of a Shangri-la in the mountains to the north-east of Chieng Mai, and I have my two flat feet and I am sure that they will last me for as long as is necessary.

POSTSCRIPT
by
Alan James

Ex-Bhikkhu Kapilavaddho, penniless and very ill, was given a home by one of his staunchest supporters, Ruth Lester. She and her daughter Jean nursed him back to health over a period of 18 months. He adopted the name Richard Randall and, whilst convalescing, wrote *Life as a Siamese Monk*.

At that time, little was known of Eastern meditation in this country. The publisher who suggested that Richard write the book hoped that he would record a tale of strange myths and incredible mental powers, then the subject of much controversy in the popular press.

When Richard presented the finished manuscript, the publisher felt that it was not sensational enough and urged him to include stranger, more amazing psychic feats (!). He suggested that all would be well if some of the facts could be 'adjusted' to make the book more dramatic. Richard refused and his work was rejected.

The manuscript ended up in the wastepaper basket. Jean rescued it and put it away for safekeeping.

* * *

The years passed. The monastic organisation Richard left behind moved into larger premises in London. It enjoyed and suffered a variety of incumbents; each new one bringing his own ideas which affected the fortunes of the Trust, not always for the better.

At a particularly low point, the English Sangha Trust asked Richard if he would return to his previous role of teacher. Aware of his earlier drive and enthusiasm, not to mention his outstanding qualification for the task, the Trustees felt that only Richard himself could revitalise the work of teaching Buddhism and Buddhist meditation for which the charity had been formed in the first place.

He accepted the challenge, with Ruth's blessing, even though it meant total disruption of the lifestyle they had established together.

In October 1967 he was ordained once again and was given his old monastic name, Bhikkhu Kapilavaddho, 'he who spreads and increases the Teaching'.

Quickly taking hold of the reins, he began to impose his own impeccable sense of order. The centre began to attract people with a serious interest in Buddhism. Some of the men entered the Order of monks, and the group grew.

Ruth died, but still the work went on. Meditation classes and lectures for lay people were introduced on a regular basis. Kapilavaddho produced a monthly journal and revived interest in The Sangha Association, an affiliation of lay Buddhists.

Bhikkhu Kapilavaddho was gaining unparalleled experience of teaching Buddhism in the West. He came to believe that the essence of the Buddha's message - as distinct from its cultural clothing - could at that time be best conveyed to Westerners through lay organisations. Always true to his convictions he disrobed, in 1970, taking once again the name Richard Randall.

He remarried. He continued to work hard - too hard - and his health began to fail as a result. He fell seriously ill on a number of occasions but always rallied and, to those close to him, seemed almost indestructible. But advancing age and the severe treatment he had given his body over the years finally began to overwhelm even his iron will. He entered hospital for the last time in December 1971 and died quietly on the19th. He was 65.

*   *   *

The legacy of the Buddha's teaching has been handed down through the centuries across many cultural and geographical barriers. In its move to the Western world, its transmission as a practical and accessible way to truth has been helped and accelerated by the singular efforts of William Purfurst, aka Bhikkhu Kapilavaddho, aka Richard Randall. His indomitable drive and determination are an example to us all of what one man can accomplish in the face of immense odds.

All profits from the sale of this book go directly to
the Aukana Trust, a registered charity (No 326938)
dedicated to the promotion of the Buddha's teaching.

Under the spiritual guidance of **Alan James**, the Aukana Trust
provides a wide range of facilities from introductory evening
classes in meditation and Buddhist philosophy
right through to full-time monastic training.
Most of the activities are held at the House of Inner
Tranquillity in Bradford on Avon; the Trust also
runs classes in London.

If you would like further information, please write to:

Aukana Trust
9 Masons Lane
Bradford on Avon BA15 1QN
England

e-mail: aukana@globalnet.co.uk
internet: www.aukana.org.uk

THE UNFOLDING OF WISDOM
The Buddha's Path to Enlightenment

Alan James

' ... it is like having lived all your life in a dark cave, never being sure where the walls, the ceiling or the exits were, never being sure of the real shape of the space around you. When at last you bring in some light to the darkness, immediately your old idea of the cave disappears. The illumination of true vision eliminates what had been total darkness, including all your speculations about the reality of the cave.

'When this occurs, there is never any need to refer to your earlier idea of how things were; it simply becomes irrelevant. Now you know things as they are. What interest can speculative fantasies have for you now?'

The Unfolding of Wisdom is uncompromising. It presents the facts about spiritual progress. It is not for those who would speculate about symbolism or metaphor but for those who would dare to approach truth directly.

ISBN 0 9511769 4 3 (hardback)   0 9511769 5 1 (softback)
224 pages   230 x 155mm

BUDDHISM: The Plain Facts

Robert Mann & Rose Youd

A clear, systematic guide to *vipassana* meditation,
the practice of insight at the heart of Buddhism.
This book focuses on the original teachings of the
Buddha and shows how they can be applied today.

This is Buddhism without history, politics or jargon -
the plain facts about the Buddha's path
to enlightenment.

ISBN 0 9511769 7 8
176 pages   216 x 138mm

MODERN BUDDHISM

Alan & Jacqui James

'The Buddha's teaching is as relevant today as it ever has been. It describes the facts of human life which are observable by anyone who cares to take the trouble to investigate.'

Presenting timeless truths in a 20th-century context, *Modern Buddhism* provides answers to questions that have always haunted mankind.

Death and dying: a wasted and terrifying experience - or an opportunity for spiritual growth? A meditation teacher describes the way she helped her mother approach the doors of death.

Family relationships: why do some families live in harmony, whilst others are constantly at war? What is the purpose of the family unit?

Sexuality: what sexual habits are most conducive to progress along the path?

Alan & Jacqui James belong to the tradition of teachers who present the essence of Buddhism in a way which is totally in tune with the needs of their own time and culture.

In a confused and dark world, the book is like a ray of light showing the path to sanity and peace -
Buddhism Today, Brisbane

ISBN 0 9511769 1 9
176 pages   215 x 135mm

BUDDHISM IN A FOREIGN LAND

Robert Mann

As Buddhism is taking root in the West, evolving new
forms to suit new conditions, much of its traditional
oriental context is being called into question.

In this intriguing and provocative collection of talks,
Robert Mann addresses many of the issues which confront
Buddhism as it adapts to modern western culture.

Rebirth and traditional cosmology, the role of ethics in
20th-century consumer society, the dangers inherent in
confusing therapy with spirituality - these are just some of
the topics included in this controversial book.

*Covers in an admirably clear manner the fundamentals of the
Buddhadharma ... a book to be recommended -*
Journal of Buddhist Ethics

A pleasure to read - lucid, unambiguous and expressive -
Buddhism Now

ISBN 0 9511769 6 X
192 pages   215 x 135mm

BUDDHIST CHARACTER ANALYSIS

Robert Mann & Rose Youd

Food, sleep, relationships, sex: do you go for quality, quantity or moderation? Or would you prefer to live without them?

Buddhist Character Analysis is a practical guide to the infinite complexities of human behaviour.

You're offered your own TV show. Do you think, 'What took them so long?' Or would you rather die?

Based exclusively on observable facts, **Buddhist Character Analysis** identifies our fundamental motives and assumptions.

Does your heart sink at the prospect of a quiet weekend? Or do you believe that the world could be a wonderful place if it wasn't for all those people?

Skilful use of **Buddhist Character Analysis** leads to a greater understanding of human nature and increasing happiness in daily life.

How do you see the enlightened person? An aloof Himalayan hermit, master of self-control? Or a charismatic leader using his powers to create a better world?

Combined with a spiritual training, **Buddhist Character Analysis** deepens insight into the true nature of reality.

ISBN 0 9511769 3 5
144 pages   197 x 125mm

These books are available by mail-order:

Life as a Siamese Monk	£8.95
The Unfolding of Wisdom	
softback	£8.95
hardback	£10.95
Buddhism: The Plain Facts	£6.95
Modern Buddhism	£7.95
Buddhism in a Foreign Land	£8.50
Buddhist Character Analysis	£6.95

Prices include postage and packing

Please send to:

Aukana Trust
9 Masons Lane
Bradford on Avon
Wiltshire BA15 1QN